Whistling Dixie

Other books on the South
by John Shelton Reed

Southern Folk:
Plain and Fancy (1986)

Southerners:
The Social Psychology of Sectionalism (1983)

One South:
An Ethnic Approach to Regional Culture (1982)

Regionalism and the South:
Selected Papers of Rupert Vance
(editor, with Daniel Joseph Singal, 1982)

Perspectives on the American South
(editor, with Merle Black; 1981, 1983)

The Enduring South:
Subcultural Persistence in Mass Society
(1972; revised edition, 1986)

Whistling Dixie
Dispatches from the South

John Shelton Reed

A Harvest/HBJ Book
Harcourt Brace Jovanovich, Publishers
San Diego   New York   London

Copyright © 1990 by The Curators of the University of Missouri

All rights reserved. No part of this publication may be reproduced or
transmitted in any form or by any means, electronic or mechanical,
including photocopy, recording, or any information storage and
retrieval system, without permission in writing from the publisher.

Requests for permission to make copies of any part of the
work should be mailed to: Permissions Department,
Harcourt Brace Jovanovich, Publishers, 8th Floor,
Orlando, Florida 32887.

First published by University of Missouri Press,
Columbia, Missouri 65201

Library of Congress Cataloging-in-Publication Data
Reed, John Shelton.
    Whistling Dixie: dispatches from the South/John Shelton Reed.
    p.   cm.
    Originally published Columbia: University of Missouri Press,
c1990.
    ISBN 0-15-696174-1
    1. Southern States—Civilization. 2. Southern States—Politics
and government—1951-   3. Political culture—Southern States.
I. Title.
[F209.R44   1992]
975—dc20   92-21658

Printed in the United States of America
First Harvest/HBJ edition 1992
A B C D E

To my parents,
   who tried to teach me to speak the truth,
   politely.

Contents

Preface

It was along about 1979 that I got in the opinion racket on a regular basis. I guess the Carter years got to me. Or maybe they just made more people interested in hearing about the South. Anyway, it's probably not accidental that I started to write this stuff while Jimmy and Billy and Ham and Jody and Miz Lillian and the whole Hee Haw gang were still riding high. They may have been politically disappointing, but they sure were culturally inspiring.

So when Thomas Fleming, then the resident classicist of McClellanville, South Carolina, founded a magazine he called the *Southern Partisan Quarterly Review*, I jumped at the chance to write a pseudonymous column for it. Dr. Fleming's "quarterly" (more like a semiannual, as it worked out) didn't last very long, as any bookkeeper could have told us it wouldn't. The title *Southern Partisan* continued, under new management, but my brief secret life as a columnist ended with the demise of *SPQR*, and I had to do a lot of tongue-biting. When Fleming moved on to become the editor of the monthly *Chronicles: A Magazine of American Culture*— think of it as the *Rockford, Illinois, Review of Books*—I sent him a "Letter from the Lower Right" (this time under my own name). Then another. And another. Now, somewhat to my surprise, I find that I've been at this for over a decade.

That's a dangerously long time. As a writer here in town observed when he packed it in to go to law school, after three or four years in this business even some of the best columnists wind up writing about crabgrass. If I haven't begun to sound like Andy Rooney yet, it probably just reflects my good luck in being able to write from the South and mostly about it.

You can't beat down-home subject matter. But I think that's only part of it. Looking at the world from this particular corner affects not just what you see but how you see it. These essays treat subjects from a Confederate monument to a music video, places from Bob Jones University to Barcelona, people from Jesse Jackson to Bill Bennett, but I hope they're informed and unified by a doggedly provincial point of view, for which I make no apologies.

If some of these essays sound a little bewildered—well, these are bewildering times for a Southerner of more or less conservative views. If some of them sound testy, I'm sorry, but not all of the changes around here have been for the better. I hope some of them are amusing, because Lord knows the South is often funny— maybe now more than ever.

For this collection, I've grouped these pieces into six sections. The first deals with Southern identity and its relation to the South's history and symbols; the second with recent developments in Southern life and society; the third with Southern ways of doing things like making music and preparing food. The fourth section includes some roundups of regional news that I've put together from time to time. (Some of these collations turn out to have themes; others just sit there and ask to be marveled at.) The fifth section groups pieces that treat American politics and politicians, while the last is a frankly eclectic bunch dealing with exotic people, places, and institutions, mostly non-Southern. Within sections, I've held to chronological order, except when it seemed a better idea not to.

Why would people want to read these? Beats me, but I'll tell you why they *should*.

It's said that when Thoreau heard about the construction of a telegraph from Maine to Texas he asked whether Maine and Texas had anything to say to one another. These days, I suspect, more people would ask whether Maine and Texas have anything *new* to say to each other. After all, aren't people pretty much the same in both places?

Well, as a matter of fact, no. Study after study, often paid for by your tax dollars, shows that. (Here's one example: Dr. James Marks of the Centers for Disease Control says of a high-priced survey of activity levels, drinking, obesity, and so forth that "the main thing we were surprised at was the amount of variation from state to state. We expected some, but nowhere near as much.") Americans need to be reminded that there are good-sized regional differences in this country, and that some of those differences are getting larger.

Of course what Carl Carmer wrote of Alabama—that "the Congo is not more different from Massachusetts or Kansas"—isn't true, and never has been. And that's just as well. If it were, then the civilized world could pay as little attention to the South as it does to Zaire. The South's not *that* different.

But it's different enough to be instructive. I think Southerners are one of those exemplary minorities—like Catholics, like Jews, like blacks, like Mormons—who ought to keep sticking their oars in, reminding "mainstream" Americans that there are other ways to look at history, other ways to do things in the present, other visions of what the future might be. So I'm volunteering to help with all this reminding. Let me be very clear about a couple of things, though.

First, these are feuilletons, reviews, dispatches from the front, what-have-you—but they are *not scholarly articles*, understand? If you use them for that, you'll void your warranty.

Second, I'm not presuming to present "the Southern point of view." The fact is that often there is no such thing. And when there is, sometimes I don't share it. But most Americans, and nearly all that are worth a damn, reflect the places they come from, so these doubtless reveal *a* Southern viewpoint—that is, mine.

Let me tell a story. One time some of us went fishing down off the North Carolina coast, and we stopped in a general store for provisions. I spied a cap for sale, emblazoned with crossed Confederate and U.S. flags and the motto "American by birth / Southern by the grace of God." Now, I wanted that cap, so I asked the trailer-camp mama behind the counter how much it cost.

My buddy Peter, a recent immigrant from Brooklyn (who, as a matter of fact, was wearing a New York Yankees baseball cap), started giving me a hard time. "No real Southerner would wear one of those things," he said, and went on to lay some heavy adjectives on me. Deracinated, self-conscious, and effete were just for starters.

The woman at the register gave the Flatbush Flash a pitying look. "Honey," she said, "a real Southerner will wear any damn hat he wants to."

And that's as explicit as I plan to get about what I'm up to.

Acknowledgments

Many friends have told me stories, sent me clippings, or otherwise helped me out over the years. There are too many to mention here, but you know who you are. Thanks.

Dale Volberg Reed has been feeding me good lines since high school, and she's a discerning and tactful critic when asked and sometimes when not. She's especially adept at spotting pomposity. But those are the least of my debts to her.

For over a decade Thomas Fleming has given me a forum and a heady measure of freedom. I'll always be grateful to Tom, no matter what his many enemies say about him.

Beverly Jarrett has contributed immeasurably to the scholarly study of the South. She gave this undertaking her personal support and encouragement, and gave me some good editorial advice, too. I hope her enthusiasm doesn't prove to be misplaced: I've never yet ruined a lady's reputation, and sure don't want to start now.

I'm indebted to Eugene Genovese for an early reading of this material. Wayne Flynt also gave me a helpful reading of these essays, and I'm grateful to Wayne, Taylor Littleton, and their colleagues at Auburn University for hospitality on several occasions. Some material in "In with the In-Crowd," pp. 114–19, has been adapted from the 1988 Draughon Lectures at Auburn, and parts of "Editing the South" and "Editing the South: The Final Chapter," pp. 67–79, were presented in somewhat different form as a 1990 Franklin Lecture there.

A few of these pieces were written while I was a fellow at the National Humanities Center, although that's not what I was there for. I appreciate that place and its staff more each year.

For permission to reprint copyrighted material I thank the following publications:

The *Daily Tar Heel* for "The Rebel Rip-off and the Yankee Dollar."

The *American Spectator* for "A Sound Dollar."

The *Raleigh News and Observer* for "Through the Stomach to the Heart of Dixie."

The *Georgia Historical Quarterly* for "The Garden of Eatin'."

The *Southern Partisan* for "Why No Southern Nationalism?" "How 'Bout Them Dawgs?" "S.O.S. (Stamp Out *Southeastern*)," "Is the White Southerner Ready for Equality?" "The Useful South," "Plain Folk of the New South," "Gentlemen, Be Seated," "The Sense of 'Southernizing'," "Precious Memories," "Hey Good-lookin', Whatcha Got Cookin'?" "All the News That Fits," "Food for Thought," "Science and Religion," and "Ole Ted."

Everything else originally appeared in *Chronicles: A Magazine of American Culture*.

Whistling Dixie

I. The Southern Nation

Rebel Yell. "Distilled, Aged and Bottled by Rebel Yell Distillery, Louisville, Kentucky, Exclusively for the Deep South."

Well, actually, they sell it in the Shallow South, too, but there is some exclusivity about it, and it is nice to have something we can call our own. I mean, after all that we've given the world—Coca Cola, Holiday Inns, Jimmy Carter, and Kentucky Fried Chicken come to mind—we're entitled to keep something for ourselves, right?

And it's not bad whiskey. When I lived in New York, we expatriates used to pick up a bottle or two when we went home. Rebel Yell had a certain cachet—sort of like Coors when people drove to Texas to buy it.

Smart marketing, I thought. Sure, sometimes they hit the "Forget, hell" chord a little hard, but I know a splendid old gentleman who was mighty tickled when he got his colonel's commission in the Rebel Yell Army. He framed it. Put it right next to his University of Chicago Ph.D. Besides, I can't be the only bourbon drinker who grins when he sees a "Get Your Heart in Dixie or Get Your Ass Out" bumper sticker. I know it's wrong, but I'm weak. (I wouldn't put one on my car, you understand.) Put us closet rednecks together with the genuine article and you've got a pretty good collection of folks who'd just as soon reach for Rebel Yell as not, when they can't afford Wild Turkey.

Well, friends, I'm here to tell you that we've been sold a bill of goods. Yessir, once again the sturdy, staggering yeomen of the South have been taken for a ride by Yankee capital. In my first effort at investigative reporting, I've turned up a sordid story worthy of Woodward and Bernstein. Brace yourself.

Last year I ran across a new advertisement for Rebel Yell, and it was too much. It was, in a word, tacky. (That word is another Southern gift to the nation. Ever notice how these things lose their savor when they go national?) "Oh," says a big headline, "the Joys of Being a Good Ol' Boy." Good Ol' Boy, indeed. Aside from the fact that that phrase has turned my stomach since approximately the 1976 election, there's something phony about the way the ad uses it. "Many joys are unique only [sic] to the South. One of them is traditionally enjoyed while the good ol' boys joyfully partake of the others." "The Good Ol' Boys' Bourbon," the ad concludes, in case we missed the point. Along the way, the copywriter offers us some facts about Robert E. Lee and kudzu, and serves up a verse worthy of the late J. Gordon Coogler: "For years there've been toasts to the Southern Belle. Who nowadays toast [*sic*] back with her"—guess what.

Aside from the grammar, the ad lacks the authentic down-home touch. It reads like whoever wrote it learned about good ol' boys from *New York* magazine. (The last revolting straw is the injunction to "Have yourself a sun belt.") It seemed obvious to me that some Madison Avenue genius confected this—probably not a Southerner at all, or else one who's spent too much time at Elaine's. I had to know, so I called Louisville information for the number of the Rebel Yell Distillery.

There is no listing for a Rebel Yell Distillery in Louisville.

I called the Yellow Pages operator, who suggested that I try National Distillery ("They make a lot of off-brands"). At National (which nation, I wondered) a pleasant lady said, no, they don't make Rebel Yell, but she thought Schenley might. I called Schenley. No, they don't make it, but I could try Brown Foreman. I called Brown Foreman. No, they don't make it; maybe Schenley's does.

By this time I was concluding that, in bourbon circles, Rebel Yell is not what you call your heavyweight competition.

When I told the lady at Brown Foreman that Schenley's had sent me to her, she went off to consult a reference book, and returned with the information that Rebel Yell is distilled by something called the Stitzel Weller Distillery—a/k/a the "Rebel Yell Distillery," I guess, but the alias seems to be used only in advertisements.

"Is that in Louisville?"

"Yes . . . yes, it is."

That's something, anyway. "Would I call there to talk to somebody in the Rebel Yell marketing department?"

"Oh, no. They're just the distillers. You'd want somebody at the parent company. That's . . . Somerset Importers."

"Are they in Louisville, too?"

"No, they're in New York."

Yes, that's right. The "host bourbon of the South," the one that claims it's "made and sold only beneath the Mason-Dixon line," is only made and sold there. What the South gets out of this is a few blue-collar jobs and a bunch of drunks. Some New York outfit with a candy-ass British name gets all the expense-account jobs and "imports" all the profits. There's a Yankee in the woodpile, and we get the short end of the stick.

Now the iron hand of Wall Street, with or without the velvet glove of Madison Avenue, has been milking the South for a long time. (That's probably why the rebels yelled in the first place. *You* try being milked by an iron hand.) But using a product called "Rebel Yell" to skim the gravy off the grits—well, I call that downright low.

Damn it, it's time to rethink secession. What we need is a Southern Nationalist movement that would promise to national-ize Rebel Yell. We could call them the Dixienats, and I'd drink to their success if I could find anything to do it with.

(January 1979)

❧ A Sound Dollar ❧

A cryptic note in *National Review* some time ago is the only mention I've seen in the popular press of a fact that insiders have known for years: the U.S. dollar has shown a dramatic long-term decline against Confederate money. (To minimize purely numis-matic considerations, I refer here to the prices asked for the garden-variety one-dollar bill printed in Richmond from 1862 to 1864, bearing the portrait of Clement C. Clay, in "average circu-lated condition." Investors should note that the prices apply regardless of the condition of the U.S. currency offered in ex-change.)

In 1865 the Confederate dollar was mere scrap paper. Even sixty years later it could be picked up for a U.S. nickel. But today, on specialized exchanges like the one run by Colonel Grover Criswell in Fort McCoy, Florida, a Confederate one-dollar bill costs eight dollars U.S. (Colonel Criswell, the former president of the Amer-ican Numismatic Association, the author of *Confederate and South-ern States Currency,* and probably the leading specialist in this market, supplied me with the information on exchange rates reported here.)

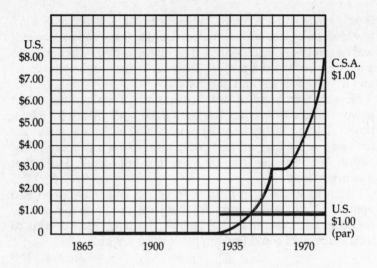

FIGURE 1. Value in U.S. dollars of one dollar C.S.A. since 1865.

The Confederate dollar's remarkable comeback began about the 1920s (Figure 1). Although FDR may have been correct when he said in the 1930s that the South was the nation's number-one economic problem, Southerners who had saved their Confederate money were holding a currency that was appreciating against a *sound* U.S. dollar at an average annual rate of nearly 15 percent, doubling in value every five years. The end of World War II saw the Confederate and U.S. dollars trading at par (a fact unknown to most Americans and unremarked even in the financial press), and after a period of stability in the late 1950s and early 1960s, the U.S. dollar resumed its decline. U.S. citizens who put their money into Confederate dollars in 1965 saw those dollars rise in value over the next fourteen years at an average annual rate of 7.4 percent, comfortably outpacing the rise in the cost of living (Figure 2).

This solid performance is bound to lead to an even greater flight from the U.S. dollar to the Confederate. As the Yankee dollar is eaten away by inflation, Confederate money should begin to attract not just currency speculators but ordinary Americans looking for a sounder currency in which to hold their savings.

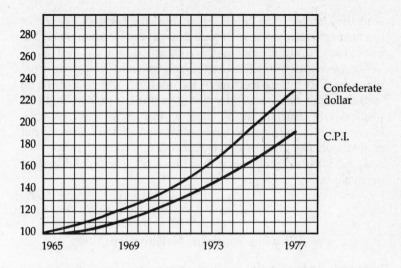

FIGURE 2. Rise in Consumer Price Index and in exchange rate of Confederate dollar (1965 = 100).

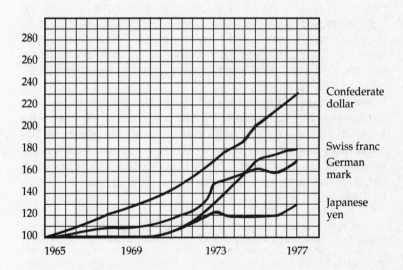

FIGURE 3. Rise in exchange rates for Confederate dollar, Swiss franc, German mark, and Japanese yen (1965 = 100).

And they couldn't do better. Since 1965 the Confederate dollar has outperformed even such blue chips as the German mark, the Swiss franc, and the Japanese yen (Figure 3).*

What accounts for "the Confederate miracle"? How can currency backed by a government defunct for over a century be sounder than one backed by the government in Washington? Confederate officials aren't saying, but they seem to have learned a lesson from the severe inflation of 1862–1865. Strict controls on the growth of the Confederate money supply are coupled with a fiscal policy that produces a balanced budget every year.

(August 1979)

❧ Why No Southern Nationalism? ❧

It doesn't do to take the South too seriously. Those who do may wind up like Edmund Ruffin, who responded to the Confederacy's defeat by writing a note about how much he hated Yankees and blowing his brains out. Or poor W. J. Cash, after the publication of *The Mind of the South:* he hanged himself in a Mexico City hotel room, leaving what must be the most pathetic suicide note ever written ("I can't stand it anymore, and I don't even know what it is"). Or Clarence Cason, author of *90° in the Shade*, also a suicide. Or John Gould Fletcher, who wrote the essay on education in *I'll Take My Stand*, ditto.

Southerners in general have a lower suicide rate than other Americans, but you wouldn't know it to look at the ones who write about their region. Self-destruction seems almost an occupational hazard, and I don't plan to court that outcome by being serious very often. From time to time an interesting semi-serious question does occur to me, though, and this is one of those times.

---

*I should note that there are anomalies in the market for Confederate currency. Unofficial exchanges often offer slightly different rates for large bills of any currency, for instance, but this discrepancy is very marked for those buying Confederate bills. Denominations of five dollars and up can sometimes be acquired at substantial discounts—even below par. There is no corresponding discount for those buying large U.S. bills with Confederate money. Amateur investors should proceed with caution.

Some time back the *Economist* of London published a lengthy, thorough, and fair-minded essay on the South, which I've just been rereading. It is a fine job, right up to the non sequitur at the end, where the author, Johnny Grimond, simply tacks on the conventional wisdom that the South is disappearing as a distinctive cultural entity—a pity, he implies, but there you are.

What I noticed on this rereading is that conclusion's context. Just a few pages earlier, *The Economist* had reported the fall of Britain's Labour government, brought down by the votes of Scottish nationalists seeking a greater measure of self-determination for Scotland.

That juxtaposition raises an interesting question, and one that nobody, to my knowledge, has ever addressed. Why is the United States assumed to be immune to the centrifugal tendencies afflicting so many industrialized nations in these decades? If Britain, Spain, and France (France!) are troubled by separatist agitation—not to mention our Canadian neighbors—why should the U.S. ship of state sail on serenely, undisturbed by rumblings of mutiny from the lower decks? Why, in particular, is there no Southern nationalism? Sectional conflict has come up again and again, over a variety of issues, and the Gordian solution has at least the virtue of simplicity. Why has no one of any consequence seriously urged it?

Southern nationalism simply isn't there, politically, and it hasn't been since 1865. But, like the little man on the stair who also wasn't there, it won't go away. Just for laughs, a 1971 public opinion poll in North Carolina asked whether the South would be better off as a separate country, if it could be done without war. Out of every eight respondents, one thought it would be a good idea and two were undecided. That may sound like pretty paltry support; a solid majority opposed the idea, after all. But at about the same time, polls in Quebec were revealing an almost identical level of support for an independent Quebec—and a higher level of opposition.

The difference between Quebec and the South, obviously, lay less in the state of public opinion than in the nature of political activity. In Quebec, a separatist movement had emerged, articulating a broadly attractive program and forcing the issue onto the political agenda. Why has nothing similar happened in the South?

One answer, of course, is that it did happen, in 1860, and the South got whipped. Whether might makes right or not, it is often an effective teaching device. The educational activities of Generals Grant and Sherman taught Southerners lessons in the meaning of the Constitution not easily forgotten. Having raised the issue and lost, fair and square and painfully, Southerners have felt the matter was settled, and few have been disposed to try again.

In addition, from the end of Reconstruction until, oh, say the 1960s, the United States was clearly a going concern, one that Southerners were proud to be part of. Just as Great Britain was not seriously troubled by Scottish or Welsh nationalism so long as the sun never set on Scotsmen and Welshmen (the Irish, of course, were a different matter), Southern nationalism seems petty, somehow irresponsible, if Americans feel that the rest of the world is relying on them. A generation ago, serious Southern nationalism would have been "un-American"—and that used to be a term of opprobrium, in the South as elsewhere.

And there's one more reason, I think, why we haven't seen American separatism of the Canadian or European type. Brother Dave Gardner used to raise a chorus of rebel yells by remarking that "The South may not always be right, but by God it's never wrong." But the South has been wrong time and again—about race. By insisting, like the Georgia historian Ulrich Phillips, that white supremacy is the sine qua non of the South, some of our region's spokesmen have made it impossible for many thoughtful and humane Southerners (black ones, of course, but white ones, too) to cast their lot wholeheartedly with the South. By defending the indefensible, by confounding the case for the South with the case for lynching, our Tillmans, Vardamans, and Bleases produced silence, equivocation, or active hostility among the best of the South's teachers, clergymen, and journalists, the very "New Class" elements that (say what you will about them in other respects) seem to be required to formulate and to propagate a serious political program, and that are in fact at the center of the European and Canadian separatist movements.

So, why no Southern nationalism? Not because the U.S. is exempt from the forces that produce such movements elsewhere, but because of several unique inhibiting factors. If I'm right, the stage may now be set for really hard-core sectional politics, for the first time in over a century, because each of these factors is now waning. (Remember: You read it here first.)

Consider, in the first place, that the old Confederates have gone, and with them the memories of the last go-round. The veterans of the Grand Army of the Republic are equally extinct, taking with them, I believe, the mystical commitment to the Union that led them to preserve it by stomping the South. Difficult as it might be to imagine another go at secession, it's even harder to imagine that the U.S. Army would burn Atlanta again to stop it. (More's the pity, some Southerners would say.) As well imagine the RAF unleashed on Edinburgh. Few Western nations any longer have the will for that sort of undertaking; certainly the U.S. does not.

Both at home and abroad the idea of Americanism has lost its vitality in recent years. As Washington finally takes on the physical trappings of an imperial capital, it's losing the international clout that alone could justify that ostentation. Our role in the world is increasingly unclear, and to our national dismay we're being told that we simply aren't wanted in many places. As in Britain when it ceased to be Great, the anticolonialist impulse has begun to surface close to home.

Deplore it or not, as you will, but it's simply a fact that insisting on the rights and interests of one's own group within the nation is no longer seen as subversive—or perhaps that subversion is no longer seen as bad form. So far the voice of sectionalism has been subdued amid the clamor of contending interest groups, but if it's heard in the future, it won't be the only one hollering.

In addition, it seems to me at least possible that the South is finally ridding itself of the incubus of white supremacy. Consider what that would mean for the cause of sectionalism. Freed of the obsession with race, freed of the necessity to treat the subject (as I am now) in every discussion of the South, those of us for whom bigotry has no charms would be able to celebrate without reservations the region's undeniable virtues. (To revise that quote from Brother Dave: the South may not always be right, but by God it's not always been wrong.)

States' rights is a self-evidently reasonable and just doctrine, with an appeal extending well beyond the South—so long as it's not a mask for the states' wrongs of racial discrimination. We in the South have asked for trouble in the past, giving exploitative and anti-Southern elements outside the region the occasion to do well, quite legitimately, by doing good. If the South's race relations have become (as I believe) better than those elsewhere, that excuse for interference no longer exists.

Moreover, if what I take to be the accidental link between Southern sectionalism and white supremacy is severed, the South can begin to profit from the reservoir of affection for it that exists among black Southerners. For good reason, most have heretofore looked outside the South for allies, but once they're assured that their hard-won rights are secure and they're guaranteed the respect due to partners in the Southern enterprise, it wouldn't surprise me to find many prepared to make common cause with whites on their homeland's behalf. There are already signs of this, and the process may well accelerate as blacks realize that they are now much more of a presence in Southern state capitals than in the U.S. Congress.

Am I serious? Well, as I said, not always. To tell the truth, I don't know that a full-blown Southern nationalism would appeal to me. Anyway, I once took an oath to support and defend the Constitution of the United States. But it wouldn't surprise me to see a separatist movement emerge, and I for one would find an American politics where the proper balance between federal power and decentralization was subject to debate preferable to one where an arrogant central government recognizes no limits on its authority.

And, politics aside, the *cultural* Balkanization of America strikes me as almost wholly desirable. I'm not one of those who feel that one New York or California is too many, but God knows one's enough.

We heard a lot a while back from "new breed" Southern politicians about what the South has to offer the nation. To hell with that. Let the others look out for themselves. But one thing they can learn from us, if we'll demonstrate it to them, is humility. Tempting as it may be to dictate to others, preach at them, and generally push them around, we Southerners of all people ought to restrain ourselves. Different parts of a large and varied country will have both different problems and different solutions to similar problems. It would be naive to expect that our solutions can be a model for other regions, even if they were disposed to learn from us, and it would be presumptuous to tell them how to run their affairs.

I take that to be the beginning of wisdom in these matters. When rulers lack that wisdom or fail to act on it, they invite the separatist response.

(Fall 1981–Spring 1982)

❦ How 'Bout Them Dawgs? ❧

The other evening I dined with some students from Chapel Hill, and listened to several of the young gentlemen complain that our university has no varsity crew. One of them told the story of the long and hard struggle to get lacrosse established as a varsity sport, and there was general agreement that, aside from baseball and the two money-making sports, North Carolina has been slow to develop its athletic teams. I listened with a growing sense of unease and annoyance.

Squash? Tennis? Lacrosse? Crew? It occurs to me to wonder why we want to import these la-di-da Yankee sports when we have fine native traditions to build on. There are, after all, many Southern sports, activities where we have abundant local talent and no need to recruit from the high schools of Brooklyn or the prep schools of New England. More than that: these are sports that interest our citizens at large, and might dispose them to think more kindly of their colleges and universities. My dinner companions were rightly proud of North Carolina's national championships in lacrosse, but do you suppose that anyone in Goldsboro will pay his taxes more cheerfully as a result?

Think about it. How about varsity bass-fishing? The university could offer a few scholarships to eighteen-year-old Bassmasters; they'd probably even bring their own boats. Or what about a grant-in-aid for some old boy from Randleman, N.C., who's been racing cars since he could see over a steering wheel? Can you imagine the Tobacco Road 500: UNC, Duke, Wake Forest, and N.C. State fighting it out at Rockingham? (Never mind that it's not really Duke's kind of thing. They could hire a team.)

Let yourself go, and imagine a varsity pit-bull team. Hooo-eeee, as we say. Some of our better schools might have to waive their normal admissions requirements and set up some special remedial courses, but I understand that sort of thing is not unheard of even now.

Other possibilities will suggest themselves to the meanest intelligence, but my point is that bringing in lacrosse and crew-racing and all the rest may be OK for them as wants it, but could be just another sorry example of a preference for meretricious imports rather than hardy, wholesome natives. Consider the homely tomato, and take a lesson from it: there's no substitute for home-grown.

While we're on the subject of higher education, let me risk offending some of my friends by asking why it is that the South has no really great university of its own. Yes, yes, we have some fine colleges and a number of pretty good universities (I won't give examples, lest I leave out your alma mater). The colleges, though, lack the libraries and faculty and mission of a university, and each of the universities is unsatisfactory in one way or another.

There was a time when North Carolina seemed to be on its way to becoming the sort of place I'm talking about. Bright students from all over the South converged on Chapel Hill, got a decent if not surpassingly excellent education, got to know one another, married each other's sisters, and went forth to be the Southern elite of the next generation. The university's faculty was composed in large measure of Southerners who were good enough to go elsewhere but chose not to. Many of them saw their job as one of interpreting the South to itself; historians, sociologists, writers—all sorts of creative and scholarly Southerners wound up on the faculty and produced a flood of remarkable work on the region, becoming in the process nationally reputable. But that national reputation was a more or less accidental side effect of their devotion to the South and their practice of casting down their buckets where they were.

I fear, though, that Chapel Hill is doomed sooner or later to subside into Generic State U. The legislature supports us pretty well, especially considering that North Carolina is not a rich state. But the legislature never has understood the university, probably never can, and isn't willing just to trust us anymore. In part, I blame the sixties for that, but it's also true that the legislature is no longer filled with loyal sons of the university. Service to the state fell out pretty much naturally from the school's old regional mission, but it is now interpreted more narrowly, and the pressure is on to admit more students, make most of them in-state, get them through, and do it cheaply.

Some vestiges of former glories remain. Largely through the generosity of a few wealthy alumni there are still things to distinguish Chapel Hill from the dozen-plus other branches of the "consolidated university." But those distinctions are being slowly eroded, and faculty members who have not become "research entrepreneurs" are increasingly assimilated to the status of civil servants—schoolteachers paid to drill the state's more or less gilded youth.

I single out North Carolina because there once seemed to be hope for it, and because I love it, but much the same thing seems to be happening to the University of Virginia. The legislative mind seems much the same at the 36th and 37th parallels. And if this is what is happening at North Carolina and Virginia—and Texas, too, to include the only other Southern state university with any reputation outside its state—how much more at the Tennessees, Georgias, Kentuckys, and Florida States of the region? These are decent schools that do the job assigned to them about as well as it deserves to be done, but none can even aspire to be a great *Southern* university. Each is too busy scrapping to remain or to become the best in its state.

I'm sorry to say that there's probably little hope for the state institutions. Since I don't see any reason to suppose that socialized education is a better idea than socialized steel mills, that doesn't surprise me. But it does make me sad.

What about the private universities? Well, look at what happens when graduate departments are evaluated. You can question that standard, but it's true that the only Southern university besides North Carolina and Texas with any sort of national reputation is Duke—and what a sad situation we find there. The school might as well be in New Jersey, and two-thirds of the faculty probably wish it were. With luck, Duke could become what it sometimes says it is: "the Stanford of the South." But what a tawdry ambition that is. Most of its students aren't Southerners to begin with, and they certainly don't become Southerners while they're in Durham. Half of its faculty, it seems, didn't get tenure at Princeton or Yale and are devoted to constructing a new, ivied Eden in the pine forests. Their reference points are outside the South, and so are the ambitions of those who haven't packed it in altogether. No, Duke hasn't even thought about being a great Southern university; it's trying—to be fair, with some success—to be a thoroughly national one.

There are other private universities that might have a shot at the role I'm describing. Vanderbilt, for instance, has a tradition to work with, and interesting things are happening at Emory. To some extent all of these schools have the same problem as Duke, but at least some of their administrators understand the concept of regional leadership and don't disdain it out of hand. That's not the dominant aspiration among faculty, though, and anyone who expects students to seize upon the idea hasn't experienced the difficulty of getting today's students to seize upon *any* idea.

Still, what the South needs, and what some far-sighted administration ought to give it, is a great Southern university: great faculty, students, and resources for scholarship; Southern faculty, students, and purpose. What we need isn't a Stanford of the South, still less a Wisconsin of the South (the phrase used to be current at Chapel Hill), but a Brandeis of the South: a fine university on all counts, but one that takes as its special mission the education of an elite for the community it serves, scholarship in the history and culture of that community, and service to it. There are gentiles on the faculty and in the student body at Brandeis, and the university serves them well, but no one would deny—or even want to deny—that it is a Jewish university. Southerners need something like that, and it can hardly be started from scratch, these days. The school with the vision to fill that need would deserve to flourish.

(Fall 1983)

✎ S.O.S. (Stamp Out *Southeastern*) ✎

In a *Charlotte Observer* article some time ago, Lew Powell remarked on the growing use of the words *Southeast* and *Southeastern*, as in "NCNB is the largest bank in the Southeast." He observed that, once upon a time, not long ago, *South* would have done instead. Powell argued half-seriously that this is a disturbing trend, but the *Observer* ran his article in the "Living" section, next to a column headlined "Some Folks Actually Like Brussels Sprouts." Is preferring *South* to *Southeast* as trivial as that? Is it like preferring broccoli?

Let's consider what *Southeast* means. To the extent that it is a synonym for *eastern South*, its use is benign. In some cases, I suspect, that is exactly what it does mean, and it reflects just simple boosterism. When the University of North Carolina claims to be the best in the Southeast in something or other, it doesn't take much intelligence to decode the message that the University of Texas is better. And "largest in the Southeast" sounds much more impressive than "fifth biggest in the South" or whatever it is when Houston and Dallas are included. (Shoot, don't expect us country boys to play in that league.)

That's probably harmless enough—fish and ponds and all that. And if the use of *Southeast* implies recognition of the South's diversity, it's downright welcome, and overdue. Fifty-odd years ago, Howard W. Odum, in his book *Southern Regions of the United States* (note the plural: Southern *regions*), argued that the Southeast and Southwest were so different economically and geographically that they ought to be treated as distinct regions, for the planning and administrative purposes that he had in mind. I think Odum overstated it, for reasons I'll get to in a minute, but certainly there are important differences. Like Kipling's marine, the Texan is "a kind of a giddy harumfrodite"—Southern and Western too.

Consequently, the Southwest has long had a sense of its distinctiveness within the South, so much so that the South risks losing the Trans-Mississippi in this century, just as it did at Vicksburg. Studies of business-naming practices show that far-western Southerners seldom use *Southern* in the names of their enterprises. They are more likely to use *Western,* and far more likely to use *Southwestern.* As for *Dixie,* forget it: that word now has no more currency in the far-western South than it does in Iowa.

Frankly, I think we in the eastern South have asked for that. Both in Southern history and in Southern historiography, Virginians and Carolinians have often given the Southwest the same treatment Jimmy Carter gave his no-'count relatives: the relationship wasn't denied, but neither was it emphasized. Sometime after World War II the Southwest's petrochemical wealth and relative lack of embarrassing racial problems put the subregional bottom rail on top, and it's not surprising that such Texans as Lyndon Johnson and Dan Rather chose to deny their Southernness. Others, more endearing, just drifted off into solipsistic communion with the armadillo, Lone Star beer, and the music of Bob Wills.

If the growing use of *Southeastern* reflected only a belated recognition by cis-Mississippians that they are not the only Southerners, it would be a healthy development. As I said, we ought to recognize the South's diversity, and we ought to cherish it. After all, we tried to set up a confederacy, not a union.

But I'm afraid that, increasingly, *Southeast* is not being used to designate a part of the South, the eastern counterpart of the Southwest. Rather it refers to a major region of the United States, a counterpart to, say, the Northeast. There's a disturbing tendency in these parts to say and to write and even, God help us, to think *Southeast*, where formerly we would have said and written and thought *South*.

This meaning was made perfectly clear by a poster I saw the other day. It announced the "Southeastern United States Premier" of some movie or other. That is, it did until I corrected it with a felt-tip marker. I thought the spelling of *premiere* was a nice down-home touch, but I changed "Southeastern United States" to *Southern*. I don't think that poster meant only that this movie had already been shown in Dallas, or Shreveport, or Little Rock.

Lew Powell suggested that this alarming trend has come about because large numbers of people who now live in what used to be known as *the South* don't know where or what or why the South is. Powell suggested that *South* is going out of cognitive fashion, that *Southeast* is being popularized by Yankee migrants with no feeling for (or, worse, no sympathy with) Southern distinctiveness and pride. He quoted Al Stuart, a Charlotte geographer: "When I mention the South to these people, they get a funny little expression on their face. They don't know what I'm talking about. I immediately have to qualify it as 'the Southeastern United States'. . . . It's as if the South is a club and they don't belong to it."

Now, many of these are good and worthy folks, with a laudable commitment to low taxes and other good things. Most will make good neighbors, and they are certainly good for Southern Republicanism. Don't get me wrong; some of my best friends are Yankees. But it's a fact that *the South* means nothing at all to many of the newly arrived. For them, the South is just a place where they happen to live, pleasant enough perhaps, but not an object of affection or loyalty. *Southeast* is more accurate—why not say it?

For others (and I'm going beyond Powell here) *the South* evokes images they want nothing to do with. (*Dixie*, of course, is even worse.) These are the people who tell their Yankee relatives that they've moved to the Southeast—something less alien, less alarming, less distasteful than the South.

And precious few of these migrants see their past, present, or future tied up with that of Texans or Arkansans. Yankee migrants to Texas and Arkansas no doubt feel the same lack of kinship with Carolinians. I mentioned earlier that eastern and western Southerners have had many things in common. Whatever their differences, South Carolinians have allowed of Texans that at least they weren't Yankees. But now there are many South Carolina residents who don't see that as a point in favor of Texans. These new Southeasterners do not in fact have much in common with Southwesterners—not history, not manners, not accents, not religion, no aspect of the Southern cultural heritage that has heretofore offset the centrifugal forces of geography and economics. (Only in barbecue do cultural distinctions between the eastern and western South become insurmountable, but in that respect so are differences even between eastern and western North Carolina.)

These are the things that the hundreds of maps in Odum's *Southern Regions* ignored. Odum's maps, in other words, ignored *the South*, which has always been more a cultural entity than an economic or physiographic one. (The Confederacy, Karl Marx said, wasn't a nation at all, just a battle cry.) We can speak, properly, of economic development in the eastern South, but Lew Powell observed that we don't speak of such things as Southeastern fried chicken, Southeastern hospitality, the Southeastern accent, or Southeastern religion. Country songs aren't written about Southeastern nights or Southeastern women, and a magazine called the *Southeastern Partisan* would have a very small audience.

Creeping Southeasternization simply ignores the cultural and historical aspects of the South. It ignores the things that make eastern and western Southerners feel more at home in each other's states than in Michigan, New York, or California. The Southeast is nothing more than lines on a map, a mere quadrant, as synthetic as anything ever devised by French Revolutionaries or British imperialists.

What can be done about this thoughtless vivisection? Well, as a rule, I don't have much patience with people who want others to jump through linguistic hoops for the sake of their principles, like some of the more frivolous feminists today, or with the sort of verbal hocus-pocus that turned Negroes into blacks twenty years ago. But by God there's something to be said for trying to make the word *Southeast* unacceptable in polite company. Defacing posters is a start. (*Southwest* is probably too well established to mess with now. Maybe later.)

Because *Southeast* is ambiguous, it's not out of line to ask someone who says it what he means. If he means the South, let him say so; if he means the eastern South—well, the extra syllable is a small price to pay for clarity and the preservation of our cultural heritage. We may have to live with the adjectival form *Southeastern* (*east-Southern* sounds a little Germanic for American tongues), but we can certainly ask whether *Southern* is what is meant, and use it if it is.

As for *Southeasterner*—well, I'd like to keep that word around. We've always needed a term for residents of the eastern South who don't want or deserve to be Southerners, and this will do nicely. It should always be printed with quotation marks, and pronounced with a sneer. For the rest of us, in nearly all circumstances, *Southerner* will continue to do service, and it should be insisted upon.

Make no mistake: the Southeast is a threat to the South. Lew Powell was only half-kidding when he wrote about the "Invasion of the Identity Snatchers." The Southeast is a sort of soul-less doppelgänger for a great, living, historic region. We must drive a stake through its heart, before it is too late.

(Winter 1986)

Some years ago, I've been told, William Buckley was patiently explaining to an interviewer that most of the African states could use additional tutelage before being given their independence. The interviewer, more responsive than Buckley to the winds of change, asked when these states would be ready for self-government. Playing his youthful role of conservatism's Oscar Wilde, Buckley smilingly replied: "When they stop eating each other."

That crack seemed a good deal more outrageous before we learned how some of the Dark Continent's field marshals and emperors stocked their freezers, and that sort of thing was enough to get Buckley banned for life from at least one of the newly independent states, a punishment he accepted philosophically with the remark that, all things considered, he'd rather be forbidden to go there than required to.

I was reminded of Buckley's thoughts on colonialism the other day when a friend gave me some pamphlets from a group called the Southern National Party, a Memphis-based outfit "dedicated to the creation of an independent Southern Republic." Why an independent Southland? Well, I'm afraid you may have guessed it: to prevent "mongrelization" and preserve "white civilization." The party's literature is the old white supremacist hash, warmed over and served with a side order of anti-imperialism.

The nature of the organization's appeal can be inferred from its newsletter. A good many letters to the editor come from inmates of various prisons, who typically complain about the behavior of their black fellow-prisoners and generalize to the black population, ah, at large. These poor bewildered jailbirds don't seem to realize that one doesn't meet the highest type of black folks in prison—or white folks either, come to that. As a former governor of Georgia pointed out, most of the problems of our prisons could be solved if we had a better class of prisoners.

According to the party's literature, "A true Southerner must have [among other things] education or training as a Lady or Gentleman." Well, it's not surprising that these particular Southern gentlemen welcome the opportunity to feel superior to someone, but I hate to see their misery politicized, and I'm at something of a loss to explain the similar beliefs of those SNP members who are not at present pulling time. It seems to me that reading their mail ought to give them second thoughts about white superiority.

This sort of thing, in fact, is even enough to give one second thoughts about the South. Of course, these loonies are not representative or even respectable Southerners. Allowing for the usual nonchalance of fringe groups where zeros are involved, perhaps we can take their claim of three thousand members to mean something between thirty and three hundred. The material I have is dated 1980, so it may even be that the party's brief hour is over; it doesn't appear in the Anti-Defamation League's current Who's Who of hate groups, and perhaps it has passed into oblivion, along with, say, William Dudley Pelley's Silver Shirts. But even if the Southern National Party is something less than an imposing presence, its name draws attention in a dramatic way to the enduring, fatal affinity between this sort of trashy ideology and the South. Hate-group trivia buffs will recall that the Silver Shirts, for instance, were headquartered for a time in Asheville. More recently North Carolina was home base for something called the White Patriot Party (the title of whose newspaper, *The Confederate Leader,* defiled the memory of some gallant men). And there have been and are, alas, many more examples.

To be sure, the South has no monopoly on racial and religious hate. I'm told, and I hope it's true, that more crosses are now burned outside the South than in it, and swastika-painting has never gone down well in a region as patriotic as ours. These days, the real hate-group heartland is apparently to be found in the Mountain States—and good riddance.

But many of the South's enemies still identify the South's culture with racism, and groups like the ones I have mentioned help them to do it. The mean-spirited impulse that animates them is something that no one with hopes for the South can ignore. If Southern cultural revival means this, or even a larger voice for this, then to hell with it.

Race hatred stands in contradiction not only to the Christian principles these groups always claim to stand for, but also to their professed devotion to the South. Someone who truly loves the South loves it for what it is. Sure, without black Southerners the

South would still be something other than a hot Midwest. But it wouldn't be the South.

Marshall Frady claims an old Georgia lawyer once told him that "It's been the Negro that's really made the white Southerner so different from whites in the rest of the country—we're much closer to them, by damn, than we are to the white folks up yonder in New York and Minneapolis. . . . We've got the same way of living close and easy to our skin, same kind of humor, same relishments in food. . . . Hell, we even got the way we talk from them. We're just a little paler in all these things, that's all."

Well, maybe Frady didn't make that up. Whether he did or not, maybe it's true. And certainly black Southerners can be every bit as conservative as white ones (racial issues aside, obviously), as many white pro-life evangelicals have recently discovered.

If "pro-Southern" comes to mean "anti-black," the South will never rise again, and it won't deserve to. Thank God that most white Southerners have come to see racism for the curse—for the insidious, soul-destroying poison—that it is. Black Southerners aren't the enemy. And the South won't be ready for self-government until we stop eating each other.

(Spring 1986)

❧ Old Times There ❧

The South is a very special place. For starters, it's special because Southerners like to believe that. In a new history of the North Carolina School of the Arts, the composer Richard Adler is quoted as saying:

> For the past twenty-five years I've been, on and off, coming into this state, and one thing particularly I've learned: that I've never yet been in a state . . . where there is as much state pride as North Carolinians feel about North Carolina. And this is to me—coming now from two eastern states, New Jersey and New York, where they are pretty blasé about things like this—something to really feel and be a little bit envious of. . . . I wish we had a little bit more of it where we come from.

And well he might. It's a precious resource.

A few years ago, when a couple of us asked a sample of

Southerners what they liked about their region, most talked about the land. They seemed to agree with William Faulkner's view that the South is lucky that God has done so much for it and man so little. A lot of them sounded something like Leroy "Satchel" Paige, who said this, to William Price Fox:

> I tell you something else and you can mark this down as a prediction. You give this country twenty or thirty more years, everybody's got any sense is going down South. Now you take it down there in the Carolinas, and over to Louisiana and then down into Florida. Why, it's like a garden. That's where a man can live. Hell, you want yourself some fish, you just walk out your back door and stick your pole in the river and you got them. That's when they're good—fresh like that. Then say you want yourself some fresh vegetables—I don't mean none of this frozen mess they're throwing at you nowadays. I said fresh vegetables. Like you want yourself some collards—you just go out in the back yard and just reach down and get them. 'Cause they right there. Then say you want some turnips or some rutabeggers with them collards, why you just reach down and scratch around and you get them, too. And maybe you got a bean vine whipping around the porch to keep the dogs cool. Why you just reach out and pick them right there.

But a good many of the people we talked to about the South mentioned something else, besides the climate and the soil and the open spaces. They said one way or another that they feel at home in the South. Even a Southerner as marginal as Woodrow Wilson felt that. Speaking at the University of North Carolina in 1909, he said:

> It is all very well to talk of detachment of view, and of the effort to be national in spirit, but a boy never gets over his boyhood, and never can change those subtle influences which have become a part of him, that were bred in him when he was a child. So I am obliged to say again and again that the only place in the country, the only place in the world, where nothing has to be explained to me is the South. Sometimes after long periods of absence I forget how natural it is to be in the South, and then the moment I come . . . I know again the region to which I naturally belong.

For all the homogenization, massification, and other ugly-ations that have gone on since 1909, Southerners still claim to understand one another better than other Americans. They still don't need to have things explained to them in the South.

In *I'll Take My Stand*, Stark Young wrote of experiences that bring tears to one's eyes because of the memories they evoke of some place. "That place," he wrote, "is your country." For many of us, the South is our country, and we just can't help it.

The South isn't unique in this respect. I know New Yorkers and Midwesterners and even Californians who feel something similar about their "countries." But certainly the South has a remarkable grip on many of its children's affections and imaginations, and some unlikely Southerners have testified to this.

Listen to a friend of mine, a self-styled Marxist who teaches at Atlanta University. Returning after a summer in California, he wrote me from El Paso: "Frankly I'm ready for home, i.e. the South—with all of its [illegible] which I bitch about but always return to." (I really can't figure out what the garbled word is; it seems to me he bitches about nearly everything.)

I remember well a New Year's Day party in London, 1978. We bought Jim Beam at fifteen dollars a bottle, tracked down greens and field peas in the West Indian market, and made do with some good English ham. Somebody's mother sent Kentucky pecans for the pie. A half-dozen Tennesseans and North Carolinians and a few bewildered Londoners drank a toast "To the liberation of our country." Fred Powledge, in his fine book *Journeys through the South*, tells about the similar party he has every year in Brooklyn Heights; I wish I'd known him when I lived in New York.

I'm going to tell a story that I've never told before—maybe shouldn't tell now, but what the hell. Here goes. In the early 1970s I wrote a book called *The Enduring South*. It argued that there are still many cultural differences between the South and the rest of the United States. A couple of years after that, I was at a sociological convention, coming down on a crowded hotel elevator, when one of the other passengers read my name tag aloud and exclaimed, "Why, you wrote *The Enduring South*!" When I allowed that I had, the man told me (and the rest of the elevator) that he had read the book while teaching in California, had asked himself "What am I doing here?"—and had thrown over his job to go back home to Louisiana, to teach in a small college there.

That was heady stuff for an assistant professor. Indeed, I believe it's rare for a sociologist of any rank to be told that he has changed somebody's life. Of course I was flattered—also somewhat embarrassed and virtually speechless. In the confusion I didn't get the man's name, and I don't think I've ever seen him again.

Ever since, I've kept this story to myself. Even now, it seems grossly immodest to tell it. Besides, I'm not sure anyone will believe it. I find it pretty unbelievable myself. But I've thought about that experience a lot, and finally it came to me that the story says less about my book than about the book's subject.

You see, *The Enduring South* didn't move that man. It's good journeyman work, not bad for a graduate student (which I was when I wrote it). But it's not really evocative; indeed, it's mostly statistical tables. That man wasn't moved by the book, but by what he brought to it: his love for the South, for his country, for the place where nothing has to be explained to him. The book only triggered a process of recollection. A plate of grits might have done the same.

James Dickey said once that he's more proud of being a Southerner than of being an American. I don't know how many would go that far, but a lot of us are just as glad that Southerners haven't had to choose between those loyalties since 1865.

(April 1987)

➳ Dulce et Decorum ➣

One of the most moving war memorials I know is on a wall outside the reading room of the British Museum. It is a simple plaque with the names of a hundred or so librarians killed in the Great War. Librarians. Think about it.

That plaque makes a point, doesn't it, if not perhaps the one it was intended to make. Are we better off because these young men died? I don't know. Maybe it would be easier to say if I were Belgian.

Here's another. A few years ago, hiking in the hills above Lake Como, my wife and I came across a little chapel dedicated to the memory of local lads who died in World War II. It was decorated with freshly cut flowers. The boys it commemorated had fought for Mussolini.

Now, to have left that beautiful place to die in the sands of North

Africa or the snows of Russia—well, obviously, the right or wrong of their cause is important, but why shouldn't their parents and girlfriends have built that chapel? Who could fail to be touched that, forty years later, they still brought flowers and burned candles?

I'm told that the Vietnam Memorial attracts more visitors than any other site in Washington. I'm sure that many who go there believe that the cause for which those servicemen died was futile, even wrong, but surely no one goes to gloat or to scoff. There are some lines—are they from Housman?—something like:

> Here we lie who did not choose
> To flee and shame the race from which we'd sprung.
> Life, to be sure, is not so much to lose,
> But young men think it is, and we were young.

The librarians, the Fascist conscripts, the Vietnam draftees—no doubt all were scared young men. But they did not choose to flee, and the memorials honor them for it. We can sympathize with their causes or not, but we shouldn't deny those who wish to remember their kin and countrymen. Maybe we should even honor them, too.

These thoughts came to mind last spring, as I was walking across the beautiful, flowering campus of the Southern university where I teach. I passed the pedestal where "Silent Sam" usually stands. Sam is a statue of a Confederate infantryman, and he is a memorial to the university's alumni who died for the Confederacy. That month Sam had been removed for a much-needed cleaning after years of exposure to pigeons and rival football fans with paint cans.

By the empty pedestal stood a young man, obviously showing a visiting couple around. All were Yankees, by their accents. "They've sent it off to be cleaned," I heard him say. "Eight thousand dollars! Can you believe it?"

Well, yes, as a matter of fact I can. In *The Last Gentleman*, Will Barrett, Mississippian, tells this story:

When I was at Princeton, I blew up a Union monument. It was only a plaque hidden in the weeds behind the chemistry building, presented by the class of 1885 in memory of those who made the supreme sacrifice to suppress the infamous rebellion, or something like that. It offended me. I synthesized a liter of trinitrotoluene in chemistry lab

and blew it up one Saturday afternoon. But no one ever knew what
had been blown up. It seemed I was the only one who knew the
monument was there. It was thought to be a Harvard prank.

Will was wrong to do what he did. But Princeton was more
wrong not to know what he'd done. Maybe Walker Percy, Mississippian, is slandering Ivy Leaguers here, but I doubt it. Say this
for the South: if somebody blows up Silent Sam, it will be noticed.

And I'm afraid, in fact, that it's only a matter of time before
somebody does come gunning for him. We're going through a spell
of Confederacy-bashing down here. Some black folks are starting to
object to state flags that incorporate the Confederate battle flag, for
instance, and the Ole Miss administration has dropped that same
flag as an official school symbol (largely, I gather, because coaches
said it repelled black recruits—first things first). Last word from
Maryland was that some schoolteacher was lobbying to change the
pro-Confederate words of "Maryland, My Maryland" ("Huzzah!
She spurns the northern scum," for example). There's even a move
afoot to change the name of the Dixie Classic fair in Winston-Salem;
the objection is apparently to the very word *Dixie*. It's nice, I guess,
that we've solved all the real problems of race relations down here
and can now take up the symbolic ones.

I'm actually more sympathetic than you probably suppose.
Maybe it is time that we recognized that to many of our citizens,
rightly or wrongly, the symbols of the Confederacy don't stand
for freedom and self-determination, or for a heritage of sacrifice
and honor and duty, or even for hell-raising, good-timing, don't-
tread-on-me rebelry, but for white supremacy, plain and simple.
Given that, they're entitled to their objections. Maybe we ought
to get government out of the act and let those who value the
Confederate heritage celebrate it privately.

But Silent Sam is a different matter. Like the Vietnam Memorial, he doesn't honor a cause; rather, he honors some brave men
who died in one. And notice I said "in one," not "for one." We
can't know what motives impelled those men, but we do know
that they were defending their families and their homes. And I
mean their homes: not the shores of Tripoli, not even the halls of
Montezuma, but, say, New Bern, North Carolina.

True, Sam was put up by the United Daughters of the Confederacy at a time when nearly all of the university's alumni, stu-

dents, and governors saw the Lost Cause as a glorious one. That's no longer so, and some want us to acknowledge that somehow. Fair enough, but surely we can find a better way to recognize that change than by denying our alumni their memorial.

Maybe we can learn from still another memorial, an extraordinarily sweet and fitting one, in the chapel of New College, Oxford. It just lists the names of the scores of graduates who died for their country in the First World War—including a half-dozen whose country was Germany. That memorial honors the dead, and speaks well of the living, too.

(February 1988)

⬿ Too Greedy to Hate ⬿

Recently there was a lot of hoo-rah in northern Virginia about a plan to build a shopping mall on part of the battlefield at Manassas ("Bull Run" to Yankees). At first, some of us down here suspected a federal plot to obliterate the reminders of two humiliating defeats, but it turned out to be just the usual crowd of developers pursuing the economic logic that seems to lead inexorably to the paving of any open space close to a major metropolitan area.

Now, there's something to be said for money-making as a goal—I'll say it in a minute—and in any case it does seem pointless to expect investors to get all misty-eyed about a piece of land they bought in good faith and pay taxes on, just because some soldiers died there a long time ago. But let's not forget that there are other ways to view life than through the cash nexus. Confederate propagandists used to argue that's what those soldiers were fighting about.

It may be that we in the South have now rejoined the Union in that respect. Back in the countercultural sixties, David Riesman observed that the only students he had at Harvard who wanted to make a lot of money were Catholics and Southerners. And survey research shows no appreciable difference in cupidity between Southerners and other Americans. But in the past some Southerners at least affected to scorn the values of tradesmen.

Consider, for instance, Colonel Robert Toombs of Washington,

Georgia. Colonel Toombs was one of the great unreconstructed rebels. When someone met him at the Washington telegraph office during the Chicago fire and asked the latest news, he replied that the firefighters were battling the conflagration heroically, but the wind was on our side. To my mind, the best Toombs story concerns the time some progressive citizens of his town proposed to build a hotel, arguing that it would give commercial travelers a place to stay and be good for business. The colonel listened with ill-concealed displeasure, then announced that any gentleman who came to town could stay with him and anyone who wasn't a gentleman shouldn't be encouraged to stay the night. The hotel wasn't built.

I admire that attitude, even if I don't entirely share it. If that had been all the Confederates were fighting for, they might have deserved to win. But old Nathan Bedford Forrest, that untutored horse-soldier from the unpolished Southwest, let the cat out of the bag. After a session of high-flown Lost Cause rhetoric at a veterans' reunion, he grumbled that if he hadn't thought he was fighting to keep his slaves he wouldn't have fought. As the title character in Walker Percy's *Lancelot* observes, "the Second Revolution in 1861 against the money-grubbing North failed—as it should have because we got stuck with the Negro thing and it was our fault." Lance does go on to call for a Third Revolution, but recall that he's in a hospital for the criminally insane.

Anyway, Toombs's attitude was probably a minority view even among rebels. Many, like Forrest, seemed to have nothing against money-making, at least for themselves. Certainly by war's end and for decades afterward there were plenty who felt like Faulkner's Jason Compson: "I haven't got much pride. I can't afford it."

A sad story: when President Davis and the Confederate government fled fallen Richmond, south to Danville, then south again into North Carolina, what was left of the Confederate Army was prevented from destroying the bridge across the Dan River—by the Danville police. The mayor and other Danville notables subsequently surrendered the town intact to the pursuing federal troops. In cash-nexus terms, the Danville boys were right, of course. The war was over. Life would go on. Why tear down a bridge if you're just going to have to rebuild it?

Maybe that's not the noblest attitude going, but we can understand it, can't we?

It's harder, though, to understand some latter-day Southerners who can afford pride but seem to have forgotten what it is. Consider, for instance, the Greater Columbia Convention and Visitors Bureau. They want you to bring your meeting to some of Columbia's four-thousand-plus hotel rooms, and they don't care whether you're a gentleman or not: you're welcome to stay the night, and they're spending the taxpayers' money to tell you so. A full-page advertisement in *Association Management* magazine shows a photograph of the ruins of Columbia, with the caption "After Sherman's March we fired our booking agent!"

Now, this strikes me as roughly analogous to a tourist ad for Japan with a mushroom cloud and the caption "After Hiroshima we cleaned up our act!" But in this, as in much else, the Columbias of the South are just following the lead of Atlanta, pacesetter of the New South, a town that billed itself in the hateful sixties as "the city too busy to hate."

Think about that. As my friend Fred Hobson once observed, that's a pretty sorry reason not to hate. Not too proud, too decent, too self-respecting, too Christian—just too busy. Compared to that, Fred remarked, even hate has a certain integrity. I once angered some Atlantans by writing that every time I look at their city I see what a quarter of a million Confederate soldiers died to prevent. Well, that's the kind of thing I had in mind.

But let's be fair. The absence of hate, for whatever reason, is rare, and precious. And, as big American cities go, Atlanta may be onto something. I once read an interview in the Pan Am in-flight magazine with a black minister from Boston who spoke of his hopes for his city. Why, he asked rhetorically, should Atlanta be "the only model city for black people" in the U.S.?

Do you have any idea how strange it is to hear a Bostonian use the capital of Georgia as a good example? True, the man was black. The millennium hasn't arrived; the lion hasn't lain down with the lamb; no white Bostonian other than Robert Coles has yet been heard to utter a good word for the South. But let's savor this anyway.

And let's hear two cheers for the materialism which certainly has something to do with that outcome. Our American polity is explicitly committed to the pursuit of happiness, which usually translates, North and South alike these days, as the pursuit of wealth. And there are worse ends for a society to pursue: strength, for example; usually, in practice, even virtue. Selling out your principles isn't bad if they're obnoxious, and principles often are.

The older I get the more wisdom I see in Samuel Johnson's observation that a man is seldom more innocently engaged than when he is making money. It can't be accidental that the most successful multiethnic society on earth is the one that probably best exemplifies stodgy, money-making, bourgeois values—I'm referring of course to Switzerland. Atlantans' smug vulgarity can be insufferable, but perhaps that's the price we have to pay for communal harmony and the envy of Bostonians.

(October 1988)

～ U.S. Out of Dixie ～

Browsing at a local newsstand the other day, I spied a startling comic book, issue #11 of *Captain Confederacy*. Its $1.95 price was even more startling (the last comic book I bought, back about aught-56, cost something like fifteen cents), but I had to take this one home, and did. Let me tell you about it.

In the book, it is the present, in a South that won the Civil War. The protagonist is an actor who plays Captain Confederacy, a superhero in Confederate television propaganda films. His former girlfriend is the actress who plays the captain's companion, Miss Dixie. There are a dozen or so incidental characters, including "Monsieur Hex," an underground agent from Free Louisiana, and Dr. Kitsune Lee, a Japanese woman, alias the White Ninja.

The story has to do with a resistance movement against a Confederacy that looks rather like South Africa. President Lee apparently freed the slaves in the 1870s, but signs still say things like "Whites Only Beyond This Point." (The Great Emancipator was the first President Lee. The current president, a woman, is a Lee, too.) Coming in at #11 as I did leaves something to be desired, but the plot does seem a little confusing.

Nevertheless, there's much to enjoy here. In particular, the letters section offers some engaging speculation from readers.

There seems to be general agreement that, in this world, the fragmentation of the U.S. didn't stop with the 1860 War. Texas soon split off from the Confederacy, and California became a separate country, too, along with adjoining parts of Mexico. To the north is the Commonwealth of Columbia, where (with no federal government to build dams) happy Native American salmon fishers have largely escaped history. Some of the letters are ingenious; one, for example, explains why the Girl Scouts are found in the Confederacy and Texas, and the Campfire Girls in the U.S. and Deseret.

There are nice incidental touches in the strip itself, too. One panel shows a can of Stars and Bars beer; the "Good Morning Dixie" television program offers an offhand reference to "the Yucatan Territory uprising"; and there's a baseball card for Fidel Castro, power-hitting left fielder for the Havana Smokes of the Confederate League.

The authors of *Captain Confederacy* are by no means the first to wonder in print about what the world would be like if the ragged legions of the CSA had swept to victory. There seem to be almost enough books on the subject for us to call it a genre, but they sure are hard to track down. A friend tells me that Ward Moore's *Bring the Jubilee* (1953) is one example, and Harry Harrison's *A Rebel in Time* (1983) is another. I gather the latter is about a twentieth-century sympathizer who travels back in time to show the Confederates how to make automatic weapons.

One of the best-known such treatments, and one I have read, is by MacKinlay Kantor, the author of *Andersonville*. In his unimaginatively titled *If the South Had Won the Civil War*, as I recall, the South wins after Grant is thrown from a horse and killed. When slavery proves economically unviable, naturally the slaves are freed. As in *Captain Confederacy*, the secession of Texas reveals the inherent weakness of the Confederate constitution—or, alternatively, the devotion of Southerners to their principles. Eventually, however, Texas, the Confederacy, and what is left of the U.S. are happily reunited after they make common cause against twentieth-century totalitarianism. Kantor's book was published in 1961, and shows it.

By now, white Southerners of five generations have enjoyed the counterhistorical fantasy of Confederate victory and Southern independence. In fact, that fantasy antedates the Confederacy itself. In 1860, Edmund Ruffin published *Anticipations of the Future*, a hostile response to the impending election of Abraham Lincoln in which the South endures eight years of Lincolnian tyranny before striking a successful blow for independence.

As time has passed, though, the image of an independent Confederate States of America has become droller. As in *Captain Confederacy*, the juxtaposition of Confederate imagery and the accoutrements of modern life makes for some odd effects. Here, for instance, is Will Barrett, in Walker Percy's *The Last Gentleman*. Will is twenty miles from Richmond:

> As he ate Ritz crackers and sweet butter, he imagined how Richmond might be today if the war had ended differently. Perhaps Main Street would be the Wall Street of the South, and Broad might vie with New Orleans for opera and theater. Here in the White Oak Swamp might be located the great Lee-Randolph complex, bigger than GM and making better cars (the Lee surpassing both Lincoln and Cadillac, the Lil' Reb outselling even Volkswagens). Richmond would have five million souls by now, William and Mary be as good as Harvard and less subverted. In Chattanooga and Mobile there would be talk of the "tough, cynical Richmonders," the Berliners of the hemisphere.

Sometimes, as here, images of an independent Southland are used only to amuse. Other times, though, as for Edmund Ruffin, they have served contemporary political purposes.

Consider, for instance, the October 1988 Country Music Association awards program. Just before Hank Williams, Jr., won his second-straight Entertainer of the Year Award, he regaled the TV audience with his then-current hit, "If the South Would Have Won (We'd Have Had It Made)." If you can leave aside the grammar (my wife can't, or won't), it's quite a song.

If the South had won, Hank sang cheerfully, he'd run for president and put the Supreme Court in Texas, so murderers would swing, "instead of writing books and smiling on TV." You wonder why Lloyd Bentsen and whatsisname were doomed before they started in the South?

Hank goes on. He'd have all the cars made in Carolina, and he'd "ban all the ones made in China." (OK, so geography's not his strong point, but all those Oriental cars do sort of look alike, don't they?) Far be it from me to give the Democrats advice, but protectionism and xenophobia à la Gephardt might have played better in 1988 than what they came up with.

There's much more where this came from, but the point is that plainly the song's subtext was a disparaging commentary on the election campaign then in progress. Surely it's no accident that a song imagining a pleasanter outcome for the late unpleasantness made it to network television and the *Billboard* country music top ten at just the time that some of us down here were biting our tongues while old George Bush went on about the Pledge of Allegiance—not because we agreed with whatsisname, but because, deep down, we're still not sure about "indivisible."

(January 1989)

II. The New South

❧ The Useful South ❧

President Carter, as you may recall, asked us to find something good to say about America. Well, if we regard the South as part of America, I think he ought to know that CBS News just isn't trying. In a single evening, three stories in a row said something bad about the South. One alluded to police brutality in Memphis, Mobile, and Houston; one reported a wave of crime in the streets of Atlanta; and one exposed gang warfare against Vietnamese immigrants in east Texas. Shortly afterward an awful baying could be heard as our nation's newshounds scented a revival of the Ku Kluxers. And the (nonunion) toiling masses of our region also seem to have become a hot topic again; the agitprop mills are beginning to grind out the kind of gritty books and grainy movies that we haven't seen since the halcyon days of Scottsboro and Gastonia. Yes sir, it looks like it's getting to be time to trample out that old vineyard once again.

Consider also the prominence of white Southern villains and fools on prime-time television. Fools first. Amos and Andy have been put out to pasture, but the Dukes of Hazzard and the residents of Carter Country soldier on as the most recent in a long series of white Southern happy darkies. Never mind that lots of white Southerners like those programs; lots of blacks were sorry to see the Kingfish go, too, but the considered opinion of the keepers of the national conscience was that "Amos 'n' Andy" fed the unfortunate stereotypes of white viewers, so—good-bye, Kingfish. But Dave Gardner never got around to organizing his National Association for the Advancement of White Trash, so it's still OK to portray Southern whites as amusing nincompoops. (Incidentally, one of the actors in "The Dukes of Hazzard" actually lived in Atlanta for five years, but the other is from Michigan or somewhere like that. At least "Amos 'n' Andy" used real black actors.)

At the same time that white Southerners are becoming established as television's prime fools, we're also making a run for the title of favorite villain. Ever since the producers of "The Untouchables" got the word that they'd be fitted for cement overcoats if Elliot Ness kept chasing criminals with Italian names, there has been a real shortage of satisfactory ethnic types to serve as villains on prime-time shoot-'em-ups. If you pay attention, I think you'll see a stable of white Southerners being groomed to

39

fill that gap. Just recently, for example, I caught your standard-issue rogue lawman on a "Charlie's Angels" rerun. I've seen a dozen other examples in the past year or so, and I really don't watch that much television. They've run from *Heat of the Night* and *Easy Rider* knockoffs to some imaginatively conceived down-home Manson Family types, and the writers are onto something, sure enough: for sheer menace, it's hard to beat the redneck villain. And, of course, no one complains about ethnic slander.

Now don't get me wrong. I'm not proposing a Dixie Anti-Defamation League. I think we can afford to be philosophical and indulgent about it. I mean, we know we're superior. I am struck by the fact that people who would walk out on anti-black or anti-Semitic remarks apparently don't think twice about the stock television portrait of Southerners as hicks and brutes, but I didn't bring the subject up to complain about the unfairness of it all. I just want to point out that not long ago, it looked as if things were going our way, for the first time since moonlight and magnolias went out of style.

As recently as 1974, for example, the *Village Voice* was peddling Sam Ervin T-shirts, having found virtues in that stalwart opponent of busing and the ERA that even us longtime admirers of the senator hadn't suspected were there. It was about the same time that the good old boy was being celebrated in such unlikely quarters as the pages of *Esquire*, and a number of movies (most of them starring Burt Reynolds) were presenting an image of the working-class Southern white that really was something quite new: no snakes, no sheets, no hookworm, but not the sentimentality and ersatz dignity of the old WPA treatment either. The last American hero was alleged to be a North Carolina stock-car driver named Junior Johnson. It looked as if the nation was ready for another of its recurrent love affairs with the South.

And when Jimmy Carter got the Democratic nomination for president the media really turned it on. You remember. Every newspaper and magazine in sight updated its "At Last—The New South" feature, interviewed a few tame Southerners to tell them what the hell was going on, and concluded that the nation was thirsting for the down-home virtues, after Watergate and Vietnam. The apotheosis of Ham and Jody and Billy and Miz Lillian was something to watch. In various combinations, they turned up on the cover of every magazine from *Time* to *Rolling Stone*, flashing (as who wouldn't?) those shit-eating Georgia grins. Meanwhile, I'm told, expatriates in Brooklyn Heights worked to recover their lost accents, and the *Washington Post* "Style" section reported that Georgetown hostesses were serving peanut soup. It all added up to a case of what John Egerton called "peanuts envy," an overdose of what George Tindall called "Southern fried chic."

Well, it was great fun. But it was just one of those things. A summer romance—it couldn't last, and didn't. Carter's kinfolk were soon pretty well consigned to well-deserved obscurity. Jordan and Powell came to be seen as key figures in the "Georgia Mafia" that supposedly exerted a baleful influence on the White House, having liquidated the legitimate claimants—Abzug, Califano, and a bunch of other New Yorkers. And we've seen what the media have to say about the South these days.

Is it just that now the Carter honeymoon is over and the South is tainted with guilt by association? Well, of course that's part of the story. The Carter buildup was so extravagant that, dramaturgically, there had to be a fall, even if the poor devil hadn't helped things along by turning out to be inept. But the idealization of things Southern preceded Carter's rise—indeed, he profited from it, with Tom Wolfe and Burt Reynolds supplying the script that Ham and Jody played—and the assault on the South now shaping up seems to me to have a larger point than just further discrediting an unpopular president.

No, I think there's more to it than that. The era of good feeling that set in early in the seventies reflected political interests outside the South. The South was being used, as it often has been. It was being used by some non-Southerners to flog others. The glowing reports of Southern progress in race relations served as a standing reproach to those Northern and Western communities that were dragging their heels on school desegregation. Senator Sam's principled integrity—newly discovered—provided a dramatic counterpoint to the moral sleaziness of the Nixon White House. The good old boy's laid-back insouciance was in striking contrast to the methodical, competitive, cost-effective style of the Best and the Brightest, a style that had supposedly bogged down in the Indochinese jungles. And the only alternative to four more years of Gerald Ford was this Baptist peanut-merchant from South

Georgia. So the mythmakers got to work, and we have seen the results.

But now there's no further purpose to be served by idealizing the South. On the contrary, the sectional interests of the "national" media dictate some hasty demythologizing—or, rather, dusting off the alternative, unflattering myth that has always been held in reserve. The seventies saw something of a hemorrhage of population and resources from the Northeast to the "Sunbelt"—mostly to the West, but partly to the South as well. The folks who are left up yonder are starting to get worried about their declining tax base and congressional representation. I think we may be in for a spell of old-timey sectional ear-pulling and eye-gouging. (In fact, we're already seeing a struggle in Congress to take the South's welfare away by redefining the formulas for urban-development grants, but that's another story; my present point has to do with injurious insult.)

Ponder this. The American Dance Theater recently moved from Connecticut to Durham, North Carolina. Isn't that weird? Durham. Shoot, even North Carolinians look down on Durham.

Still, there it is. When a friend of mine heard about that, he wrote me: "Here's my plan: First we take their textile mills. Then we take their toe-dancers. Then we reopen Andersonville Prison. . . ." You can bet the Yankees don't like them apples one damn bit. So how about a few stories on the Klan revival? And maybe throw in something on brown lung while you're at it. It may not be too late: "Hey, folks—There's no New South. Honest! Don't go!"

(Fall 1979)

❧ Plain Folk of the New South ❧

I've been reading two books that examine two of the most misunderstood groups in America, Southern women and Southern blue-collar workers. Each book is a letdown in its own way, but you might want to read them both—not buy them, necessarily, just read them—because when the authors get out of the way some interesting people get to talk.

Sharon McKern, "an Austin-based writer and free-lance photographer," has written the less objectionable book because, bless her heart, she means well. *Redneck Mothers, Good Ol' Girls, and Other Southern Belles: A Celebration of the Women of Dixie* is indeed a "celebration," relentlessly so, and early on a male reader is ready to acknowledge that Southern women really do deserve the veneration we've always said they did, if not exactly for the reasons we thought. Along with McKern's insistence that Southern women are strong, liberated, trustworthy, loyal, helpful, friendly, courteous, kind, etc., are some insightful observations, but they tend to get lost in a sort of "Hee Haw" style that's got more colorful turns of phrase than a blue-tick hound has fleas in July. McKern is also big on the portentous one-sentence paragraph.

Like this.

In the early going, before the style begins to cloy, the book is often downright funny, although if you didn't like Florence King's *Southern Ladies and Gentlemen,* you won't like this one either. Larry King, Paul Hemphill, Peter Gent, and Liz Carpenter say they loved the whole thing, and maybe they did, but it began to get to me about page 25.

That was enough, however, to get me through a fine chapter called "New Strains of Scarlett Fever" (see what I mean?), which offers a typology of modern Southern women to set alongside the good old boy, the redneck, and the Southern gentleman. This exercise in the identification of what a sociologist would call "social types" is a useful field guide to the feminine fauna of the South; Southerners will recognize them on sight, and maybe Yankees will learn something.

About the time McKern's prose gets tedious, thank goodness, we start to hear from an incredible variety of women—ladies and otherwise—ranging from socialites and hard-driving businesswomen to country-music singers and a New Orleans hooker. All agree with the author, each other, and me that Southern women are neater than cat doo. There are some surprises, though, that make the book worth reading. For my part, I loved it when a black social worker came out of the closet as a Southern chauvinist: "In certain ways we've been more integrated here than [Northerners] have ever been. But they seem to feel superior to all Southerners, black and white."

Miz McKern is a feminist, but she's not doctrinaire about it. A good many of the women she talks with have no use for the ERA, for instance, but she lets them present their point of view. Her politics are liberal, in a Southern way, but they're not obtrusive. She's marvelously tolerant, also in a Southern way, of people whose views she doesn't share. She does draw the line at the opinions of Mrs. Dizzy Dean, but she doesn't insist that her reader do so. And she does a fine job of appreciating some women who tend to get underappreciated these days: mothers, politicians' wives, and garden-club ladies.

Robert Botsch, on the other hand, is doctrinaire. In *We Shall Not Overcome: Populism and Southern Blue-Collar Workers* he has a nasty way of putting down people whose views he doesn't share with the highfalutin' social-science cheap shot, from-the-hip psychology and sociology. Basically, he wants to know why Southern workers don't behave the way he thinks they should—that is, join hands, black and white, and smite the bosses. He sees nothing good about racial or regional conflict, but believes that class conflict is self-evidently laudable.

Speaking of smiting, though, I ought to let up on the boy. He's young, and maybe we should make some allowances. This was a Ph.D. dissertation, and criticizing the prose or thought in most dissertations is like killing Japanese beetles with dynamite.

Tell you what: Ignore everything in the book that isn't indented and direct your attention to the long excerpts from his interviews with fifteen North Carolina furniture workers (all male, five black, ten white). You may be as surprised as Botsch was. You'll find testimony to the continued importance of religion in Southern blue-collar life. (Botsch, coming on like a manipulative elitist, finds a silver lining, suggesting that populist politicians can adopt the style and rhetoric of preachers, so long as they don't take up their retrograde views about pornography and dope.) Several of these men value their family lives above economic advancement (which Botsch thinks is because such advancement is closed to them). Most of them want higher wages, but they steadfastly refuse to see this as a matter of greater equality: the Tenth Commandment is in pretty good shape. Nearly all take pride in their independence and self-reliance and don't think much of the government's helping people who won't work, although they are genuinely compassionate toward those who can't. They believe hard work and merit should be rewarded and seem to favor national health insurance because sickness can wipe out the savings of hardworking folks and keep people from getting what they deserve.

A separate chapter on their racial views defies easy summary but ought to be read by anyone who cares about Southern race relations. For the most part, the whites believe hardworking and meritorious blacks ought to be rewarded, too, although some doubt that blacks are as hardworking and meritorious as whites, on the average. They don't have much use for busing or quotas, but they don't have much use for segregation either. Most have black friends; few are racists, and fewer still bigots.

For most white readers, perhaps the greatest surprise will be the range of views held by the five black workers. One is virtually a segregationist, and another is so resentful about taxes and government intrusion that he'd probably vote Libertarian if he voted at all. One is something of a militant (now retired, but he still speaks the language), while another supported Carter enthusiastically in 1976 because he was getting tired of "listening to all these slick Yankees who think they know everything and have all the answers," and felt he could understand and trust a fellow Southerner.

Unlike McKern's book, this one's not a celebration. You get the feeling Botsch doesn't like most of his informants, and you won't like all of them either. There are soreheads, a redneck of the old school, a couple of all-around losers. But, by and large, these are decent men, doing their best to support their families, do right in the sight of God, and have a good time once in a while. Botsch finds them disappointing, but I'm proud to have them on my side.

Two books, then, with some good talk from good people, worth putting up with some tedious (McKern) or tendentious (Botsch) "analysis" for. And there are some lessons here, for the do-it-yourselfer. If you want to know why the ERA didn't make much headway in the South, read McKern. If you want to know why Southern workers aren't flocking to join unions, read Botsch. If you want to know why I like it here, read them both.

(Fall 1981)

∾ A Mississippi Homecoming ∾

Chauvinistic Southerners like me are hard to please. We don't like it when visitors pop in and out and say that the South has changed so much that it looks like everywhere else; but we don't like it when folks come calling and say that nothing important has changed, either. In an article in the *American Spectator*, an expatriate Mississippian named James Harkness did just that. He really should know better.

Harkness grew up in Greenwood, but now he lives in upstate New York. He clearly wants us to recognize that he's come a long way from his Mississippi roots, and, for better or for worse, he obviously has. But origins will tell: he writes like an angel. I just wish I agreed with more of what he has to say.

Harkness went back to his hometown for a visit and was apparently ticked off to discover that Mississippi is not an equitable, color-blind society. Like (one might ask) where? He does not vouchsafe to tell us what part of the U.S. he would have Greenwood emulate, and I doubt very much that he could be pleased by the white attitudes to be found in any American town with a significant black presence—much less any, like Greenwood, with a substantial black majority.

Now I've never been to Greenwood. I've never done more than briefly visit the Deep South. Maybe Harkness is right and things in the Mississippi Delta are pretty much what they always have been. Maybe race relations and conditions for blacks are better in upstate New York, or in Chicago or Detroit or the other cities to which black Mississippians have historically migrated. Maybe so.

But you wouldn't know to read his article that since 1970 or so more blacks have been moving to the South (in most cases returning there) than have been leaving it. You wouldn't know from his article that the South is the only part of the country where the percentage of black families living in poverty has decreased in the past few years, or that that percentage is lower now than in the Midwest. You wouldn't know that Mississippi now has more black elected officials than any other state in the country, or that a higher proportion of blacks hold public office in the South than in any other region. You wouldn't know that an increasing number of Southern politicians, black and white, have been elected by biracial coalitions. You wouldn't know that a majority of Southern whites now tell the Gallup Poll that they'd vote for a black for president. (OK, so some of them are lying, but what they think they *ought* to say is important, too.)

No, the South isn't a color-blind society. What some of us hope it is becoming is a working and relatively decent biracial society— a rather different thing. If that can be done, it will be no small accomplishment: I remember a college political science course about 1962 that held up as examples of successful multiethnic societies Switzerland and . . . Lebanon.

Not all whites share that goal. Not all are happy about the prospect. But a good many of us are. Harkness has little use for what he calls the "old, humorous, relentlessly superficial affability" of our region, but I suggest that it's close kin to the quality known elsewhere as civility, and that it will get us through this if anything can.

I'm not one of those who feel that Southern whites are uniquely fitted to instruct the world on race relations. Harkness makes fun of those who see something of value in the South's unhappy history on this score, and he may be right to do so. But for whatever reason—luck has something to do with it, and so do the good will and political skills of black Southerners—things are looking up in those parts of the South that I know best. And they may even be looking up in Greenwood.

There's no evidence in his article that Harkness talked to any blacks at all during his short visit, much less to any who had come back from the cities of the upper Midwest. On his next visit, he might try that. He could ask them whether they think anything of importance has changed.

It's OK to talk to black folks now, James. They'll even tell you what they think. And maybe that's the most important change of all.

(September 1986)

∾ Life in the Rust Belt ∾

August 1986 marked the fiftieth anniversary of the first field trials of the Rust cotton picker, an occasion little noted outside the pages of *Forbes*, where I saw it. Somebody should have made a bigger

deal about it. For better or for worse, that machine has trans-
formed the South in my lifetime, and maybe yours, too.

Oh, sure, you don't want to give Mr. Rust (whoever he was) as
much credit or blame as, say, Eli Whitney, whose invention got us
into cotton monoculture in the first place. Southern agriculture
might have diversified in any case, driving tenant farmers and
sharecroppers off the land. And, in time, industrialization would
probably have lured them off, with or without mechanized agriculture.

Besides, it's not obvious to some people I know that Mr. Rust
did us any favors. Are we in the South better off now that less
than 5 percent of us are farmers than we would be if half of us
were, like fifty years ago?

Well, there's no question that we're collectively better off in
economic terms. Getting out of cotton agriculture has done good
things for the South's per-capita income; fifty years ago it was
about the same as Venezuela's today. The good people of one Deep
South town even put up a statue of a boll weevil, in gratitude for
that bug's suggestion that they find some other way to make a
living. A blessing in disguise, they felt.

But a lot of individual Southerners suffered to make the average
Southerner better off. The collapse of cotton tenancy wasn't pain-
less, and we shouldn't forget that. Moreover, my agrarian friends
would say, Southerners of all people ought to recognize that man
doesn't live by bread alone. Have we sold our cultural birthright
for a mess of economic pottage?

Maybe so. But let me tell a story.

Last fall I was driving north from Sumter, South Carolina,
headed back to Chapel Hill on a pretty two-lane highway. It was
about 8:00 on a beautiful, crisp morning, with (believe it or not)
Beethoven's *Pastoral Symphony* on the car radio. I was feeling good,
soaking up the rural scenery, and watching for the notorious
South Carolina speed traps when, behold, I came upon a cotton
field, to the right of the road, where the crop was being harvested.
A solitary black man in a camouflage jacket and a cowboy hat was
perched high above what I now assume to have been a Rust cotton
picker. As I said, it was 8:00 in the morning, but he had already
covered half the field.

Was this sad? Did I miss the rank of cotton pickers, men,

women, and children, inching their way across the field, dragging their long picking sacks? Did I miss their sweet singing, evidence of their vibrant folk culture? Did I regret the passing of the ordered, traditional society that guaranteed them their humble living?

Not a chance.

Anybody inclined to nostalgia on that score needs to read James Agee's *Let Us Now Praise Famous Men* on cotton agriculture as experienced from the bottom. Better yet: pick some. I never picked cotton myself, but as a teenager I did work burley tobacco one summer for dinner and four dollars a day and I'm still resting up from the experience.

But there is the question of what those folks are doing these days instead of picking cotton. Some of them, as you may have noticed, have left South Carolina to seek opportunity in the North, where some have found it but many have not. The answer for others, though, was evident just across the road from that cotton field, on my left as I drove by: a one-story brick building with a sign identifying it as a factory producing bearings (I think it was). In the parking lot were a couple of dozen cars, vans, and pickup trucks: Pontiac, Chevrolet, Dodge (not a Volvo in sight).

This is the kind of rural industrialization that has been coming—slowly, slowly—to much of the South. It's not the sort of whizbang, high-tech, high-wage industry that advanced thinkers get excited about. It's the kind of industry that finds low-wage, poorly educated, grateful-for-a-job, displaced cotton pickers attractive workers. It's also often the kind of industry so economically marginal that it needs tax breaks and subsidies of various sorts to survive. It doesn't do much for our average industrial wage, or our image. Some say we're basically competing with the Koreans, on equal terms, and that's uncomfortably close to the truth. But it beats picking cotton, and Mr. Rust's machine does that these days, anyway.

Hamilton Horton pointed out in his contribution to a symposium called *Why the South Will Survive* that because industry came to us late, it offers some interesting, desirable features to offset its obvious shortcomings. Most of all, it doesn't uproot its workers. These factories don't have to be located in cities, near harbors or railheads; they form instead a sort of archipelago along the Interstate highway system. Their workers don't have to move to within streetcar distance either (recall those Toronados and Firebirds in the parking lot); they can stay in the rural communities where they were raised, and they do.

Just down the road from my cotton field and bearing factory were two Baptist churches, almost within sight of one another. I presume that one was black and one white, but I couldn't have said which was which. Both were modest brick buildings of recent vintage; both stood on carefully maintained grounds; both had large gravel parking lots. Both were obviously very much in business.

Who goes to those churches? Well, not cotton pickers. There aren't any left in that county, as far as I could see. Some farmers, to be sure, and perhaps a few agricultural wage-laborers. (The machine operator I saw could have been either.) But most members of their congregations would probably fall in the category the census bureau calls "rural, non-farm"—a quarter or more of the South's population, and a higher proportion here than elsewhere. These are folks who live in the countryside, generally own some land there, but work at blue-collar jobs in rural factories or commute to such jobs in the South's towns and small cities.

These are the children of yesterday's cotton pickers. A few years ago, when Howell Raines went to Alabama for the *New York Times Magazine* and tracked down some of the tenant children Agee wrote about, that's what he found: men and women living in mobile homes not far from where they grew up, working at jobs like welder, meat packer, nursing-home attendant.

I know a couple who live about an hour from here, in an unfashionable direction. They're ten miles from the nearest small town, and close to fifty from the nearest cities. Both grew up on farms, but she's now a receptionist and he's working as a mechanic while trying to get a job as a rural mail carrier. Each commutes an hour to work (in opposite directions)—an hour there and an hour back. They're certainly not rich, or even well-off; I presume they're in debt up to their eyebrows. But they have a comfortable new double-wide on six acres with a garden, deer, and wild turkey. He's got a boat that I covet, two cars, and a four-wheel-drive truck. A country boy can survive.

They have relatives nearby, and will soon have one even nearer; a son who just got out of the army is probably going to put his mobile home on their property. They seem to feel this arrangement beats apartment living, and I agree with them. They also believe their lives are better than they would have been fifty years ago; they work very hard, but I don't know anybody less nostalgic.

This new pattern of industrialization—made possible only by the automobile and decent roads—does have cultural consequences. In particular, it avoids the sort of "proletarianization" that is supposed to result from yanking people out of the villages and countryside and jamming them together in an urban working class. It allows for the possibility of blue-collar workers as individualistic and conservative as the farmers and peasants Marx had in mind when he groused about "the idiocy of rural life." Certainly, in much of the South it has produced factory and service workers who support their churches, clean their graveyards, tend their gardens, hunt and fish, and generally manifest that vibrant folk culture we were talking about.

Of course it wouldn't do to romanticize this new pattern, any more than the old one. The South's rural, nonfarm population is more amiable than an urban mob, and contributes more to social stability. But we're not talking here about a happy industrial peasantry, miraculously preserved from the acids of modernity. To judge from the number of satellite dishes, a good many spend a lot of time watching television. We can hope they're watching Jerry Falwell, but it's probably the Playboy Channel.

(June 1987)

❦ The Forsyth Saga ❧

You may recall the events of January 1987 in Forsyth County, Georgia, when a newly arrived Californian announced his presence by attempting to organize a march in Cumming, the county seat, to honor Martin Luther King. That bait wouldn't tempt an undiscriminating catfish, but a few of the local old boys rose to it anyway, displaying once again the simplicity that is one of their simultaneously endearing and infuriating traits. The reflexive

threats they proceeded to issue were enough to persuade the
newcomer to change his plans.

Now, many of us think folks ought to be able to march for any
damn-fool reason they please, or none at all, for that matter. One
Forsythian who felt that way, a white man named Dean Carter,
said he was going to march, with his family, whereupon the
threats got a little more serious. Carter, too, had second thoughts,
at which point the Reverend Hosea Williams, a veteran of the civil
rights movement who is now an Atlanta city councilman, heard
what was happening and showed up with 75 marchers. Williams's
party was met with bottles and rocks thrown by a mob of 400
(most of them Klansmen, according to the newspapers), and the
fat was in the fire.

The next week, Williams was back with more than 15,000 marchers. (As many as 4,000 more were left in Atlanta, forty miles south,
because there weren't enough buses for them.) A number of speakers addressed the marchers on the general subject of the unrigh-
teousness of Forsyth County—which does have an undeniably
sordid past. This time about 1,000 counter-demonstrators showed
up, many of them from out-of-state, but there was no violence; the
march's critics stuck to shouting insults and making obscene ges-
tures. Everybody went home and the media settled down to tell us
what it all meant. (The next week, the whole business dissolved
into farce as Williams insisted on going to jail because Oprah
Winfrey wouldn't let him on her television program.)

The national media seemed torn. Some wanted to treat both
this affair and the New York City lynching that took place about
the same time as signs of resurgent white racism, somehow
adding up to an indictment of the Reagan administration. Others,
I suspect, saw the Forsyth County episode as a welcome return
to tradition, with white racism back in the Deep South where it
belongs. Either way, most observers treated the event as (in the
Wall Street Journal's words) "an old-fashioned civil-rights march."

But, of course, an old-fashioned civil rights march is the last thing
it was. (If you wanted to see one of those, you could have watched
the splendid PBS documentary series "Eye on the Prize," which
debuted just as all this was happening.) For starters, the odds had
changed, radically. The rabble opposing the march were wise to
stay nonviolent since they were outnumbered not only 15-to-1 by

the marchers but better than 2-to-1 by the law. And added to the usual celebrities—Andrew Young, Coretta Scott King, Dick Gregory, Gary Hart (briefly, but long enough to find a television camera)—were two very significant ones: both of Georgia's U.S. senators.

But the big story, it seems to me, was that even many white Georgians without presidential aspirations were sympathetic—although the networks, the wire services, the major newspapers, *Time*, and *Newsweek* seem largely to have ignored that fact. (OK, I didn't see them all; the ones I saw ignored it.) For that angle, I'm indebted to Rocky Rosen, a reporter for the Duke University *Chronicle* who had the honesty and good sense to write his story *after* he went to Cumming.

I haven't seen a geographical breakdown of the marchers themselves, but most of those who talked to Rosen seem to have been Georgians. Certainly most of the marchers were white, and Hosea Williams had the grace to notice. Rosen quoted him: "There is not a more important moment in the history of America than today," said Williams in his speech (perhaps exaggerating just a little bit). "We never had a demonstration, from Montgomery to Memphis, that got more white folks out there standing up for justice than black folks." Rosen also noticed the "Cumming residents, mostly elderly, [who] waved to the march from inside their homes," and reported that the Forsyth County Board of Commissioners welcomed the marchers with a banner across the parade route and a full-page advertisement in the *Atlanta Journal*. Did you read about that in your newspaper?

Now, I don't want to go overboard. Those hateful counter-demonstrators were there, and not all of them were outside agitators. Maybe the banner and newspaper ad reflected merely the Board of Commissioners' fear that all this fuss is bad for business. If so, it would be in what is now an old Georgia tradition, pioneered by Atlanta, "the city too busy to hate."

Nevertheless, what went on in Cumming wasn't the relatively simple story that we saw repeated time and again in the early 1960s. The new story may be dramaturgically less satisfying, and it's harder to tell in ninety seconds on television, but it's a story that, on balance, strikes me the way it struck Hosea Williams, as good news.

By coincidence, at just about the same time all this was going on, *Rolling Stone* carried an interview with the immortal Bo Diddley, who had just been inducted into the Rock & Roll Hall of Fame. Bo wasn't talking about Forsyth County, but he could have been. After answering a question about the hard times he had faced as a black performer in the Jim Crow South, he observed:

> It's different now. The people down here in the South now is got their shit together. Everybody's fine; everybody gets along beautiful, and I'm so happy that that's what happened. But you can always find a fool—you can find a fool in church, you understand?

If everyone had Brother Diddley's true, fine sense of proportion, our national conversation would be healthier. Of course, the nation's op-ed pages would be emptier.

(July 1987)

❧ Fightin' Words ❧

Perhaps you heard something of the furor evoked down here when it was reported that a speech pathologist in Chattanooga, one Beverly Inman-Ebel, was conducting a class for those who wished to shed their Southern accents. (That's how the news stories put it. One could as well say, of course, that they wanted to acquire a Northern—or, as it's known in the speech biz, a "Standard American"—accent.) On investigation, it turned out that Ms. Inman-Ebel's course was just one of many; such courses were available in several other Southern cities.

Alas, despite ridicule and abuse from regional chauvinists like me, this abomination continues to spread, showing how irresistible is even a bad idea whose time has come. I'm embarrassed to say that my own university got in the act, when our department of "speech communication" offered such a course. When I inquired whether the taxpayers of North Carolina knew that their money was being spent to deracinate their children, the department's chairman tried gamely to put the best face on it. She offered the pragmatic argument that actors and media personalities and businessfolk need to be able to speak Standard American. (My buddy George observes that it's too bad our alumnus

Andy Griffith didn't take such a course. No telling what he might have amounted to if he could speak properly.)

People should take these courses, in other words, for the same reason that people teach them: because there's a mess of pottage in it. Or, if *mess* is on the list of condemned Southernisms, we can say: because it will help them make a buck. My colleague the chairman did not venture to say whether it is right that there are occupations where this is so, or whether students should be encouraged to enter them. She just offered it as a fact of life.

And, unfortunately, she's correct. Some non-Southerners—prospective employers, customers, clients, and voters among them—simply find Southern accents unpleasant. Billie Sue Knittel of Atlanta, for example, enrolled in a lose-your-accent course taught by an Ohio migrant named Shelly Friedman, and told a UPI reporter that the Yankee dentist she works for made her do it. "I talked too Southern for him." This jerk didn't want her answering his phone until she clipped her vowels and pronounced her terminal *g*s.

But at least he gave her the job in the first place. It was revealed a few years ago that some congresspersons had specified "no Southern accent" as a criterion for hiring folks to work in their offices. You know, some Southerners find non-Southern speech ugly, too; in a 1971 survey, about one white North Carolinian in eight and one black in six agreed that "I don't like to hear a person with a Northern accent." *Chacun à son goût*, and perhaps someone's entitled to have his phone answered in whatever accent he prefers. But recall that these are the same legislators who pass federal antidiscrimination laws.

And there's more to this than aesthetics. Apparently some believe that slow speech indicates slow thought—or so we might conclude from laboratory studies showing that the average non-Southern college sophomore assumes a Southern speaker to be less bright than a non-Southern one, even when the two are saying exactly the same thing. Since college sophomores occasionally grow up to be employers, their prejudices are of more than academic interest, and it may make sense to take them into account.

While it may be canny to cater to somebody else's bigotry, though, it's a risky business, and if you come to accept someone

else's standards for your own it can be downright degrading.
Maybe the miserable wretches who engage the services of speech
pathologists know what they're doing, in a sense. But maybe
black folks who invest in skin-lightener or hair-straightener do,
too. When it comes to regional accents, I side with Atlanta
journalist Lewis Grizzard, who wrote that "if you are going to
classes to lose your Southern accent you are turning your back
on your heritage and I hope you wind up working behind the
counter of a convenience store with three Iranians and a former
Shiite holy man."

So what can we do about it? Well, Mike Royko inadvertently
suggested an answer, in a column written at just about the same
time that Ms. Inman-Ebel's sinister activities were being exposed.
Royko wondered idly why it is that Joseph William Namath of
Beaver Falls, Pennsylvania, has a Southern accent and was known
for a time as "Joe Willie" Namath. He speculated that since
Namath's longtime occupation "involved being chased and fallen
upon by gigantic linemen, most of whom seem to be either black
or white Southerners," perhaps "Namath thought that if he
talked like them, they wouldn't fall on him as hard."

Royko also noted the prevalence of Southern speech patterns
in popular music, pointing to the career of Bob Dylan, a Jewish
boy from Minnesota who did all right once he learned to sound
like an Okie, and to the delightful spectacle of English rock
singers bawling, "C'mawnn all you pee-pull, let's git togayder."
(Royko's attempt to reproduce a Southern accent as rendered by
English rockers may not be entirely satisfactory, but you get the
idea.)

Finally, Royko wrote, one of his co-workers affected "Yup-
pabilly dialect" because he "discovered that he could impress
more females in singles bars if he spoke with a drawl. It provided
him with a more rakish, macho, good old boy personality than
did his Yale background."

Now, frankly, I find Royko's picture of big-city MBAs in Tony
Lama boots saying "Mah pu-laise or yores?" about as pathetic as
that of Billie Sue Knittel trying to enunciate. But the basic point
remains. When Southerners are good at something—football,
singin', picking up women—they don't have to shed their accents. If anybody's at a disadvantage, it's those who don't drawl.

Shelly Friedman's course is for the Billie Sues of this world. You don't see Ted Turner signing up for it. And I look forward to the episode of "Dallas" in which J. R. Ewing meets Beverly Inman-Ebel.

The best solution for us all would be pluralism. Why should all radio announcers sound as if they come from Iowa? Why should Shakespeare sound less strange in Standard American than in a Southern accent that's probably closer to the Elizabethan anyway? But if pluralism isn't realistic—if non-Southerners continue to give Southerners a hard time about our accents—our only alternative may be to take over. Then we could set up some courses to teach Yankees how to talk right.

[LATE NEWS FLASH: The *Wall Street Journal* reports that the Equal Employment Opportunity Commission has prohibited "job discrimination because of a person's accent or manner of speaking." The story goes on to say that "an employer must show a nondiscriminatory reason for denying a job because of a person's foreign accent or manner of speech." I can hardly wait for the first test case.]

(September 1987)

❦ Still Fighting the Civil War ❧

The influx of Northern migrants to these parts continues to produce misunderstanding. Some years ago the good people of Hillsborough, North Carolina, gave up their right to shoot marauding vermin in their own backyards in exchange for the town's designating an official municipal squirrel-shooter. Citizens whose nut trees were being sacked, gardens despoiled, or houses chewed up (it happens) could call police officer William King, who would come over with his .22 and take care of the problem.

This arrangement worked fine until a pushy newcomer objected to it. "This is just pagan, to be out there shooting squirrels," this troublemaker told the *Chapel Hill Observer,* and she took her case to the town council, which responded by hedging the practice about with bureaucratic restrictions. Now, owners of all adjoining property must be notified before a squirrel is shot, and the person requesting the shooting must be given a leaflet describing nonlethal methods of squirrel removal. Am I the only one who finds it weird when it's harder to kill a squirrel than to get an abortion?

This woman suggested in the newspaper that the long-term solution may lie in importing owls to control the squirrel population, but it's not clear why that's preferable. I think if I were a squirrel I'd prefer a .22 slug in the eye to being torn limb from limb by an owl. In fact, I'd prefer it even though I'm not a squirrel. Moreover, I don't understand why an owl is a natural predator and Officer King is not. But then, like most natives, I don't share this lady's Disneyesque view of rodents. As one Hillsborough man said of squirrels, "They ain't nothing but a rat with a bushy tail."

My solution would be to kill two birds with one stone (as the pagan expression has it): I'd arm welfare recipients and encourage them to forage. They could eat what they shoot, or sell it. Squirrel-based Brunswick stew is $7.00 a bowl at one fancy Chapel Hill restaurant.

Anyway, that story illustrates a problem I have, living where I do. I don't want to leave the South, and don't plan to, but I'm afraid it's leaving me. Let me explain.

There's a letter from Robert Frost in which he tells a friend of his plans to move back to New England and get "Yankier and Yankier." That's just about what he did, too, and most of us are glad of it. America's a better place because he did that.

Twenty-odd years ago, living in New York City, my wife and I came to a similar resolve about the South. Unlike poor, tormented Thomas Wolfe, we knew we could go home again. We did it a couple of times a year, and we wanted to do it for good. New York's a great city, but—well, I just had a letter from one of my former students who says she's had enough, too: "It's definitely not a good place for decent, polite Southerners, not even high-strung ones like myself."

But living in the North had changed my idea of where "home" was. I'd come to realize that I could find balm for my Yankee-jangled sensibilities not just in my particular East Tennessee hometown, but 'most anywhere in the South. Driving home, my chronic heartburn always let up somewhere around Hagerstown, Maryland, on old U.S. 11—about the same place it started up again on the trip back north.

Walker Percy wrote of a similar experience in *The Last Gentleman*. When Will Barrett and Jamie headed south, they would park their camper at night in Carolina and

> stroll to a service station or fishing camp or grocery store, where they'd have a beer or fill the tank with spring water or lay in eggs and country butter and grits and slab bacon; then back to the camper, which they'd show off to the storekeeper, he ruminating a minute and: all I got to say is, don't walk off and leave the keys in it—and so on in the complex Southern tactic of assaying a sort of running start, a joke before the joke, ten assumptions shared and a common stance of rhetoric and a whole shared set of special ironies and opposites. He was home. Even though he was hundreds of miles from home and had never been here and it was not even the same here—it was older and more decorous, more tended to and a dream with the past—he was home.

So I finished my studies in New York, shook the Northern dust from my feet, and moved South just in time for my first child to get "Durham, North Carolina" on her birth certificate—important to me, if not to her.

But now I look around and find that the North seems to have followed me. Our town and those nearby, like Hillsborough, have recently been flooded with immigrants seeking economic opportunity, gracious living, and year-round golf. I don't blame them. But please don't blame me for being less than wild about this development.

Northerners are nothing new in these parts, and in small numbers they used to provide a pleasant leaven. Some of them worked at fitting in (which isn't all that hard), and many more adopted a becoming diffidence. Even the ones who remained defiantly Yankee offered a stimulating counterpoint to the prevailing, easygoing ways. But there was no question whose region we were in.

Sometime recently, though, we passed a tipping point that's as easy to recognize as it is hard to define. There are now so many newcomers that they're no longer just the seasoning in the stew; they've become a lumpy ingredient in their own right, one that shows no signs of dissolving. People from places like Ohio and Michigan are moving into neighborhoods full of other people from Ohio and Michigan, and they all go down and get the *New York Times* on Sunday. Flannery O'Connor liked to tell a story about an Atlanta real estate salesman showing a migrant couple around. "You'll like this neighborhood," he says. "There's not a Southerner for miles." I used to find that funnier than I do now.

No offense, Northern folks, but I like the South because it's full of Southerners. You all are fine people, but you make me *tired*. I came here to be with people I don't have to explain things to, you understand? People who share my views about things like squirrels.

We've almost reached the point around here where Southerners are the ones who have to worry about fitting in. One of our students, a local boy, complained recently in the college paper that people are always coming up to him and saying, "I just love to hear you talk." "Let's get one thing straight," he wrote. "We are in the South. Therefore, I do not have the accent." Besides, it's impolite: "If we were sitting around the beach house in Cape Cahd discussing clam chowdah or Uncle Joe's haht cahndishen, I wouldn't stand up and say, 'Hot damn, you boys shore talk funny.' It just wouldn't be gentlemanlike." What really bugged him, though, is what bugs me: "There's something about having to defend my region when I'm still in it that I don't like."

Students aside, Chapel Hill looks more and more like Princeton these days. Some people think that's fine, and not all of them are from New Jersey, either. Our local realtors apparently love what's going on, and even some people who aren't making money off it seem to have bought the view that it's impolite to complain about the increasing presence of unassimilated Northerners.

Not long ago a reporter from the *Charlotte Observer* asked what I thought about the fact that someone can live in the South now and never have to come to terms with it. I told her I thought it was a shame. Soon thereafter, the long-suffering chairman of my department got a telephone call from an irate reader, a native North Carolinian (she said) who objected to my opinions or, anyway, to my expressing them. She insisted that I was "still fighting the Civil War" and demanded that he fire me. When he wearily told her that it's too late—I have tenure—she said she'd take her case to the president of the university and to the governor, if necessary.

Now, I'm not worried about that; both of those worthies are adept at dealing with cranks, as I have reason to know, having dealt with them in that capacity myself. And there's a nice irony in the fact that the last member of my department whose head was demanded by angry citizens was a gentleman and scholar whose offense was believing fifty years ago that black folks were entitled to be treated like human beings and American citizens.

But let's think about that accusation: still fighting the Civil War. Non-Southerners are never accused of that, no matter what they say about the South. Neither are Southerners who make it clear that they prefer the Northern way. You get charged with that offense if and only if you are a Southerner who would like to see the South stay Southern. And it's a sorry fact that the charge is often filed by other Southerners, like my accuser. Some of us like to joke about suburban Washington's being "Occupied Virginia," but let me tell you it's no fun living in Vichy North Carolina, either.

Look, I don't want to impose Southern ways on the world; I just want to hang on to them in the South. I don't think that one Princeton is too many, just that one is enough. I even feel that way about California: I'm glad it's out there, for all sorts of reasons. If the Great Wen, D.C., were just another unpleasant East Coast city—why, I'd say let it be. It's like food: when I go to New England, I want to eat broiled scrod and Indian pudding; I just don't want them on every menu down here. And I think it would be nice if New Englanders in these parts would eat Brunswick stew and okra, or at least keep their opinions about Southern food to themselves.

If that's still fighting the Civil War—make the most of it.

(May 1988)

∾ Bad Sports ∽

Football season is a depressing time of year, at least for me. Autumn Sundays are all right: football's an interesting game and the NFL plays it superbly. But Saturday afternoon always makes me blue. I try to be a good citizen, so I cheer for my university's team, but we really have no business trying to beat Clemson.

Look, I hate to be a walking cliché. Few things are more banal than professors wringing their hands about the scandal of college athletics. Especially in the South, there's not even much point in it. Down here, most folks seem to care more about sports than about anything else that goes on in our colleges. Few Southerners would agree with the Columbia history professor who said that he found his university's record football losing streak reassuring because it suggested to the world that Columbia's priorities were in order. We like winners down here, maybe because we got a bellyful of losing a century and a quarter ago.

But we really have lost our sense of proportion, so much so that I teeter on the edge of being embarrassed for the South. I mean no disrespect for Southern higher education, but few lists of top colleges and universities overrepresent our region; one that does, though, is the list of schools that raise the most money for athletics, where half the entries are Southern. Nor has publishing ever been a Southern specialty, but 19 of the 24 universities that published sports magazines in 1982 were in the South. There was an outcry a while back when the attorney general of Georgia removed the state troopers who had traditionally escorted Coach Vince Dooley on and off the field; and when the president of the University of Alabama hired a football coach with an unimpressive win-loss record, he got death threats.

All this may sound like good clean fun, but I don't think it's accidental that 12 out of 22 colleges under NCAA sanctions in the fall of 1987 were in the South; for violations having to do with football, it was 8 out of 11. The truth is that to field nationally ranked teams in the "money sports" (football and men's basketball) requires highly skilled, highly recruited, highly paid mercenaries, both athletes and coaches. To enlist them and to keep them happy and working seems often to require a measure of corruption.

Stories are legion, and there are new ones each year. One of my favorites involves the avid booster at Texas (get this) Christian University who sequestered a recruit in a motel room to keep him away from the competition until signing time, and arranged for prostitutes to entertain him. A friend who knows about these things says Texas Christian is unusual only in using professionals. Perhaps that's why TCU, when nailed on this and several other counts, had the shameless audacity to complain that the penalties imposed by the NCAA were too severe. (TCU, by the way, is the alma mater of Shake Tiller and Billy Clyde Puckett in Dan Jenkins's novels *Semi-Tough* and *Life Its Ownself.* I once thought Jenkins was writing satire.)

Another, less colorful example comes from the University of Virginia. Recruiters there, being smarter than your average TCU booster, did an end run around NCAA regulations. Finding that the athletic department had used its full quota of basketball scholarships, they offered a hot young blue-chipper a football scholarship instead, with the understanding that he would be allowed to "change his mind" about what sport he wished to play once he was enrolled at Charlottesville.* Now I ask you: Is this honorable? Is this gentlemanly? Is this building character? Is this what Mr. Jefferson had in mind?

I pick on Virginia not because it's the worst but because it's one of the best, one of the few major state universities for which there ever was much hope. Most schools that seem to have things in perspective are either poor or private. (Rice is one example, and Emory is another.) But even some private universities with aspirations to academic respectability bend to the cultural wind.

Tulane, for example, after its most recent scandal, had a chance to do the right thing. A committee set up to look at the athletic program could have called for the school to return sport to its proper place as an extracurricular activity slightly less important than debate. The trustees would have been unhappy, though, and no aggregation known to man is more pusillanimous than a faculty committee, so of course they blew it. Tulane is still going head-to-head with LSU.

Wake Forest also competes with much larger and less selective colleges. (People used to alter the road signs around here to read things like "Interstate 85 / Wake Forest 0.") Wake could have taken pride in fielding teams where every player could count to eleven with his shoes on. But, no, the Deacons recently hired a coach who used to work at my university, where he holds a record for

---

*When this was first published, I had a courteous letter from Mr. Terry Holland, Virginia's basketball coach, pointing out that the player in question was actually a second-string football player as well as a starter for the basketball team. If that's good enough to have earned him a football scholarship legitimately, I apologize for my error, but taking out this paragraph would have messed up my transition.

recruiting a player (subsequently in the NFL) with the lowest SAT scores ever reported for an entering freshman.

But this is football, I hear you say. To get within a hundred yards of the drug-crazed animals some colleges put on the field, maybe you need an IQ about par for eighteen holes. Well, basketball seems to be about as bad. There's a land-grant institution near here (which shall remain nameless, since it has enough ongoing troubles without being reminded of past ones). When one of its star players was arrested for theft, an enterprising reporter discovered that the lad's SAT scores totaled 470 points, out of a possible 1,600. Three of him, in other words, might add up to one MIT freshman (which raises the question of whether three MIT freshmen could handle him on the court, but never mind). This "student-athlete" was in fact illiterate, but that didn't matter to the schools that recruited him. Duke has gotten uppity since the *New York Times* called it a "hot school," but it was one of them; *Sports Illustrated* published a passionate mash note from its coach to this talented juvenile delinquent.

Some schools, including mine, point to graduation rates for athletes that equal or exceed those for run-of-the-mill students, but that's a two-edged sword. Even allowing for tutors, mandatory study halls, and guidance to easy courses and faculty groupies, if young men without much in the way of scholastic aptitude can hold down what amount to full-time jobs and still get through, maybe the curriculum is too easy.

Moreover, lack of intellect isn't the only problem. Most college athletes I know are self-respecting and/or God-fearing young men and women, but apparently it's hard to win ball games consistently these days without at least a few specimens of low-grade human material, young men who tear up parking tickets, beat people up in bars, steal bicycles (these are all cases I know firsthand)—and who expect, correctly as a rule, to get away with only slaps on the wrist, if that. Consider Mr. Jeff Burger, starting quarterback for Auburn in 1987. In a little over two months Burger was suspended once for plagiarism, once for accepting a free plane ride from a booster (to go dove hunting), and once for taking money from an assistant coach (to post bail on a concealed-weapon charge). Each time he was unsuspended on appeal in time for the next game. Auburn's vice-president for "academic affairs" let him off on the plagiarism charge; the ever-obliging NCAA winked at the others.

Now, it's not athletes' fault that the system works the way it does. Given how it does work, though, it's almost surprising that so many are decent, earnest, and hardworking. It may even be that thugs, liars, petty thieves, vandals, and unwed fathers are no more common among football and basketball players than among late-adolescent American males in general. But, frankly, I don't believe that. The adulation and special treatment—not to mention the steroids—meted out to big-time college athletes don't exactly breed humility and self-restraint. Consider the football player (also at the nameless nearby university) who was charged with rape: part of his defense was that a star like him wasn't used to girls who said no, and he didn't think this one really meant it.

I could go on and on. Memphis State, Oklahoma, Maryland, Georgia, Kentucky, SMU, Florida—I get them confused. Not long ago some Arkansas alumni lobbied to pull their state university out of the Southwest Conference, pointing out that it was one of only three schools in the conference *not* in trouble with the NCAA. Coach Broyles reportedly vetoed that move. College presidents come and go—sometimes for countenancing abuses, sometimes for opposing them—but athletic departments seem to go on forever. At Clemson a few years ago the president gave the trustees an ultimatum to the effect that it was either him or the athletic director, whereupon he was wished the best of luck in his new job, whatever that might turn out to be.

I can't be smug about that. A half-century ago, my university's sainted president, a man remembered in these parts as a sort of male Eleanor Roosevelt, proposed to do away with athletic scholarships. When it was made plain to him that he was going to be president of a university with big-time athletics or he wasn't going to be president at all, he had a change of heart. One consequence, if you want to look at it that way, came fifty years later when we fired our football coach; or, rather, when he was allowed to resign with a $900,000 settlement to make up for the years on his contract that, we were told, he had freely chosen not to work. (I know it doesn't make sense, but that's how they said it happened.) There had been an "erosion of confidence" among some "elements of the community": this is what a modern university administrator says when members of a booster club are unhappy.

Now, I've served on the committee that considers the admission of students with "special talents," and it certainly seems that our team should have won more games than it did. I won't get into specifics; let's just say that committee admitted a few large students whose special talents apparently didn't include schoolwork. If our coach couldn't win with that material, maybe there was something wrong with his coaching. I don't feel sorry for him—for $900,000 I'd leave, too—but I am sorry he lost his job, because it makes it too plain for comfort what the conditions of his employment were. It's hard to mouth the old platitudes about why we have an athletic program when losing coaches are let go without reference to how much character they've built.

Enough. I'm starting to rant. Foaming at the mouth is the next stage.

Can anything be done? Well, probably not. The NCAA continues to tinker with its pathetic regulations, trying to palliate what even a few coaches and college presidents have come to recognize is a smelly situation. But rule changes won't help. For a college or university, assimilating semiprofessional athletics is like building a perpetual-motion machine: some do better than others, but the undertaking is impossible in the first place.

Ideally, professional football and basketball would have farm clubs, like baseball's. If it were up to the athletes, I'm sure they would. There's no reason novice professionals shouldn't be paid for their labors, and no reason they should have to struggle with Western Civ as a precondition for plying their craft. But of course there's also no reason for the NFL and NBA to have their own minor leagues so long as colleges are willing to provide them.

The Ivy League with its characteristic, superb arrogance has chosen in effect not to play that game. Its attitude seems to be: let the Dukes, the North Carolinas, the Texases, Nebraskas, Michigans, and UCLAs—all the academic no-hopers of the world, the intellectual Siberias—let them train players for the professional teams; we'll just play with real universities. Down here, though, folks won't buy that approach. We want our colleges, by God, to *compete* with Valley State and Nevada–Las Vegas.

Well, call me an effete snob, but I like the Ivies' attitude. The Harvard-Yale game seems to be no less hotly contested just because all the players have SATs higher than their body weights.

As someone once said, athletics are to education what bullfighting is to agriculture. (That's an analogy, son—like on the SAT, you know? Don't worry if you don't understand it. What was that bench-press weight again?)

(October 1989)

∾ Editing the South ∽

I've written for a few Southern magazines, written about a couple, cribbed from some more—one way or another a few subscriptions and the odd newsstand purchase wind up as deductions on my income tax. Even the most banal of these magazines is interesting, if only because it's part of the image machine that exploits and celebrates and burnishes Southern difference and self-consciousness. Month after month, year in and year out, the very titles even of such humdrum trade magazines as the *Southern Sociologist* and the *Southern Funeral Director* say that the South exists, that there's something different (and usually at least by implication better) about it. One reason I follow these magazines is to keep track of what that something is supposed to be.

A few examples and maybe you can draw your own conclusions. Consider, for instance, *Southern Living,* an extravagantly successful house-and-garden magazine out of Birmingham that celebrated its silver anniversary in 1990. I'll have more to say about *SL*; for now, simply note that over 2 million subscribers make it not just the most successful Southern magazine but the most successful regional magazine, period, leaving the West Coast's *Sunset* far behind and inspiring imitators that include the recent *Midwestern Living.*

The publishers of *Southern Living* have acquired a number of other magazines, among them *Travel South,* essentially an expanded and freestanding edition of *SL*'s travel section, and *Southern Accents,* sort of a Southern *Architectural Digest. Southern Accents* appeals to a more upscale market than its parent magazine, but the basic message—that Southerners have both a different idea of gracious living and a special knack for it—is approximately the same.

In the interests of science, I read another magazine with pretty much that same view of what the South is about. "The days of Scarlett O'Hara may be gone," says an ad in *Southern Bride* (subtitled *The Magazine of Traditional Weddings*), "but that same graciousness and majesty, that same elegance and style so steeped in tradition live on in the Southern weddings today." No Kahlil Gibran here, in other words, and the magazine's letters column provides a forum for aggrieved traditionalists like the minister who wrote to complain about a couple who wanted "She's Having My Baby" played at their wedding. The advertising in *Southern Bride* is often more interesting than the editorial content. Regional chauvinism sometimes provides a potent hook, as it does for a Birmingham engraver who gushes that "There's Just Something About a Southern Wedding—Something Only a Southern Engraver Can Capture!" But usually the pitch is a little more subtle, like: "Thanks to her grandmother, her hair is red, her eyes are green and her flatware is silver."

A somewhat less old-fashioned image of the South is presented by *Southern Style*, a big glossy women's magazine from the Whittle Communications empire of Knoxville. "The Southern woman stands apart from her neighbors to the north and the west," the first issue proclaimed. "She is proud, she is dedicated, she is capable and she has the courage to live life, not merely observe it." I have no idea what this means, but clearly the editors hope that "the Southern woman" stands apart at least enough to want a magazine of her own.

One way she stands apart, allegedly, is in what she wants to look like. According to the magazine's market director, "Editors in New York don't know [Southern women's] taste in clothes or hairstyles and they don't understand their pride in the region." Before *Southern Style* came along, he says, many Southern women had given up on Yankee fashion magazines: "They either didn't want to look like that or it was unattainable." Maybe so. Anyway, the attractive women pictured in *Southern Style* are not the killer androgynes one finds in *Vogue*—although few are as unandrogynous as Dolly Parton, who graced the first issue's cover and allowed inside that "I'm always defending us. I'm quick to jump in when somebody tries to make light of the South."

If you've ever picked up a magazine only to find all the cents-off coupons already clipped, *Southern Style* has found the answer: each ad for Duncan Hines cake mix in its special "Salon Edition" (distributed free to beauty parlors throughout the South) is accompanied by a dozen coupons. This sounds tacky, but *Southern Style* is actually well edited, pleasant to look at, and surprisingly literate.

When you've had as much gentility as you can stand, though, turn for a purgative to a magazine that's one of my personal favorites: *Southern Guns & Shooter.* A recent cover shows two pistols superimposed on the Confederate battle flag and headlines an article entitled "The Threat From Up North—They're Still Trying to Take Our Guns Away." In the same issue another article reviews the "45 ACP: S—t Kicker of a Gun," and a regular feature is the "Sheriff of the Month." This is not some low-budget lunatic-fringe newsletter. At $2.50, it is chock-full of advertising and color photographs with captions like "Jan likes the feel of a long barrel, something she can get her fingers around and caress like a fine collector's item." Eat your heart out, Howard Metzenbaum.

Right now the question of Southern identity, what it means to be Southern and who qualifies, strikes me as up for grabs, and regional magazines offer a remarkable variety of answers, some only implicitly, others more forthrightly. The *Southern Partisan*, for instance, a fire-eating quarterly out of Columbia, South Carolina, still stoutly maintains the classic "Forget, hell!" position. The *Partisan* never apologizes, seldom explains. Its views on current politics could be characterized roughly as New Right, but the issues that really excite it are old ones. Very old ones. Its sections have headings like "The Smoke Never Clears," "From Behind Enemy Lines," and "CSA Today," and its habit of referring to Richmond as "our nation's capital" lets you know exactly where the *Partisan* is coming from. Personally, I'd enjoy the magazine more if its editors would stop giving their Scalawag Award to friends of mine, but the *Partisan* may be valuable the way an old musket is valuable: as a reminder of valor long ago, in simpler times, and maybe still serviceable in a pinch.

For something entirely different, check out *Southern Exposure,* a somber organ of the aging New Left from Durham's Institute for

Southern Studies, an organization spun off some years back by the pinko Institute for Policy Studies. The *Utne Reader* (a sort of countercultural *Reader's Digest*) recently gave *Southern Exposure* an "Alternative Press Award" as "an enduring catalyst for social change in a place defined by tradition"—you get the idea. *Southern Exposure* is the favorite Southern magazine of non-Southern progressives, since it tells them that the South is still primarily about oppression, injustice, and struggle. Occasionally, though, *Southern Exposure* takes time off from its favorite causes to appreciate the culture of the Southern common folk. Its appreciation is selective (voting for Jesse Helms is not an acceptable folkway), but it has published some good stuff on Southern religion and music, for example.

Oddly, *Southern Exposure* resembles the *Southern Partisan* in some ways. For one thing, neither magazine is a barrel of laughs. *Exposure* is deadly serious, while the *Partisan* sometimes tries to be funny, but I almost always wish it hadn't. Both magazines are usually predictable, but each tells you things that you won't learn anywhere else, some of them even true. Finally, both represent authentic, indigenous Southern traditions. The *Partisan's* tradition is the obvious one, but perhaps you can link *Southern Exposure* to the Populist movement of a century ago or even to Marse Tom Jefferson himself; at the very least it's working a field well plowed during the Depression by the writers and photographers of the WPA and the Farm Security Administration. *Southern Exposure* isn't the only remaining outlet for proletarian testimonial and hardscrabble documentary photography, but it may be the only one with ink that doesn't come off on your fingers.

If the Southern thesis is stated by the *Southern Partisan* and the antithesis by *Southern Exposure*, I think a magazine that came out of Little Rock a few years ago can be seen as the late-twentieth-century synthesis. In a book called *Myth, Media, and the Southern Mind*, Professor Stephen Smith of the University of Arkansas documented the emergence in the 1970s of a new and different "myth" of the South (Jimmy Carter had a lot to do with this, and so did Burt Reynolds)—not the Old South, not the South of "We Shall Overcome" either, but rather a down-home sort of place that had its problems, but that also offered good music, good food, good people, and good times. That was the South of *Southern* magazine.

Folks with loyalties to other myths, or vested interests in them, could not have been expected to like *Southern*, and they didn't. It quickly earned the *Southern Partisan's* Scalawag Award for an article asking whether the South needs a new flag, and the editor of *Southern Changes* (a *Southern Exposure*-like magazine published by the Southern Regional Council) dismissed it as mere entertainment, nostalgia, not serious. But *Southern* quickly became a quirky, engaging, unpredictable magazine.

Southern wasn't the first general-interest Southern magazine (*Southern Voices* and *Southern World* each lasted a year or so in the 1970s), but it was better financed and better edited than its predecessors. Linton Weeks, its editor, enlisted dozens of talented Southern writers, well-known and obscure, black and white, most of them young. He published Lee Smith's fiction, John Egerton's culinary essays, Roy Blount's humor, Florence King on Southern women, Fetzer Mills on stock-car racing.

Discerning readers will have noticed that I write about *Southern* in the past tense. It is no longer with us, but not for lack of readers. When it ceased publication in 1989 (not for any reason you're likely to suppose, but that's a story I'll get to later), it had a paid circulation of nearly three hundred thousand.

And that's very interesting. *Southern's* motto was "The South, the whole South, and nothing but the South." If it was Southern, whether good or bad, *Southern* was interested. This led to occasional false steps (I thought an article on upper-middle-class homosexual life in Birmingham was especially ill-advised), but the magazine's success proved conclusively that many Southerners of a certain age (roughly, well, thirtysomething or a little older) have moved beyond the old defensiveness on the one hand, the old guilt on the other. They don't object to portraying the South warts and all—as long as it's made clear that Southern warts are more interesting than anyone else's.

(January 1990)

∾ Editing the South: The Final Chapter ∾

Howell Raines once griped in the *New York Times Book Review* about "the *Southern Living* disease," an affliction he claimed leads Southerners to depict their region "as one endless festival of barbecue, boiled shrimp, football Saturdays, and good old Nashville music." Now, Raines was right when he described that house-and-garden magazine as "relentlessly cheerful"; other than that, though, the man doesn't know what he's talking about. Sure, *Southern Living* offers recipes for tailgate parties, but its shrimp are usually tarted up with some fancy sauce, Nashville music seems to be infra dig, and as for barbecue—well, let me tell a story.

If you ask me, one of the best pieces *Southern Living* ever ran was an article by Gary Ford on barbecue. When I said as much to a *Southern Living* staffer, though, he grinned. "You know, Emory [Cunningham, the founding publisher] really didn't like that piece," he said. "He almost killed it."

I asked why on earth he'd want to do that.

"Too down-home. Too low-rent."

Raines claims that "always with the South, things circle back around to race and class," but he's strangely tone-deaf when it comes to the social pitch of *Southern Living.* This is one genteel magazine.

Take his description of the *Southern Living* disease, though, give the blues equal billing with country music, add a dash of cultural anthropology and a touch of political reportage, remove the contemptuous tone, and I'd buy it as a description of the magazine called, simply, *Southern. Southern,* out of Little Rock, was also written and edited for a Southern middle-class audience, but for one that was interested in more than portraits of itself.

In fact, while it lasted, *Southern* epitomized a novel idea of what the South is all about, one that since the 1970s has been struggling for the region's soul with the traditional—what we might call the "Old South"—view. (*Southern Exposure*'s workers-and-peasants approach is a nonstarter, while *Southern Living* and most other regional magazines aren't in the soul-winning business.) Among the regional magazines published today, the *Southern Partisan* articulates the old idea of the South most starkly.

Southern differed from the *Southern Partisan* in many ways, but nowhere more obviously than in its treatment of black Southerners. As a rule, neither magazine preached on the subject; the two simply presumed quite different things. At best it might be said that the *Partisan* finally adopted the expedient urged in the Confederacy's last desperate days: blacks can be citizens if they're willing to bear arms for the cause. (More might find those terms appealing if the *Partisan* would quit stuff like running ads for reprint editions of *Little Black Sambo.*)

Southern, on the other hand, worked conscientiously to portray and to celebrate a biracial society—definitely not a color-blind one, rather one that both blacks and whites have built and must share. It sought black writers (successfully) and subscribers (I don't know), and it was surprisingly candid about the South's remaining and emerging problems of race relations. It comes down to this: when the *Partisan* says "Southerners" it usually means white Southerners; when *Southern* meant white Southerners, it said so.

Over a quarter-million of us found *Southern's* approach appealing enough to subscribe. But the magazine, like the fellow in the country song, lived fast and died young.

In the winter of 1988–1989 I heard rumors out of Birmingham that the publishers of *Southern Living* were preparing to start a general-interest magazine of their own, to go head-to-head with *Southern*. They coveted *Southern's* audience. Compared to *Southern Living*, *Southern* drew proportionately more young readers and more men, and some advertisers like that. Moreover, *Southern's* circulation was growing rapidly; *Southern Living* had pretty well saturated its market, reaching as it did a substantial fraction of the Southern middle class.

I was happy to hear these rumors—the more regional magazines the better—and unhappy to learn in March 1989 that they were wrong. *Southern Living* didn't start a competing magazine; it just bought out the 70 percent interest in *Southern* held by a Little Rock investment banking firm. The new owners promptly sacked *Southern's* publisher, editor, and staff and moved its editorial offices to Atlanta. In short order they announced that *Southern* was being killed, to be replaced by something called *Southpoint: The Metropolitan Monthly.*

Well, the move to Atlanta should have been a warning. Any magazine edited from there would have to be very different from the old *Southern* magazine. As an executive of *Atlanta* magazine told the Cox News Service: "The South that is Atlanta, the South that is Florida, bears little resemblance to the South that is Little Rock." This statement, meant as a criticism of Little Rock, is the kind of thing that makes Atlanta despised elsewhere in the South, except maybe in Florida. It is true, though, if only because there's some question of how many white folks in Atlanta are Southerners to start with. This same obnoxious yuppie argued that *Southern* "had this real outdated romanticism about the South." Well, *Southpoint*'s promotional literature made it clear there'd be no romance about this new magazine. It wasn't going to struggle for the South's soul: it was looking to sell it.

Speaking of souls, you've probably heard the one about how Satan approaches a lawyer and offers him wealth, power, and fame in exchange for his. "What's the catch?" the man asks—just the sort of subscriber *Southpoint* seemed to be looking for. (A sample cover advertised an article on the ten best lawyers in the South. No kidding.)

A promotional mailing threatened that *Southpoint* would be a magazine that "demands your attention." It would offer "a probing, candid look at the region's big changes, new players, shifting currents." It would have "more about the hot issues directly affecting your career," as well as "revealing close-ups of the coolest players and fastest comers who shape today's South, the big winners (and losers)." I found myself wondering what the lukewarm outcome might be when a cool player meets a hot issue. And, oh, it's hard to leave that phrase "fastest comers" alone. You know that Conway Twitty song about the "man with a slow hand"?

Anyway, the flier said that someone like me, "who works, lives and plays (to win!) in today's South," has "the greatest need for a magazine like *Southpoint,* written for and about the 'thought' leaders who drive our fast-moving, quick-changing region." Now, it seems to me that if parts of the South have become "fast-moving" and "quick-changing" the least we can do is preserve a decent silence about it. And who wants to live in a "driven" region, much less one driven by "'thought' leaders"?

In short, this new magazine was not promising. One contrast sums it up nicely: where *Southern* had articles on barbecue and biscuits, *Southpoint*'s brochure promised a story on good airport food.

This is just embarrassing. Yankees do this stuff so much better, I say let them do it all.

To be fair, when *Southpoint* actually appeared it was better than this mailing had led me to fear. In its first issue, an enlightening cover story put the financial affairs of Southern college football coaches under the lens. There was a pleasant article about Olive Ann Burns, author of *Cold Sassy Tree*, and a promising column on urban planning. All of the material I liked could have appeared in the old *Southern*, though, and the rest was either boring or silly. Real sundowners of articles dealt with banks and business and "cool players," as promised. The sort of flagrant advertising tie-in that has made *Southern Living* so much money was represented by an article on a bunch of expensive hotels (the "five best" were in New Orleans, Dallas, Houston, Miami, and—Washington!). There was a poorly researched article on the supposedly best bookstores in the South, and one I couldn't judge on Oriental restaurants. And there was absolutely no whimsy about this new magazine.

What we had here was a combination of *Fortune* and *New York* magazine in a Southern setting, a magazine for people who work, live, and play (to win!) in Southern cities—not at all the same thing as a magazine for Southerners. If *Southpoint* survives in its present format, I'll be curious to see how many of its readers are migrants to the South and how many are natives. I'm not sure what to predict, though. Will many migrants care about a Southern magazine? Will many natives care about *this* one?

Frankly, I believe that the *Southern Living* folks have made a big mistake with *Southpoint*, and that it reflects a generation gap of some consequence. Consider the reasons for *Southern Living*'s success.

Back in the early 1960s some genius at the Southern Progress Corporation, the publisher of *Progressive Farmer*, noticed that farmers, progressive or otherwise, had become an endangered species in the South. The South's economic development was making it hard to find Southerners who were worse off than their parents had been; migrants to the South had just begun to outnumber migrants from it; and the 1960 census had just shown that, for the first time, most Southerners were city folk. Wasn't there a place, this genius asked, for a magazine that would tell all these new-comers to Southern middle-class life how to spend their money appropriately? Something like the West Coast's *Sunset*, but for the South?

Southern Living got off to a shaky start; one early article was on helping your daughter choose her first bra. It soon hit its stride, though, and its four sections—travel, gardens, food, and home improvement—began to offer middle-class Southerners what *Playboy* used to offer adolescent males: a version of the good life, tied to consumption of the goods advertised nearby.

To be sure, *SL* hasn't been all recipes, garden tips, and advertising tie-ins. Over the years its "Books About the South" section has given respectful treatment to a great many books, some of which deserved it. A section called "Southerners" has profiled a number of admirable folk doing admirable things. Lately the magazine has lobbied quietly for downtown revitalization and historic preservation. But *SL* doesn't force the pace of social change. Its occasional references to Southern tradition have generally mentioned black-eyed peas on the table or azaleas in the yard, not, say, getting rowdy on Saturday night or going to church on Sunday morning—and certainly not any of the really troublesome Southern traditions.

Black faces have been rare enough in *Southern Living* to be striking when they do appear, but give *SL* a break, folks. How many blacks do you see in *Better Homes and Gardens*? *Southern Living* is, after all, just a "lifestyle" magazine, looking to attract the largest possible (Southern) audience. In that search it has not only avoided controversy, but prided itself on doing so. I hear that when the financial people from Southern Progress came to Little Rock to look over *Southern*'s books, one asked whether the magazine got many angry letters.

"Sure," *Southern*'s accountant replied. "We've had a lot of them."

Well, he was told, *Southern Living* doesn't get angry letters.

"Kind of hard to disagree with pecan pie," he observed.

To say that *SL*'s formula has been successful is grotesque understatement. The magazine's Silver Anniversary in 1990 found it on over 2 million Southern coffee tables, and its advertising revenues put it in the top dozen or so magazines in the country—not bad for a little old regional magazine. In fact, by 1985 *SL* had become so successful that it attracted the ravenous attention of Time, Inc., which bought Southern Progress for a cool half-billion dollars. (Time, of course, then got itself bought by Warner Communications, and at this rate Southern magazine journalism will soon be controlled by someone like Mitsubishi.)

Anyway, the growth of the South's middle class obviously gave *SL*'s founders a great demographic wave that they caught and rode for all it was worth. But they also had some help from current events. After all, in *SL*'s first years images of the South in the national media ran to stuff like mobs abusing little schoolchildren and fat tobacco-chewing deputy sheriffs on trial for murdering civil rights workers. I suspect that many early subscribers were folks just glad to see a glossy magazine that didn't paint their homeplace as the moral mudsill of the nation.

Of course *Southern Living* has never been explicitly defensive (that would be controversial), but for twenty-five years it has unceasingly portrayed Southerners as normal middle-class Americans who play tennis at the country club, live in nice houses, vacation at the beach, entertain graciously, eat well, and don't have those old backwoods hangups about liquor. If we, ah, deconstruct that portrait, we find a defensive subtext whispering that, really, the South is (at least) just as good as the North. And notice that this comparison is essentially in the North's own terms. We have every good thing they have, and some other things they want but don't have. You want gourmet food? By God, we've got gourmet food— and we can play golf all year around, too.

Given *Southern Living*'s success, it's not surprising that when its founders set out to devise a general-interest regional magazine they came up with—more of the same. When *Southpoint* portrays hip young urban fast-trackers who just happen to be doing their hip young urban thing in Southern cities, the implicit message is: just being in Charlotte doesn't mean you're out of it.

Now, I think there's a better response to real or imagined outside criticism, more effective and more accurate, too. It goes: "You bet we're different, and we like it that way, and if you don't like it, that's your problem." As Hank Williams, Jr., puts it: "We say grace and we say 'ma'am.' / If you ain't into that, we don't give a damn." (The only drawback with this approach is that you can get carried away, like Brother Dave Gardner—"I love everything about the South; I even love hate"—or Roy Blount, Jr., when someone at a Manhattan dinner party mentioned a *New York Times* article about Southern dirt-eating—"Hell yes, we eat dirt! And if you haven't ever tried blackened red dirt you don't know what's good!")

Southern magazine took this line by simply assuming what *Southern Living* had been implicitly denying for twenty-five years: that the South was different, that in its soul it was down-home, funky, country; that we do stuff down here that outsiders can't understand, and wouldn't like if they could.

I suspect—as a matter of fact, I know—that some people at Southern Progress were puzzled and annoyed by *Southern*. When they killed it and replaced it with *Southpoint* they weren't just reinforcing their monopoly of ownership; they were also crushing a competing myth of the South.

Maybe *Southpoint*'s variation on the *Southern Living* theme will work for it, but I think *Southern* had the right idea. I think the guys who invented *Southern Living* are looking at a new generation of Southerners that they don't understand. If they're not careful, they may wind up peddling a myth as irrelevant and dated as Hugh Hefner's pipe-smoking dream of jazz and sports cars and Playboy bunnies.

They have two problems, as I see it. For starters, many of the acquisitive yuppies that *Southpoint* is targeting barely think of themselves as Southerners. Whether they're homegrown or drawn here by our flourishing metropolitan economy, these folks are ready to move to Minneapolis if it will help their careers. Why would they want a Southern magazine? A city magazine, maybe, to keep up with the social scene, but I bet they'll take their business news and career advice straight, from *Savvy* or *Inc.*, *Working Woman* or *Forbes*.

And *Southpoint* is likely to have a different problem when it comes to the majority of young middle-class Southerners, to whom the South still means something. For some years now I've been teaching undergraduates who have no personal recollection of the civil rights era, to whom it's news that the South was ever the nation's number-one economic problem, who don't understand why the South might have trouble with its image. Unlike their parents (that is, unlike *Southern Living* readers), they're not going to care about *Southpoint*'s lists of the South's best hotels, bookstores, and Oriental restaurants. These lists are only superficially consumer's guides; at least half the point is, look here, the South has decent hotels and bookstores and Oriental restaurants. But my students have never known a South that didn't.

Moreover, unlike their parents, who often found all that old trashy Southern food and music and speech an embarrassment, some of these kids enjoy all those things, even value them as badges of regional identity, at least once in a while. When Emory Cunningham almost killed Gary Ford's article because he thought barbecue was too low-class, how could he have guessed that someday there'd be a two-hour wait to get into a blues and ribs joint in Alexandria owned by the chairman of the Republican National Committee?

We've got an example here to support what's known in ethnic studies as the "third-generation hypothesis": ethnic revival occurs when the confident, acculturated grandchild remembers what the anxious, acculturating child forgot. Another case in point (from the pages of *Southpoint*, actually): Ted Turner's son, Robert Edward Turner IV, has left the shop of his cosmopolitan, globe-trotting dad to work for Nashville's Country Music Network, where the motto is "We don't just play country . . . we live it."

Young Turner isn't alone; lots of young Southerners like to live country now and again, to dress down and raise hell to the music of Emmy Lou Harris, the Allman Brothers, Maurice Williams and the Zodiacs, or Howlin' Wolf. Even more interesting: some of them don't know who Howlin' Wolf is (their mamas and daddies didn't play that sort of music around the house), and they're willing to pay to find out.

Southpoint ought to tell them. After all, these are the people who've made a surprise best-seller, at $50 a copy, of the *Encyclopedia of Southern Culture.* Nearly three hundred thousand of them subscribed to *Southern* when that magazine expired. But *Southpoint* saves its music coverage for the likes of REM, an Athens megaband that is as much a commercial as a musical phenomenon.

After all, the Wolf's not a cool player. *Southpoint* saves that accolade for Atlanta desk-jockeys in pin-striped suits, and that's its real problem.

(February–March 1990)

[In May 1990, the Southern Progress Corporation folded *Southpoint*, after nine issues, citing declining newsstand sales and "lack of ad support in crucial categories."]

III. Southern Culture

Some time back, in *New York* magazine, Michael Korda wrote about the time he and his wife were dining in a London restaurant and some drunks at a nearby table got offensive. They threw bread balls at his wife and finally passed her an obscene note. Korda, who seems otherwise something of a wimp, flung an ashtray at them.

So far, so ho-hum. You can witness pretty much the same scene nightly in a few hundred roadhouses, and the outcome is usually predictable, unless somebody's carrying a gun (in which case, come to think of it, the outcome is also predictable). But this was London, remember, and this wasn't some urban cowboy and his girlfriend. Korda's wife blew up at him: "If you ever do that again, I'll leave you! [T]o be treated like a chattel, to be robbed of any right to decide for myself whether I'd been insulted, or how badly, to have you react for me because I'm your woman . . . that's really sickening, it's like being a slave." And so forth. Korda apparently stood there and took it—not because he was out of ashtrays to throw, but, he says, because he saw that she was right.

Now, that story was on my mind for a long time after I read it, because I was a lot less ready to see Mrs. Korda's point than her husband was. Not even all New York literati would agree with her. When asked to comment, Nora Ephron, sensible woman, remarked that no one ever propositions her in restaurants, but that if someone did she'd prefer that her husband handle it—and I'm sure she'd be too decent to second-guess the poor devil later.

Anyway, it's not obvious to me that a husband who defends his wife is treating her like chattel, much less that a wife *is* chattel. Such a man's behavior might well have less to do with what he thinks of his wife than with what he thinks of himself. It might be that he would do the same, or feel he should, for anyone—male or female, relative, friend, or total stranger—who was being abused and bullied.

But of course the fact that the abused in this case was a woman, and presumptively a lady, is not irrelevant. Those of us who were raised properly can be identified by the little dances we do to stay on the streetward side of women; if we go to that extreme to protect them from hypothetical mud on their hypothetical crinolines, how much more to protect them from real bread balls and figurative mud thrown by louts in restaurants?

And if this be "sexism"—make the most of it. Hodding Carter wrote once that Southern manners, men-women manners, are simply the rules of an endlessly amusing game. Like all games, this one is based on difference, but hardly on inequality. Sure, the game could have other rules. It might even be a better game with different rules. But it happens to have these rules, and so far, like that old-time religion, they've been good enough for us.

The rules have nothing to do with the attitudes of the players; they existed before the players learned them. For instance: a gentleman stands up for ladies. He may love them, admire them, respect them, hardly notice them, despise them, like boys better—it doesn't matter. If they are ladies and he is a gentleman, he will stand, and they will expect it. Never mind that an anthropologist I know argues that the custom represents a symbolic erection, that Javanese males in the same situation explicitly cover their genitals. To my mind, that only makes it more insulting for a man not to stand.

What makes the American, non-Southern, cult of spontaneity and sincerity so treacherous is that what someone does depends on what he feels—so you never know what to expect. Walker Percy wrote somewhere that Southerners know what manners are for: they exist so no one will not know what to do. Everyone *will* know. In that sense, a code of manners is marvelously democratic.

Getting along without manners is like playing a game where you make up the rules as you go along, and change them whenever you feel like it. The inevitable result is frustration, discord, and ill will. Some agreement has to exist before we can do anything.

Of course, it can be almost any agreement, so long as everyone understands. Let me give you an example. American visitors to Israel sometimes complain about Israelis' "rudeness." The behavior that occasions that comment is nowhere more evident than in bus queues, which appear to operate on Darwinian principles. But let the stranger approach a bus stop carrying a baby, as I once did, and the Israelites will part like the Red Sea. Old ladies will stand and insist that one take their seats. The driver will seem almost embarrassed to accept the fare. There are rules—yes, indeed. They're just different from ours. Once that's understood, we usually hear less about "rudeness."

What prompts all of this is something that happened—or rather didn't happen—on an airport bus in Dallas. The bus was full and I had a seat toward the front, when a man and two women got on. They looked around, saw there were no seats, and grumbled to one another about having to stand. I started to offer my seat to one of the women, but Michael Korda's story flashed into my head and I froze. Their accents were 100 percent New York. What if the woman was Mrs. Korda, or someone who thought like her? Every stand-up-for-ladies reflex screamed against it, but I buried my face in my book and kept my seat.

Ordinarily, I'd have said to hell with them: let them sit. When in Rome they can damn well do like Romans. But I was just too tired. Better to ignore them, I thought, better to let them think Southern men are as boorish as New Yorkers, better anything than to invite a feminist lecture in a crowded bus with a long way to go.

I swear that if they'd had Southern accents, I'd have been on my feet. Southern women—even Southern feminists, this side of Ti-Grace Atkinson—understand how these things work. They would know I learned my manners from my mother. But a New Yorker might think I'd made them up on the spot to imply that women are inferior (forgetting that in cultures where that's really believed, the *women* stand).

Courtesy comes in many forms, and perhaps at this unhappy point in our cultural history the courteous thing for Southerners to do is to practice our brand among ourselves, and wait for other folks to figure out what the hell they want us to do about them.

(Summer 1981)

∾ The Sense of "Southernizing" ∾

For as long as people have been writing about Southern character—and that's getting to be a pretty long time now—they've been inclined to mention Southern individualism. From Thomas Jefferson's letter to the Marquis de Chastellux, to Charlie Daniels's "Long-Haired Country Boy," Southerners have been inclined to mention this trait themselves. W. J. Cash probably discussed it most thoroughly, in *The Mind of the South*. He didn't entirely or even mostly approve, but his description strikes me as right on the money.

Things might have been different if history had given the proslavery theorist George Fitzhugh a couple more decades to work on the ideas he was developing in *Cannibals All* and *Sociology for the South*. Might have been, but I doubt it. To the extent that Southerners bought Fitzhugh's anti-individualist philosophy in the 1850s, I suspect it was because it gave them an elegant rationale for holding onto their property. Certainly the variety of proslavery thought that took off from Jeffersonian premises—that is, individualistic ones—was more influential, if less interesting to the intellectual historian.

George Pullen Jackson, in his book *White Spirituals in the Southern Uplands*, has given us a sort of parable for how Southern individualism works. He introduced me to the verb *to Southernize*, current in the nineteenth century. Many of the Southern gospel songs Jackson studied had their origins in the North, he shows. But when they were reprinted for use in the South the arrangements were often Southernized. (Often the publication indicated who did it: "Southernized by John Doe.")

What this meant was that each of the nonmelody parts was made more complicated, and more interesting. The bass, for instance, instead of droning away on three or four notes as the New England version had him doing, was given something like a different melody of his own to play around with down under the melody proper. Same for the other backup parts: none was entirely subordinate; none was boring. Everyone got to show off sometime.

Jackson points out that this often worked to the detriment of the ensemble. It was less harmonious, more chaotic than the original, un-Southernized version. But what the hell—these people weren't singing for an audience. They were singing for themselves and for the glory of God. If someone wanted to sing with them, instead of standing aside and finding fault with the harmony, he'd soon realize that the Southern way was more fun for the singers, whatever impression it might make on observers.

The Southern way in many things has been to make allowances for individuals. Nothing can make a bass into a tenor, but that doesn't mean he can't do something interesting. There has never been a shortage of critics to point out that this arrangement is, really, sort of messy; that it could be made more pleasant for the audience with a little more coordination, some regulation here and there, some small sacrifices of individuality on the part of the subordinate choristers. But Southerners just won't see their parts as subordinate. If it comes to that, we'd just as soon not sing at all. And if our critics knew as much about singing as they claim to know about music, they'd see why Southernizing is something the whole country could use more of.

(Summer 1982)

❧ Precious Memories ❧

George Garrett, in a splendidly cranky and very wise essay, observes that a nearly universal characteristic of Southern writers is their sense of loss, of "the dimming of many bright things and the falling away of familiar certainties." He notes that this is one of Southerners' most attractive traits, but that "it is mildly strange that what the very youngest generation of Southern writers laments and regrets the passing of has to be, in fact, among the crowd of new things whose arrival and presence on the scene was roundly deplored by the previous generation."

I know what he means. Older readers may not believe me, but I swear it's possible to be nostalgic about white bread and lunch meat sandwiches. For me, a Dolly Madison cupcake can set off a Proustian reverie of driving through a steamy Southern night, with WLAC blasting Hank Ballard songs. One can actually believe, deep down, that the decline of Western civilization dates from the death of Buddy Holly. I know. I do.

At the same time, I can be scornful about those younger folks who feel the same way about Simon and Garfunkel. And I am absolutely distraught when I think about what my own children may remember fondly. Izod shirts? Disco? The new Episcopal prayer book? (Actually, I may have inoculated my kids. "What's in life jackets, Daddy?" my daughter asked one day. "It used to be something called kapok," I told her. "I don't know what they use now." "But it's not as good, is it?" she said.)

Of course, Garrett's point is that we need to remember that our own parents looked on Buddy Holly much as the Romans must have regarded Alaric. Indeed, that was part of Buddy's appeal.

Our folks, in their turn, were given to lamenting that nothing had been the same since the War—meaning World War II, by which time the Golden Age was long past, according to *their* parents. This elegiac stance was certainly evident in the aftermath of Appomattox. Oscar Wilde, during his American tour, remarked that you couldn't admire the moon in Georgia without being told how much better it looked before the War. I gather, though, that antebellum Southerners harked back to Ole Virginny, of the seventeenth and eighteenth centuries, if not to Merrie Englande.

Maybe Garrett is right when he traces this trope to the Anglo-Saxon ballad. Lord knows it's alive and well in the latter-day Anglo-Saxon ballads of country music, where vanished scenes of our childhood and home make up much of the subject matter. Coupled with that pervasive nostalgia is a celebration of continuity, sometimes disconcerting, as when Hank Williams, Jr., rejoices that Florida girls still don't wear underwear, folks still get drunk at football games, his woman "still looks good in her T-shirt, standin' in the Georgia rain"—and "the New South, thank God, is still the same." It may be significant that one of the few songs even somewhat skeptical about the singer's own rose-colored memories is sung by one of the very few black country-music singers around. In "I Wonder Could I Live There Any More," Charlie Pride doesn't deny the feeling, but he does recognize that actuality was grimmer than he realized at the time.

There are really two sides to Garrett's anthropological observation: on the one hand, Southerners' regret at the passing of familiar things; on the other, our readiness to adopt new things, to naturalize them and turn them into familiar things—Southern things—whose passing we shall regret. It's startling to consider how many of what seem bedrock Southern institutions are actually recent innovations. In *The Strange Career of Jim Crow,* C. Vann Woodward even argued that that was so for racial segregation. Maybe he exaggerated, for rhetorical effect, but there are other examples. For instance, I dare say few of us now could imagine the South without stock-car racing, although we know, deep down, that it didn't exist before stock cars did. A happy historical amnesia can help this tendency along. I don't doubt that there are younger Southerners who think the Atlanta Braves were founded about the same time as the Ku Klux Klan.

Joe Gray Taylor has some nice examples in his informal history of Southern foodways, *Eating, Drinking, and Visiting in the South.* Heavily sweetened iced tea, for instance, the staple potation of the Southern summer, wasn't widely consumed until there were reliable supplies of ice in the Southern countryside. And however great Grandma's biscuits were, you can bet her grandmother didn't bake many of them: she didn't have the wheat flour and baking powder to do it with.

No, particulars come and go. I'll lament the passing of most of them as loudly as any man or woman here, but perhaps there's some comfort in the persistence of the lamentation itself, and in the great ability the South has shown to roll with the economic, social, military, and technological punches—taking over new things and domesticating them, getting cozy with them, missing them when they, in turn, are gone.

A fragment of speech I recently overheard in a local grocery store seems somehow to the point. One of the checkers, responding to an inquiry from a high-toned lady customer, turned toward the manager's booth and hollered: "Hey Bobby—where's the couscous at?"

(Fall 1982)

❧ Did You Ever . . . ? ❧

The eighties were not good years for Southern comedians (some of our politicians aside). First we lost the Reverend Grady Nutt, whose gentle Baptist humor was one of the high spots of the syndicated television program "Hee Haw." Southern Baptist preachers drink a lot of iced tea in the line of duty: it was Grady Nutt who taught us to refer to the sugar-loaded Southern variety as "40-weight" tea. His untimely death in a plane crash left his church, his region, and the world sadder and grimmer.

Not long after, we lost another "Hee Haw" regular, Junior Samples, dead of heart disease at fifty-six. Unlike most Southerners, Junior wasn't a storyteller. He wasn't even much of a talker; his inarticulateness was part of the joke. But when the camera came up on this salt-of-the-earth, good-natured fat man in overalls, lying in the front yard with his dogs—well, you laughed before he said anything at all. And whoever wrote his material got a good line off from time to time. Like: "Them folks is so poor their little baby has to sleep in the box the color TV came in."

Between these two deaths, there was still another, less noted. Brother Dave Gardner was not on "Hee Haw"—indeed, he hadn't been on television for twenty years. But to a generation of Southerners—my generation—he stood for good times and happy days. Rejoice, dear hearts, for his life and work.

Long ago, before assassinations, urban riots, jungle warfare, student unrest—before the sixties began in spirit, if not chronology—this down-home free spirit delighted us and puzzled Yankees in appearances on Jack Parr's television show and with his weird, zany records. He was surely the most off-the-wall comedian of a time before the phrase *off-the-wall* was current, a time that saw such formidable competition in the weird zaniness category as Lenny Bruce.

In retrospect, it's easy to recognize much of Brother Dave's humor as debris from his blown mind, a product of the reefer madness that was then pretty much confined to the black ghetto and the world of jazz musicians. (Brother Dave started out as a drummer and, after a fashion, a singer.) But this was before the great American middle class turned to dope, fulfilling the prophecy that it would in time make vice as banal as it had long since made virtue. Few of us then knew the signs, and Brother Dave was not as explicit as Cheech and Chong. All we knew was that he was a very funny man, and he was as much a part of campus life circa 1960 as Ray Charles, Bo Diddley, or Doug Clark and the Hot Nuts.

Surely no one who has heard Brother Dave's stories will forget the city cow and the country cow, or the Down-Home Players' production of *Julius Caesar*, or Little David versus the Philadelphians, or (best of all) the famous motorcycle wreck. Some of his one-liners were priceless, too, especially when he talked about the differences between the North and his beloved South: "The only reason people live up there, dear hearts, is because they have jobs there. Did you ever hear of anybody *retiring* to the North?"

As the sixties got less funny, so did Brother Dave, and by some accounts he went completely around the bend into paranoia, incoherence, and hate. We didn't hear from him for many years, but his memory became sort of the private property of Southerners of a certain age. We'd drag out those old records when the mood was just right, and laugh ourselves to tears, missing a man, a time, old friends, old selves. Not long before his death, I heard that an enterprising Atlanta journalist had tracked him down somewhere in Texas and had written a story that set up glorious comeback performances in a couple of Southern cities. I heard that Our People turned out in droves, chanted the old stories along with Brother Dave, laughed and hollered, and had the sort of good time that once seemed to have gone out of style forever about 1964. I wish I'd been there. Shortly after that, though, while driving through Mississippi, I heard the inimitable voice on a Memphis radio station, doing a commercial for a hamburger chain—and I almost drove off the road.

I'm glad that Brother Dave went to glory knowing that lots of us here in the mundane sphere (he talked like that) hadn't forgotten him. I guess there won't be any albums of new material, but that's probably just as well. The old stuff has done so far and ought to get us into the twenty-first century just fine. Ain't that a weird thought?

So long, Brother Dave. Goodbye, Reverend Grady. Farewell, Junior. I sure do hope there are more where you all came from.

(September 1985)

❧ The Garden of Eatin' ❧

The fact that snow is important to Eskimos is supposedly indicated by the seven or twelve or however many words they have for it. What, then, are we to make of the hundred-plus expressions for cornbread of various kinds that one folklorist uncovered in South Carolina alone? Obviously food is important to Southerners—perhaps in part because some have never had enough, and there have been times when no one had enough.

In *Eating, Drinking, and Visiting in the South: An Informal History*, Professor Joe Gray Taylor uses menus, recipe books, memoirs, travelers' accounts, even social science research to document what different sorts of Southerners were eating at different times in the past, and to discuss how hunting, gathering, raising, preparing, and devouring food have shaped the everyday life of Southern families.

Professor Taylor's book is organized more or less chronologically, with chapter-long digressions to discuss the food of special populations. An opening chapter treats the Southern frontier, where an abundance of game guaranteed that no one went hungry and where an early and lasting preference for corn in various forms (including distilled) was established. (As recently as 1960, nonfarm households in the South spent two and a half times the national average on cornmeal—and twice the average on lard.) Two chapters examine plain eating in the antebellum period, when hogmeat and various garden vegetables came to supplement and partly to replace the staples of the frontier period. The folks in the Big House and their slaves were working from opposite ends of the hog (each group gets a chapter), but they were employing pretty much the same raw materials as the white yeomanry. And everybody ate better at home than on the road: a revolting chapter describes the generally ghastly food encountered at antebellum places of public accommodation.

Even that, however, would have looked good to most Southerners during the Civil War, when agricultural manpower shortages, the depredations of looters and thieves, and an appallingly inefficient distribution system combined to produce hard times in the countryside and food riots in some Southern cities. The list of substitutes for coffee—parched rye, wheat, corn, peanuts, persimmon seed, okra seed, watermelon seed, and sweet potato—will give some idea of the desperate expedients to which Southerners were reduced. Taylor offers some interesting speculation on the effects of semi-starvation on the morale and fighting efficiency of the Confederate army.

After Appomattox, things returned more or less to normal— which for most folks sounds pretty good. Mass-produced Midwestern wheat flour, baking soda, and cookstoves meant that biscuits were no longer an upper-class luxury, and iced tea was brought to the Southern countryside when reliable supplies of ice became available. Coca-Cola, of course, was another New South innovation.

But at the bottom of the social scale, among the quarter of the South's population caught up in the sharecropping system, things were worse than ever. A steady diet of cornmeal and fatback, supplemented for some with clay, had its predictable consequences, which can still be seen today in much of the Third World.

Taylor ends his book with a chapter on the contemporary South. Although the incidence of pellagra is greatly reduced and the hookworm may turn up on the next list of endangered species, in general Taylor's picture of the cuisine of the newest New South is not a cheering one. There are more—and, it must be said, better—restaurants, but they run to fast food at the bottom and what Calvin Trillin calls La Maison de la Casa House, Continental Cuisine, at the top. Taylor observes that even at home, to judge from cookbooks, beef Stroganoff has become a traditional Southern dish. Still, there are survivals (in the barbecue and ribs department, for example), and some households haven't succumbed altogether to the blandishments of the frozen food section. There are also revivals: my wife has discovered that beaten biscuits (largely gone with the wind and with cheap domestic help) can be made with a food processor. And the natural affinity between beer and the Southern climate has at last been recognized, even made notorious by a presidential brother.

Taylor's engaging account is spiced with his own recollections of several decades of eating. The book is often thought-provoking and always diplomatic. (He takes no side in the Carolina-Texas barbecue wars, or in the uplands/low country question of whether "grits" is singular or plural—sometimes it's one, sometimes they're the other.) The book has pleasant illustrations, and it would make a good present for any cook or serious eater.

(Fall 1982)

～ Hey Good-lookin', Whatcha Got Cookin'? ～

I don't know much about cookbooks from a user's point of view since I don't cook much, from books or otherwise. Nevertheless, as an on-again, off-again dieter, I'm an inveterate cookbook reader. Like a taste for pornography, it's a habit that probably doesn't bear close examination, but whenever I'm in a strange town with time to kill, I hunt up a bookstore and see what the local Junior League has put together.

I recently came across a book called *White Trash Cooking*, by Ernest Matthew Mickler. Please understand that I wanted to dislike this book.

Let's start with the title. *White trash* is one of the very few epithets that no one ever uses sympathetically. Brother Dave Gardner, a possible exception, had such a unique spin that you couldn't tell *what* he meant when he talked about the National Association for the Advancement of White Trash, but for most of us "Smile when you say that" doesn't even apply. People will call themselves rednecks, but not, I believe, trash. So the sensitive may detect at least a whiff of bigotry. Just to get an angle on this, would you call a book of recipes collected from poor, rural black folks *Nigger Cooking*?

Well, I guess you might, but you'd better have the right credentials, and, even so, you'd have to be careful to strike exactly the right note. Mickler comes from hardscrabble North Florida roots, but he picked up a Master of Fine Arts degree in California along the way, and he doesn't quite pull it off. He doesn't scorn the unsuspecting country people who gave him many of his recipes and posed for his photographs, but he sometimes patronizes them, albeit amiably. They don't deserve that.

The book's foreword, written by the publisher in a sort of L'il Abner prose, doesn't help. And the plot thickens when we turn to *Vogue*, usually a reliable negative bellwether, and find a favorable review down there with the Calvin Klein ads, the pedophilia, and the high kink. (Please don't ask why I was reading *Vogue*. Just don't ask.)

For some inexplicable or at least unexplained reason, a number of the author's photographs are stuck in the middle of the book. They look about like what you'd expect from a California M.F.A. turned loose with a camera in the rural South. A blurb inside the front cover from the editor of something called *Aperture* praises them; personally I liked them better when Walker Evans did them in black and white fifty years ago.

But the book also has blurbs from Roy Blount and Ed McClanahan, who know Southern humor, and from Judith Olney, who knows good food, and from ex-Governor Jim Hunt of North Carolina, who knows—who knows? Anyway, curious, I paid my thirteen dollars, took the book home, and started reading the recipes—what a cookbook is all about, after all. And, bless my soul, it's pretty good.

There are actually three cookbooks here. The first presents Southern white soul food—hopping john, corn pone, and other staples, as well as exotica like possum and 'gator. This cuisine is mostly indistinguishable from the black variety, which would stand to reason even without interracial recipe trading. In both cases we're talking about the food of poor country people, making do with what's at hand; for both races, that has meant corn, pork, game, molasses, and so forth.

If you're only after soul food recipes, there are better sources. (My favorite is the *Buster Holmes Restaurant Cookbook*, from the New Orleans establishment where I first ate red beans and rice. As I recall, a bowl was thirty-five cents in 1968; last time I went, alas, it was closer to two dollars.) Besides these traditional entries, though, *White Trash Cooking* offers some recipes for modern poor folks. That still means inexpensive food. It also means easy food—one reason these recipes are regarded as trashy. But to infer that only a lazy, slatternly housewife would stoop to something like Freda's Five-Can Casserole is unfair, not to mention unkind. These are recipes devised by unliberated women who put in eight-hour days at shift work, come home exhausted to families that expect hot suppers, and only send out to Pizza Hut on special occasions.

Since women like these aren't the only Americans who appreciate cheap, easy, decent-tasting grub, I'm sure many others could use these recipes, too. Graduate students come to mind, as do yuppies saving up for a new set of speakers or a dinner at Chez Panisse (although they'll probably want to take the empty mushroom soup cans and Velveeta boxes to a dumpster in the dark of night). If you can ignore the cultural connotations of this food, in other words, you can eat well out of this book. I wish I'd had some of these recipes when I was single.

But those cultural connotations are sometimes hard to ignore. The third set of recipes in this book is the culinary equivalent of pink flamingo yard ornaments. These recipes are presumably what Blount and McClanahan find funny, and they ought to be ashamed of themselves; sneering at these dishes is too easy. But how else can you respond to something like Tutti's Fruited Pork-

ettes? Tutti's own granddaughter remarks that you can't get trash-
ier than a Hawaiian recipe with Southern ingredients.

Southern readers, at least, will probably end up by entering
into the spirit of this enterprise, however much they may hate
themselves for it in the morning. They'll note the omission of
some traditional favorites. There's no recipe here for chitterlings,
as I'm sure the author has heard from Salley, South Carolina,
home of the annual Chitlin Strut. Nor is the corndog mentioned;
like barbecue, but with less reason, corndogs are seldom prepared at home—why not, I wonder? The most conspicuous omission is the Vienna sausage sandwich (*petit saucisson en bidon*,
Michael Hicks calls it). Half a dozen little links right out of the can
between two slices of white bread, slathered with Miracle Whip
and dressed with pickle relish—now, *that's* eating. (In emergen-
cies, just Viennas and soda crackers aren't bad either.)

Once you get rolling, you can devise your own recipes. I recall
squirming with embarrassment for my political party when Tricia
Nixon once supplied some woman's magazine with her recipe for
Twinkie Surprise. (Hide a Twinkie beneath vanilla ice cream and
serve. Surprise!) Thinking about it now reminds me of another
regional favorite that Mickler doesn't mention: anyone for Moon
Pie Surprise?

White Trash Cooking deserves at least a look. It may even deserve
a place on your kitchen shelf next to Bill Neal's *Southern Cooking*
and John Egerton's *Southern Food*—the first a fine recent contribution to the upscale side of Southern cuisine, the second probably
as close to a definitive treatment as the subject is ever likely to
receive.

And while I'm plugging cookbooks, let me direct your attention to one called *The Famous Writers' Cookbook*. It is notable less
for the recipes (well, would you read *Short Stories by Famous
Cooks*?) than for the letters that accompany them. It's worth it if
only for Roy Blount's "Ode to Grits," which concludes:

> True grits, more grits, fish, grits, and collards.
> Life is good where grits are swallered.

(Summer 1986)

∾ Through the Stomach to the Heart of Dixie ∾

Recently, my wife and I ate at a restaurant in Macon, Georgia, where the menu proudly proclaimed, "Best Food in the South." Well, it wasn't even the best food in Macon, but the $3.25 plate lunch wasn't bad: country-fried steak, three well-cooked vegetables, banana pudding. I'll go back next time I'm in Macon, which is more than I can say for the place our hosts proudly took us that evening, a fern bar that might as well have been in Sausalito. If you know what I'm talking about, you'll love John Egerton's book, *Southern Food: At Home, on the Road, in History.*

As a matter of fact, everyone who eats—I mean *eats,* not just stokes, or grazes—ought to enjoy Egerton's compilation of Southern foodlore. Even those whose doctors have spoiled the fun will find vicarious pleasure here, if they can stand it. Egerton's way to the heart of Dixie is through its stomach, and he comes closer by that route than a good many explorers who have taken the high road.

His crafty idea was that Alfred A. Knopf should stake him to a gastronomic survey of the South, collecting recipes, visiting restaurants, picking the brains and writings of various Dixiologists, past and present. He ate in 335 varied restaurants and talked food with some four hundred varied Southerners. I envy him the conversation almost as much as the eating; among the names I recognized in his acknowledgments were John Lewis, Tom T. Hall, Reynolds Price, and Lee Smith. (Egerton even talked with me, which I hope doesn't preclude my plugging his book.)

This hefty book (nearly four hundred large pages) is like a good country dinner: overwhelming. After some preliminary appetizers, it gets serious, with a forty-page side-dish historical essay, full of pungent morsels on the relation of food to Southern culture and society. Two nourishing entrees follow: a section on "Eating Out" treats Southern restaurant food, and one on "Eating In" deals with home cooking. The book's margins are garnished with seventy-five of Al Clayton's tasty photographs of food, cooks, and eaters, and with close to two hundred excerpts from the works of Southern writers, nearly all of whom seem to have had something to say about food.

For dessert, an annotated bibliography offers more than three

hundred selections, ranging from scholarly monographs to Junior
League cookbooks. This is not to be consumed at one sitting
without risk of indigestion, but it's hard to stop.

"Eating Out" recounts the highlights of Egerton's eight-month,
27,000-mile tour of Southern restaurants. (Southern restaurant
food is often maligned by carrot-juice fiends, gastroenterologists,
and other subversives, but Egerton reports that his cholesterol
and triglyceride levels and blood pressure actually went down in
the course of his research.) He tells of the restaurants' histories
and settings, waitresses and countermen, customers and cooks,
and writes of great barbecue pit-men.

But mostly he tells about the food. One chapter recalls outstanding breakfasts (biscuits and gravy, brains and eggs, fried
tomatoes), another examines the universal meat-and-three-vege-
tables plate lunch, a third deals with memorable dinners. Other
chapters describe good family places and fish restaurants. Still
another treats the food of Louisiana, which has certainly earned
a chapter of its own.

Reading this book in North Carolina, of course, I turned immediately to the chapter on barbecue, and naturally I found much
that native Tar Heels could argue about. But we transmontane
Southerners (Egerton's from Kentucky) rise above these intrastate
squabbles, eat the barbecues of eastern and western North Carolina with impartial gusto, and even like the South Carolina stuff
with mustard, on rice. As a matter of fact, I've never met a
smoked pig I didn't like, and Egerton seems to agree.

An index to restaurants, by state, makes this section look like a
guidebook, but Egerton claims that's not his intention, and it's not
a good idea anyway. Half the fun of traveling in the South is
discovering these secret treasures for yourself. Still, Egerton does
write about many of my favorite restaurants, and his judgment is
almost always sound. There are a few serious omissions, and I
started to catalog them, but then asked myself: Do I really want
any fool with $22.95 to spend on this book to know where to get
the best catfish in North Mississippi, the most succulent ribs in
Knoxville, or the tastiest fried pies in Atlanta? Of course not, and
I bet Egerton held out a few places, for his personal custom.

So don't take this as a guidebook. Read it as a protracted essay
about continuity and change in Southern culture, and don't

complain if it neglects the best barbecue joint in the Western Hemisphere. Fame wouldn't be good for it anyway.

The second entree, "Eating In," offers some 150 recipes for sauces, gravies, jellies and jams, drinks, breads, main dishes, side dishes, and desserts. The recipes are good ones, but "Eating In" isn't just a cookbook, any more than "Eating Out" is just a restaurant guide. Egerton uses the recipes as occasions for mini-essays on corn whiskey, country ham, grits, muscadines, okra—this is starting to sound like one of Grandpa Jones's menus on "Hee Haw," but, here again, the message is sometimes that "progress" offers new ways to do old things.

Egerton asserts, in this regard, that "the South, for better or worse, has all but lost its identity as a separate place." Not a surprising claim from the author of *The Americanization of Dixie*, but many of us disagree, and now we can use Egerton's new book against him. He makes it plain that the South's distinctive foods survive, and that is not immaterial.

Maybe the great ceremonial dishes of the South are now produced only for ritual occasions. Maybe few drink mint juleps now save on Derby Day, or even think about hog jowl except at New Year's. But how many Scots eat haggis, as a regular thing? Yet they wolf it down on Burns's birthday, and their identity, if not their digestion, is the better for it.

And the more ordinary cuisine of the South is still a living reality in homes and restaurants and cafeterias throughout the region. True, in cosmopolitan parts like mine it survives more and more like the American Indian—on reservations, segregated in uptown eateries like Bill Neal's Crook's Corner (two stars) and kitschy chains like Bill Anderson's Po' Folks. ("What will it be tonight, dear? Szechuan? Mexican? Thai? Southern?") But I'd rather see it survive that way than not at all, and the lines at Crook's and Po' Folks suggest that lots of people agree with me.

John Egerton agrees, too. Just because he predicted the Americanization of Dixie doesn't mean he's looking forward to it, and this book should help to prevent that catastrophe.

(July 1987)

A wise man once observed that the existence of a nation requires that many things be forgotten—in particular, those things that divide its people. Maybe that's why the South never quite made it.

Black and white Southerners have had their little disagreements in the past, of course, and so have flatlanders and hillbillies, rednecks and gentry. Politics and religion have usually been at least as good for an argument here as anywhere else. But if you want a topic with real divisive potential, something really fissionable, let's talk barbecue.

In this respect (others, too, of course) barbecue is unlike grits. Grits glue the South together, if you'll excuse the image. Black and white, uplands and lowlands, everybody likes grits. A few years ago, a fellow named Stan Woodward made a marvelous movie called *It's Grits*, an hour or so of heartwarming grits lore, with testimonials from illustrious Southerners like Strom Thurmond and Craig Claibourne and from common folk including the entire crowd at a South Carolina Gamecocks football game ("Give me a G! Give me an R!"). The last time I saw Stan, though, he was starting to film a movie on barbecue, and he hasn't been heard from since. I'm afraid he's a casualty. Reporting Southern barbecue is like reporting Lebanon: risky business.

Smoked meat is a subject folks can get excited about, you know what I mean? Barbecue drives a wedge between Texas (beef) and the Carolinas (pork), and completely isolates those parts of Kentucky around Owensboro (mutton). Even porcivores can't agree: barbecue divides western North Carolina (tomato) from eastern North Carolina (no tomato), not to mention from South Carolina (mustard). You might say barbecue pits Southerners against one another. (Sorry.)

Now, personally, I don't regret these hard feelings. If they keep the South's proud local barbecue traditions alive—well, long may they wave. When a "Texas-style" barbecue joint opened in my Carolina hometown, I was delighted to see it go out of business within a year. Not that I don't like brisket; I love it, in Texas. But eating that stuff here was like drinking Dr Pepper in Munich—just not *right*, you understand? Southern barbecue is the closest thing we have in the U.S. to Europe's wines or cheeses; drive a hundred miles and the barbecue changes. Let's keep it that way.

Anyone who cares about barbecue needs to see a savory book by Greg Johnson and Vince Staten, called *Real Barbecue*. This is one important book, a cultural landmark. Remember a movie called *The Endless Summer*? This book does with barbecue what that did with surfing.

Johnson and Staten are reporters in Louisville, and they are fanatics. They are, in other words, just the men to travel 40,000 miles and eat roughly 200 pounds of barbecue (629,200 calories) in order to compile a sort of *Whole Barbecue Catalog*: 260 pages, with annotated listings of barbecue joints, sources for flash-frozen air-freight barbecue, recipes for side dishes, and plans for monster cookers guaranteed to capture your neighbors' attention. Boxed here and there are some tasty barbecue quotations (although not the raunchy testimonial from the North Carolina-born novelist Tom Robbins that the prurient can find on page 57 of *Another Roadside Attraction*). The book also includes nice little essays on such topics as the names of barbecue joints ("Bubba's" is indeed a favorite) and why Cincinnati doesn't have good barbecue.

Inevitably, the book has a Southern slant, since nearly all of the great pit-folk come from the South, and most are still in it. But Greg and Vince have worked real hard to include the rest of the country. Maybe too hard: their affirmative action has turned up what they claim is semidecent barbecue in Vermont and a mail-order sauce from Castro Street, San Francisco, that I think I'll pass up. When I know what these guys are talking about, though, they do have pretty close to perfect pitch (I'd thought the fact that O'Brien's in Bethesda was actually good was my very own secret discovery), so I want to try some of the places I don't know. As a matter of fact, I was reading the book while visiting Chicago, and tried to promote an expedition to Lem's or Leon's for some Southside ribs, but my Hyde Park quiche-eating hosts thought I was out of my mind. Next time.

I do confess to mixed feelings about the book's list of great joints, because it's almost a law that fame isn't good for such places. As Greg and Vince point out, for example, after Calvin Trillin wrote about Arthur Bryant's in Kansas City, it started selling its sauce in bottles with *price codes* on them. But since the cat is out of the bag, or the pig out of the poke, let's quibble (that's part of the fun).

I could show off by complaining that the book doesn't mention the Wild Horse BBQ, in Sallisaw, Oklahoma: drinks from a machine, no health certificate in evidence, a side order of jalapeños, and sauce on the beef ribs that seared my effete Eastern taste buds before I could tell much about the meat, but my Fort Smith friends swear by it. You'll probably get to Atlanta before Sallisaw, though, so I'll plug the Auburn Rib Shack, also unaccountably omitted. I don't know if Greg and Vince missed the Shack, or just hit it on a bad day, but it's on Auburn Avenue near the Ebenezer Baptist Church and SCLC headquarters, which ought to count for something. Harold's, near the prison, gets the book's highest rating ("As good as we've ever had"); I ate there once back-to-back with the Auburn Rib Shack, and I'd rate the outcome a draw.

If you get over our way, we could check out Allen and Son's, which the boys rate "Real good." Their hushpuppies went to hell about the time they put the hanging plants in, but lately they've come back strong. Or we could drive thirty miles to O.T.'s, outside Apex, which isn't in the book. O.T.'s barbecue is standard-issue Piedmont pig—that is, merely transcendentally wonderful. What keeps me and my wife going back are the accessories: great hushpuppies, and Brunswick stew that rivals the best burgoo I've ever had. (As a Tennessean, frankly, I find that Tar Heel Brunswick stew is too often just a peppery mush.) O.T. is a Baptist preacher and serves no beer, alas, but for a buck he'll give you an enormous plate of "skin"—pork rind. You can feel your arteries clog as you crunch your way through it. Both Research Triangle yuppies and construction workers find O.T.'s worth the drive for lunch. Once I watched the News5 helicopter plop down in the lot and fly off with several plates to go.

I could go on, putting Scruggs's unrated Knoxville ribs up against Brother Jack's ("Real good"), for example. But you get the idea. If all of this means nothing to you, I'm sorry for you. If you enjoy it, you can subscribe to a barbecue newsletter that Greg and Vince have started. (A recent issue included, among other things, the itinerary of a three-day, two-night, eleven-barbecue-and-one-fried-pie-joint tour of Kentucky. Between that and Joe Bob Briggs's *News of the*

Weird, my mailman has started to look at me funny.) Better yet, get the book. Give it to your aerobics instructor for Christmas.

(December 1988)

❧ Poetic Gems ❧

> Alas, for the South! Her books have grown fewer—
> She never was much given to literature.

Thus, South Carolina's J. Gordon Coogler—"the last bard of Dixie, at least in the legitimate line," as H. L. Mencken put it in his scathing essay "Sahara of the Bozart." Mencken's essay has by now introduced several generations of readers to the Songbird of Dixie. No doubt many of those readers have assumed that Mencken made him up, but he did not: the Bard of the Congaree was all too real, the author of *Purely Original Verse* (1897), nearly all of it every bit as lame as his immortal couplet on Southern belles lettres.

Coogler is a splendid example of what we might call a primitive poet, the verbal equivalent of the folk artists whose paintings have lately come to command critical acclaim and inflated prices.

My region boasts many others. Heck, my state does. I place in evidence *Nematodes in My Garden of Verse,* subtitled *A Little Book of Tar Heel Poems* and edited by Richard Walser. Walser culled a number of these things from turn-of-the-century North Carolina newspapers, which often printed their readers' verse, dealing with presidential assassinations, train wrecks, the coming of spring, and other subjects of civic or personal interest. But the centerpiece of *Nematodes* is six poems from a little book called *Little Pansy* (1890), by the Poetissima Laureatissima [*sic*] of Bladen County, North Carolina, Miss Mattie J. Peterson, in whose masterwork "I Kissed Pa Twice After His Death" are found the priceless lines:

> I saw him coming, stepping high,
> Which was of his walk the way.

Perfect.

I don't know why—or even whether—the South has produced more than its share of primitive poets. (These days, of course, we have more than our share of the high-toned sort.) Even if we have a quantitative edge, of course, this folk-bardic tradition is not a Southern monopoly. In fact, the all-time record for sustained badness without surcease, year in and year out, a record unsurpassed and unsurpassable, must belong to a nineteenth-century Dundee weaver named William McGonagall. The inimitable McGonagall retired the cup.

A short summary of McGonagall's career may have some inspirational value for those not familiar with it. In 1877, by his own account, McGonagall was seized by a "strange kind of feeling [that] seemed to kindle up my entire frame, along with a strong desire to write poetry." He promptly penned a testimonial to a local clergyman, in verse that concluded:

> My blessing on his noble form,
>   And on his lofty head,
> May all good angels guard him while living,
>   And hereafter when he's dead.

The reverend gentleman responded tactfully that "Shakespeare never wrote anything like this," and it was onward and downward thereafter for McGonagall.

There was no stopping him. He didn't take hints. When he stepped up to recite his verse in pubs, people jeered him, threw peas at him, dumped flour on him. . . . His persistence amounted to a species of heroism, diminished only slightly by the fact that he seemed not to recognize ridicule and abuse for what it was. After the publication of his first book, *Poetic Gems,* for instance, some students wrote him a hoaxing letter from the "King of Burma" proclaiming him a "Knight of the Order of the White Elephant of Burma"; thereafter he signed himself, in perfect faith, "Sir William."

It is simply impossible to convey the effect produced by an entire book of McGonagall's verse. It is all dreadful. I swear to you that I have just now opened at random to this stanza, from a lengthy account of the Johnstown flood:

> The pillaging of the houses in Johnstown is fearful to
>   describe,
>   By the Hungarians and ghouls, and woe betide
> Any person or party that interfered with them,
>   Because they were mad with drink, and yelling like tigers
>   in a den.

There are pages and pages of this stuff.

It is estimated that a half-million copies of *Poetic Gems* have been sold since McGonagall's day—not, alas, to the profit of the author and his long-suffering wife and children. In 1965 the BBC held a competition to find a worthy successor to McGonagall, but the judges called it off. None of the entries, they said, was in the same league.

But of course none could have been. The BBC's contest was like asking people to do primitive paintings. People who paint the Apotheosis of Hank Williams do not think of their work as folk art. This kind of thing can't be done tongue-in-cheek. It must be turned out in dead earnest. (And by people who ought to know better: children can write like this, and sometimes do, but the effect isn't the same at all.)

So I proposed a different competition for the readers of my monthly letter in *Chronicles: A Magazine of American Culture.* I asked them to submit McGonagallisms from the work of poets who are or at one time were well-regarded. Even Homer nods, and isolated passages almost as bad as the ones I've quoted have been written by people who made better livings off their verse than poor Sir William ever did.

My candidate, to get things started, was from Whittier's eulogy for John Randolph of Roanoke:

> Too honest or too proud to feign
> A love he never cherished,
> Beyond Virginia's border line
> His patriotism perished.

(True, it scans, and the rhymes aren't bad. But you must admit that it has that Coogleresque quality, that Petersonian je ne sais quoi. William McGonagall would not have been ashamed of it.)

The contest elicited some truly dreadful entries, although none of them was awful in just the right bathetic way. The winner was this, from Byron's "Song to the Suliotes":

> Up to battle! Sons of Suli
> Up, and do your duty duly!
> There the wall—and there the Moat is:
> Bouwah! Bouwah! Suliotes,
> There is booty—there is Beauty,
> Up my boys and do your duty.

The Atlanta man who submitted that got to shake his booty; his prize was my copy of Whittier, which had cost me thirty-five cents some years back.

The runner-up was a Chicagoan, who submitted the entire text of Browning's "Why I Am a Liberal." (Look it up: it's every bit as sappy as it sounds.) A curious fact, for the record, is that this man was the only non-Southerner who entered the contest. Could he be the only non-Southerner who reads this sort of verse? In any case, he averred that Chicagoans do not have to yield to Southerners when it comes to *writing* it, and placed in evidence the work of Alderman John J. "Bathhouse John" Coughlin, author of "Ode to a Bath Tub," "Why Did They Build the Lovely Lake So Close to the Horrible Shore?," "They're Tearing Up Clark Street Again," "She Sleeps by the Side of the Drainage Canal," and many other works.

"Like Wallace Stevens," my correspondent wrote, "Bathhouse John had to devote most of his time to his career—in his case, political corruption—but surely his shade has earned the right to enjoy the company of Coogler and other immortals." Surely, indeed, as this sample of his verse attests:

To a Hod Carrier

'Tis not a ladder of fame he climbs
This rugged man of bricks and mortar;
The mason gets six for laying the bricks
While the hod carrier gets but two and a quarter.

Two other readers received, ah, Honorable Mention, although their entries didn't exactly meet the criteria. A Nashville lady sent a specimen of her own original verse (as well as several entries from her grandmother's 1860 edition of Longfellow which were, Lord knows, pretty bad). Did I say Coogleresque verse can't be written on purpose? This lady did it, thus:

In 1865 we tried to forget the Late Unpleasantness,
But the Reconstruction laws imposed were dirty as a pheasant
    nest.

Finally, among the many crimes for which anarchism must answer are some poems from *The Illustrious Life of William Mc-Kinley: Our Martyred President,* sent in by a reader in Savannah. The editor of this memorial volume observed that many of these samples from the spontaneous outpouring of folk verse evoked by McKinley's death express "the feeling that by too indulgent toleration of the infamous doctrines whose disciples slew the good President the nation has fallen into disgrace and incurred a stain upon its honor which must be effaced." Refreshing.

These verses had me wondering why John Kennedy's assassination produced no comparable effluence—until I suddenly realized that it had. Indeed, my state legislator at the time, the Honorable R. L. "Bobby" Peters of Kingsport, Tennessee, not only wrote something called "A Sunny Day in Dallas," but set it to music, and recorded it too. The tradition of McGonagall and Coogler (and, yes, of Coughlin) continues—where else but in country music?

(July 1986)

❧ How to Get Along in the South: ❧ A Guide for Yankees

Right now, down here, we seem to be experiencing an influx of Northern migrants. There are so many of them, and misunderstanding is so frequent, that I fear a new wave of sectional hostility may be shaping up. I offer as evidence the fact that some of my less tolerant brethren have taken to referring to Northerners as "'rhoids"—short for hemorrhoids, from a rude joke with the punch line, "If they come down and stay down, they're a pain in the ass."

But these new invaders are friendlier than the last bunch, and some of them apparently even want to fit in. At least so I surmise from the fact that the University of North Carolina at Charlotte sponsored a well-attended adult education course not long ago on "The South for Non-Southerners." (This goes to show how thoughtful we are down here, by the way. When I lived in Boston and New York I don't recall anyone offering a course on the North for non-Northerners, although I could have used one a few times.)

If I were running that course I think I could boil it down to elaboration of a single theme, and I offer it at no charge. Reed's Rule for Successful Adjustment to the South is simply this: Don't think that you know what's going on.

William Price Fox puts the basic problem well: "No lie, the average Yankee knows about as much about the South as a hog knows about the Lord's plan for salvation." The thing about the hog, though, is that he doesn't think he knows. Believing they know what's happening is probably the most common mistake Northerners make. Most other problems stem from that. Heck, half the time Southerners don't know what's going on here; why should someone who just unloaded his U-Haul?

It's funny, but real foreigners often seem to have an easier time of it than folks from Wisconsin or Massachusetts or California. Brits and Germans and Japanese and Kuwaitis are likely to recognize that things in the South aren't what they're used to, and can't be made that way by complaining loudly.

One common problem is that Northern migrants often ethno-centrically insist that we mean what they think we said when what we mean is—well, what we *really* said. Choong Soon Kim, author of *An Asian Anthropologist in the South* (I'm not making this up), observes that Southerners very seldom say what they mean. He finds us, in a word, inscrutable. Maybe Northern migrants should just accept that fact, as Kim does. But if you insist on trying to understand Southern conversation, here are a few examples that may be helpful.

Surely you know that "You all come see us" doesn't mean that you all should actually drop in. That ought to be Lesson #1 in any Introductory Southern course. An intermediate course might teach that it almost always does mean "Come see us if you have to for some reason"—although that usually goes without saying. And an advanced course would teach the student that sometimes it actually does mean you all should drop in. Depending.

Similarly, as in the North, "Where's your husband today?" can be nosiness plain and simple or, from a male, a cautious inquiry before making some moves. In the South, though, it can also be just a polite expression of interest in your kinfolks; the questioner may not really care.

See? These things aren't simple. Take the question "What church do you go to?" Many newcomers find it offensive when brand-new acquaintances ask that. They assume it's the prelude to some serious witnessing, and it may be. On the other hand, it can also be just a conventional pleasantry, like "What do you do?" (a question

Southerners sometimes find offensive) or "What's your sign?" (a question I always answer "No Trespassing"). "What church do you go to?" can also be an insult, especially if the emphasis is on the word "you." Again, it depends. Migrants should just recognize that they don't have a clue, and hope for the best.

Reed's Rule has an important corollary: Since you don't know what's going on, be very careful about offering advice. I once hired a couple of men to tear down our old garage (a job the termites already had well in hand). I was watching them slam away with crowbars and sledgehammers, when my neighbor's father, who was visiting from Michigan, came over. "You know," he said, "up North we'd get some heavy machinery in there and we'd have that baby down in a half an hour."

Well, now. Here's another rule for getting along in the South. If you must give unsolicited advice, pretend it's something that just occurred to you. *Never, under any circumstances, tell us how it's done up North.*

Never mind that you think the Northern way is superior. Even if it is—maybe especially if it is—we don't want to hear about it. Even the most cosmopolitan Southerner is likely to bristle at that. Lewis Grizzard puts it eloquently: "Delta is ready when you are."

Now my neighbor's father meant well; she and her husband are nice folks, and they are my neighbors. So I did not say "Eat hot lead, Yank." Neither did I say: "Well, down here we get a couple of old boys in with crowbars and save us some money and keep 'em off the welfare." (It's true that heavy machinery could have done that job quicker than the guys I hired, but I paid them $60 instead of the $75 minimum it would have cost me for a machine and an operator. And my county's unemployment rate is under 3 percent. What's Lansing's?)

As a matter of fact, I didn't say much of anything at all, just mumbled something. But I did a little better when a New York acquaintance who was thinking of retiring to our area asked if there had been much Klan activity lately, a question just about as appropriate as my asking him about the Mafia—no less, no more. It's a fact that the Klan exists. It's an unpleasant feature of our cultural landscape. But there's less activity than there used to be; it doesn't affect most of us in our daily lives (I go whole months without thinking about it); and it's trifling enough that most of us are content to let the police worry about it.

I guess I could have said all that, but I actually said something like: "Well, some of the boys act up now and then, but if you keep your opinions to yourself and don't let 'em hear your accent, they won't bother you none."

I'm afraid that New Yorker now thinks he knows what's going on. Anyway, he retired to Arizona.

(January 1987)

∾ Songs of the South ∾

I like that old-time rock and roll. I'm sure nostalgia has a lot to do with it (the older I get the better the fifties look), but there's more to it than that. I like what the music says about America, and especially about the South. Let me explain.

Some time ago, a geographer at Oklahoma State mapped the birthplaces of country-music notables: singers, songwriters, and musicians. The resulting map makes his entire career worth-while. Not surprisingly, it shows that country music has been *Southern* music. Give or take a speck here and there in Canada or Montana or Okie-land California, the people who make it have come overwhelmingly from the South. But they're not from just anywhere in the South. Most are from a fertile crescent that reaches from southwest Virginia through Kentucky and the eastern two-thirds of Tennessee, over into northern Arkansas, southeast Missouri, Oklahoma, and Texas. Country music, in other words, is a product of the fringe, of the margins of the region proper, of Appalachia, the Ozarks, the Southwest. The map defines the South by sketching its boundary: the Deep South appears as a near-vacuum (although not a black hole like New England).

But when one of my students did a similar map of the origins of blues singers and we overlaid it on the country-music map, it filled in the Deep South nicely. The two maps together clearly showed the South—black and white, separate but equal—to be the great seedbed of American music (what John Seelye used to say "AM" stood for; FM, of course, stood for "foreign music"). But

the two maps also made it plain, as I said, that for a long time
white folks didn't do much singing in the Deep South, perhaps
because they had blacks to do it for them. (The image of Slim
Pickens in *Blazing Saddles* comes irresistibly to mind, as does the
similar scene, not at all funny, in James Agee's *Let Us Now Praise
Famous Men*.)

When Deep South white boys did start to sing, though, along
about 1956, they showed that they'd been listening. What they
gave us was "rockabilly"—half hillbilly, half black rhythm and
blues, a wild half-breed music. Along with some black folks who
were mostly Southerners, too, Elvis and Carl Perkins and Jerry
Lee Lewis and Charlie Rich and Ronnie Hawkins and Conway
Twitty and the Everly Brothers gave us rock and roll.

And although it has been little noted, the musical influence
went both ways. Everyone knows how Elvis grew up listening to
Rufus Thomas and Big Mama Thornton, thus becoming the answer to Sam Phillips's prayer for a white singer with a Negro
sound. Just so, his fellow-Tennessean Bobby Bland talks of how
"we used to listen to the radio every morning to people like Roy
Acuff, Lefty Frizzell, Hank Williams and Hank Snow," and says
"I think hillbilly has more of a story than people give it credit for."
Bland, of course, is black.

With this genealogy, rock and roll really was something different. It made for one of the few experiences shared by young
Southerners across the racial divide. Opinions differed about rock
and roll (they were meant to), but not along racial lines. Black or
white, most Southerners now of approximately menopausal age
grew up making out to the same music, on the same radio stations. In the Carolinas and Virginia it was gentle "beach music."
Over the mountains, in my part of the South, it was tougher,
meaner, raunchier—and WLAC, Nashville, was the place to go for
it. I was pleased when Don Williams included a reference to
WLAC's John R in his nostalgic country song "Good Old Boys
Like Me," and I was amused when Bobbie Ann Mason wrote in
the *New Yorker* (of all places) about listening to WLAC while
growing up in Kentucky. But I was actually moved when Steven
Millner, a black professor at Ole Miss, mentioned WLAC on
William Buckley's "Firing Line." Listening to WLAC's juxtaposition of Hank Ballard and the Midnighters with suggestive ads for

White Rose Petroleum Jelly was a mere thread across the chasm of segregation, but it was that.

Some saw rock and roll as a threat to Western civilization, and that was part of its charm. Preachers preached against it. Pious teenagers took to the platform to witness against it. Sanctimonious small-town radio stations banned it. But it was no threat—just the opposite. Consider what it replaced.

Browsing in the record bin at a local thrift shop one day recently, I came across an old Phil Harris LP. Two of the songs on it were "That's What I Like about the South" and "The Darktown Poker Club," sides A and B of an old 78 that I must have worn out sometime in the early 1950s. For fifty cents I bought the record and took it home.

I used to love those songs. I remember playing them over and over. But listening to them now, I realize that they are horrible: musically, culturally, in every way. Phil Harris, this white man from Ohio, was working in the coon-song tradition. From the middle of the last century until the middle of this one, that tradition produced literally scores of demeaning songs that white folks apparently found inexhaustibly amusing. We need to be reminded of how awful they were, if only so as to understand that black folks really do have reason to be ticked off.

For my part, listening with embarrassment to these songs that I once loved uncritically made me glad that God sent rock and roll when He did, sometime during my junior-high years. Even a screaming, eye-shadowed flamer like Little Richard was a more wholesome influence on American race relations than Phil Harris. Rock and roll was a definite improvement, and I don't care what Allan Bloom says.

But the Golden Age of biracial Southern hegemony in rock and roll was short-lived. By 1960, it had given way to the era of the teen idols: Ricky Nelson and Fabian and Dion and the Bobbies—Vinton, Darin, Vee—meretricious, marketed, mediocre. (About the same time, as I recall, something similar happened to the presidency.) When the Beatles came along, they probably got a better reception than they deserved because these guys were so bad. The Fab Four were OK when they did old Chuck Berry and Jerry Lee Lewis numbers (Ringo tended to sing them), but "Norwegian Wood"? Come *on*.

I guess the sixties were OK for those who were stoned the whole time. For the rest of us, though, "A Whiter Shade of Pale" just didn't hack it. If we worked at it, we could find songs worth listening to, and not all of them by Southerners like Delaney and Bonnie, either. Soul music was still worth listening to (there weren't that many black hippies). Eric Clapton and Joe Cocker and some of the other English rockers knew where the bodies were buried. And the Rolling Stones were arguably the greatest rock and roll band ever. But the dominant, drugged-out stream that flowed from the Beatles and wound up at the Fillmore left me cold.

And sometime in the seventies I lost it altogether. Now I can't tell the difference between New Wave and heavy metal—and frankly I don't care. I can recognize that Prince is the Little Richard of the '80s, but even that recognition doesn't make him any easier to listen to. Some of my contemporaries claim that the torch has been passed to Bruce Springsteen, but I don't see it. For starters, how can you take someone named Bruce seriously as a rocker? (No offense, you Bruces out there, but it is a lot like Bobby.)

So where does an old rock-and-roller turn these days? Country music is where I go, back to the source. To me, these days, it often sounds more like rock and roll than rock and roll does. Listen to Hank Williams, Jr.'s *Born to Boogie* album, for example. The words of the title cut aren't much, but it's got a good beat and you can dance to it. "Honky Tonk Women" goes up against the memory of Mick Jagger and pummels him to a draw. "Keep Your Hands to Yourself" covers a hit by the Georgia Satellites, a neotraditional group I wish well, if only because their leader told *Southern* magazine that "The last vestiges of regionalism should be hung onto like a Doberman with a sweater." My favorite may be a solid rocker called "Buck Naked" (which Hank pronounces "nekkid," of course, in keeping with Lewis Grizzard's observation that, in Southern English, "naked" means you ain't got no clothes on, while "nekkid" means you ain't got no clothes on and you're up to something). And that's just Side A: five songs, four of them pretty fair rock and roll.

Like the rock and roll of thirty years ago, the rocking country of Charlie Daniels and Waylon Jennings and Hank Williams, Jr., should be listened to in smoky dives, on crowded dance floors, or in steamy parked cars. This is, in short, good-time music. Ignoring that fact is part of what was wrong with the sixties, and I've come perilously close to doing it here. Rock and roll shouldn't be treated solemnly. But that doesn't mean it can't be taken seriously.

(February 1989)

❧ In with the In-Crowd: ❧ Talkin' Trash, Spendin' Cash

A joke going around down here asks why Southern women don't like group sex. Give up? Too many thank-you notes.

I wouldn't besmirch these pages with such smut, of course, if it didn't speak directly to my topic. (No, not group sex, for crying out loud.) I want to say a few words about regional differences in manners. I want to look at the uses of Southern gentility, and at how criticism is understood in the South and elsewhere.

Southern expatriates have always traded on the region's stereotypically courtly style, but the exchange value of that currency probably peaked during the Gilded Age. So I conclude at least from William Stadiem's recently remaindered *A Class By Themselves*. That one of Stadiem's earlier books was *Marilyn Monroe Confidential* may suggest that he's not really the man to write the Southern *Our Crowd* that his subject calls for, but nevertheless I'm in his debt for introducing me to a fascinating little creep named Ward McAllister, the self-styled "Autocrat of Drawing Rooms."

McAllister, from Savannah, became the social arbiter of post–Civil War New York not just despite but partly because of being conspicuously a Southern gentleman. McAllister didn't disguise his Southern origins. Not at all: he played them for all they were worth, becoming an early example of the sort of Southern expatriate for whom the advantages of being Southern outweigh the disadvantages.

McAllister's affection for his native region didn't extend to fighting for it. He prudently sat out the Civil War in Newport and Delmonico's, and his memoir, *Society as I Have Found It*, barely mentions the War. (Readers of the copy in my university's library have graced his lengthy account of a wartime costume party with rude comments in the margins.) But Stadiem says that McAllister really did like the South—indeed, that he was "enraptured" by it—and suggests that this was because "McAllister was inordinately fond of himself and all that he represented."

Be that as it may, McAllister worked hard to establish a Southern presence in New York high society. He enjoyed the patronage of Mrs. Astor, whom he called his "Mystic Rose," and his famous list was The 400 because that was the size of her ballroom. Southerners were on that list in good numbers, and New Yorkers' stereotypes helped put some of them there. A presumption of gentility attached itself—still does—to presentable Southerners, overcoming in some cases backgrounds that wouldn't have withstood close scrutiny. As observers from William Faulkner to Billy Carter have remarked, Yankees can be remarkably gullible where Southerners are concerned.

Consider, for example, McAllister's friend Richard T. Wilson. A former traveling salesman from Loudon, Tennessee, Wilson made a shady wartime fortune selling purloined Confederate supplies in Europe. But he was a tall, handsome man with elegant manners, and McAllister presented him to New York society with such success that his daughters married a Goelet millionaire, a Vanderbilt, and "Mungo" Herbert, brother of the Earl of Pembroke, while his son married Carrie Astor, daughter of the Mystic Rose herself.

The "marrying Wilsons" were an extreme case, but the point is that some Southerners have done well by acting the way Northerners expect Southern gentry to act. Ordinary Southern manners have made many middle-class Southern girls and boys into putative ladies and gentlemen once they've left the South.

Sometimes Southern gentry are allowed to be impolite, too; a certain hauteur is almost expected. Another story, this one about the English branch of the Astors: Lady Astor (the former Nancy Langhorne of Charlottesville) disapproved of the fast set around King Edward VII. It's said she once declined to play cards with him, saying she couldn't tell the difference between a king and a knave. Her friend A. L. Rowse explains that since she began her life as a Virginia belle she never felt inferior to anybody.

Certainly Nancy Astor was proud of her origins. Rowse writes that she was "an unreconstructed Southerner, a Virginian first and last." When she entertained Virginia soldiers at Cliveden during World War II, she always told them, "When you get drunk and disorderly, tell people that you are from New York." She died at age eighty-five, in 1964, and was buried with a Confederate flag in her hands.

Like Richard Wilson, Nancy Astor got away with a lot, in part because she was a Southerner and acted the way people expect Southerners to act. If you're not Lady Astor or one of The 400, though, acting out somebody else's idea of what Southerners are about can be a risky business. You risk your dignity and self-respect, in the first place; there can be an element of Samboism in all this. In the second place, you risk becoming something of a house Southerner, subject to dismissal when folks don't find the act amusing anymore.

Ward McAllister found that out the hard way. His memoirs, published in 1890, turned out to be his undoing. His chronicle of dinners, cotillions, and fancy-dress balls was seen in some quarters as a betrayal, a portrait of rich Yankees as insecure tradesmen in need of Southern guidance, specifically McAllister's. Mrs. Astor abandoned him, and Stuyvesant Fish announced that "McAllister is a discharged servant. That is all."

The Astors and Fishes were wrong about McAllister. He was a silly, vain, self-absorbed little man—sort of a Truman Capote, a proto-Capote, without the talent. But his book wasn't malicious; he wasn't smart enough for that. He didn't mean to offend his rich and powerful friends; he just miscalculated.

Capote may have done the same with his book *Answered Prayers*, but it's hard to say. Some Southern expatriates, and Capote may have been one, have set out quite consciously to trash the Northern society they saw around them. To be sure, it's usually pretty tiresome when some Southerner goes on about how awful the North is. But the impulse has produced some fine country music, and when someone with real gifts of observation and expression succumbs to it the results can be wonderfully pungent social criticism. And a surprisingly large number of talented Southerners have had that response to living in the North.

Take the Vanderbilt Agrarians, for instance, the authors of a slashing attack on industrial—that is, Yankee—society, *I'll Take My Stand*, published in 1930. I believe that all twelve of them had lived outside the South before they came to write that book, and a number of them still did as the book was being written. Living outside the South had inflamed their Southernness; their Southern-bred distaste for Northern ways gave them their theme, and their considerable literary talent means the book is still worth reading.

Funny thing: within a few years, several of the Agrarians had teaching jobs in the North—pretty good ones, too. Can't Yankees read?

Consider the similar, more recent, case of Tom Wolfe (the New Journalist, not the Tar Heel novelist). Here is a studiedly Southern boy, a graduate of Washington and Lee, wearing the custom-tailored white suits of a real Dixie dandy. This pose, of course, disguises a brilliant writer and an acute social critic, with both his literary style and his criticism rooted in traditions that Southerners, at least, ought to recognize as Southern. The writing is strikingly innovative—but in an ornamented, particularistic way that reminds me of James Agee, that premature New Journalist from Knoxville. And the criticism is profoundly conservative.

Look at what Wolfe does: he savages nouveaux riches social climbers, shallow left-wing trendinistas, fast-track yuppies, Third World rip-off artists, and other denizens of modern New York and California. Who is presented as admirable? Well, a North Carolina stock-car racer and a West Virginia test pilot, for starters—the "last American hero" and exemplar of "the right stuff," respectively.

And Wolfe still gets invited to the right parties. What's going on here?

George Garrett has written about this in his contribution to a collection of essays called *Why the South Will Survive*, suggesting that the answer lies in those regional differences in manners I mentioned earlier. Southern critics of the North such as Wolfe and the Agrarians and (in their own ways) Truman Capote and James Dickey have exploited those differences. The element of real hostility in their criticism goes largely unrecognized outside the South, because criticism is understood differently there.

Southerners generally regard outsiders' criticism as offensive, never mind whether it's fair or not. Unless guests mean to be offensive, they don't criticize their hosts. It's bad manners, and

Garrett observes that, for Southerners, "A violation of the code of manners [can mean] the same thing as a fist in the face or a blade between the ribs." So when Southerners outside the South criticize what they see around them, they are, by their own lights, being very rude indeed—and on purpose. As somebody once observed, Southerners will be polite until they are angry enough to kill you. Thus, as Garrett puts it, by Southern standards, "Wolfe's satirical assault on both the intellectual hypocrisy and the bad manners of the New York scene . . . is just about as violent an attack as he could make, short of tossing around a case of fragmentation grenades."

But Northerners simply don't seem to understand that their Southern critics are shooting to kill. They admire Wolfe's style, Capote's wit, the Agrarians' vision—and don't recognize that these men don't like them very much. Garrett implies that if the Northern establishment ever figures that out, these men will wind up like poor, silly Ward McAllister, discharged servants. (Garrett's own novel *Poison Pen* makes the point much harder to miss, but he published it only after moving back to the South from Michigan, and, whether by design or not, it is damned hard to get hold of a copy. Don't wait for the paperback.)

I'm not sure Garrett's entirely right, though. The "Northern establishment" he's talking about is basically the New York literary crowd, and their code of manners, unlike ours, rewards even malicious, grotesquely unfair criticism, provided it's sufficiently clever or amusing. That's why New Yorkers fight all the time: they enjoy it, and nobody winds up actually dead.

Some survey data are to the point. Asked some time back what the best American state was, over 90 percent of native North Carolinians picked North Carolina. Other Southerners were almost as enthusiastic about their states. But less than half of the residents of New York and Massachusetts said they were living in the best states. Think about that. Of course, North Carolina really is the best American state, and other Southern states are almost as good. I wouldn't want to deny that. But they're not *that* much better than New York and New England. Surely the explanation of these findings lies at least partly in regional differences in manners. Southerners expect each other to show state loyalty and pride. Yankees expect each other to complain—and they don't seem to mind if Southerners complain, too, so long as they do it eloquently or amusingly.

In other words, as long as Southern expatriates criticize Northern society *well*, they can be surprisingly successful. Right many talented Southerners have been moved by living in the North to do exactly that, and the literature of American social criticism is richer for it.

(June 1989)

❧ Billy, the Fabulous Moolah, and Me ❧

When I first heard that V. S. Naipaul was writing a book about the South, it made me nervous. What would the author of *Among the Believers* make of Jim and Tammy? Could we look for *Louisiana: A Wounded Civilization*?

Well, when I finally read *A Turn in the South*, I saw that Naipaul had taken it easy on us. His characteristic way of working (harder than it looks) is to go around and talk to people, and he found some good Southerners to talk to. He was properly impressed with our religiosity, and he even kind of admired rednecks—although he may just have been saying that to tease the readers of the *New York Review of Books*.

So it's ungrateful of me to complain. But I have to say that Naipaul's book made the South just the teeniest bit—well, boring. And that's not right, because boring is one thing the South has never been and, please God, never will be.

I'm reminded of another pleasant book called *Journeys through the South*, written by a journalist named Fred Powledge back about 1977. Powledge spent part of the sixties pinned down by sniper fire at the University of Mississippi while covering the matriculation of James Meredith, so he was struck by how much Ole Dixie had changed. In 1977 he traveled all over and nobody shot at him, despite his beard. (One of my all-time favorite bumper stickers, by the way, is one from South Carolina that says: "Don't Shoot, I'm a *Local* Hippie." Think about that.)

Anyway, Powledge's book was upbeat, reflecting the South's mood in those early days of the Carter administration, when the idea of the "Sunbelt" had just begun to catch on and people were talking seriously about silly ideas like how the rest of the nation was going to learn from the South. Roy Blount reviewed Powledge's book for the *New York Times* and gave it pretty good marks, complaining only that the picture it painted was so relentlessly normal. Blount said something like, "I kept wishing Harry Crews would run by with an armload of snakes."

For those who don't know him, Crews is one of the foremost latter-day practitioners of the Southern grotesque, my candidate for the job of successor to Erskine Caldwell, and author of a book of essays with the great title *Blood and Grits,* which I wish I'd thought of first. And Roy Blount's *Crackers* is, to my mind, one of the funniest and truest books ever written about Our People.

But this is turning into a bibliographical essay. Let me get back to the point, which is that the South is an odd place, and any portrait that implies it isn't, lies.

Both Powledge and Naipaul did run into typically weird Southern stuff, but each chose to downplay it—for different reasons, I suspect. For instance, Powledge ran across Alvis Lassiter drying a parachute in his front yard. Now, Fred grew up in Raleigh, so he knew why Lassiter kept a parachute around: "he just liked the way it looked," that's all. In other circumstances he might have paused to savor that, but in his book he quickly passed over the subject, presumably because dwelling on it would have interfered with the "South Rejoins Union" story he was trying to tell.

On the other hand, when Naipaul found himself being driven around Mississippi by a black man in a hair net, with shaving cream on his face, it was all he could do to maintain his sangfroid. He didn't have the advantages of a Southern upbringing to help him just accept the fact that folks have their reasons. Naipaul's a good sport, but he seemed to find the episode rather sinister. Apparently he likes to know what's going on, and his book moved right along to characters more easily understood.

My point is that a true portrait would not only report that the South is an odd place, but revel in it. Any picture of the South in the late twentieth century, that is, should save a prominent place for the likes of the Reverend Billy C. Wirtz.

The Reverend Billy is a Raleigh boy, a former special-education teacher turned boogie-woogie piano player, 6'4" with a spiky punk haircut, tattoos on most of his visible parts, and a silver earring in the form of a chain saw. He writes his own music, which he describes as "middle of the rude," or "queasy listening." His songs have titles like "Mennonite Surf Party" and "Your Greens Give Me the Blues"; his lyrics run to "Stick out your can / 'Cause here comes the garbage man." His first album, "Salvation through Polyester," went nowhere at all; his second, "Deep-Fried and Sanctified," got reviewed in *People* magazine—and still went nowhere at all. He seems to be an acquired taste.

Anyway, I caught the reverend's act one evening and wrote an appreciative review. He called to thank me.

"Want to be in show business?" he asked.

Is a wild Indian Catholic? Does the Pope . . . Of course I want to be in show business.

It turned out Billy's record company was flying a film crew into Raleigh from Los Angeles to make a music video of "Teenie Weenie Meanie," a love song addressed to—uh, well, to a lady wrestler. A *midget* lady wrestler. Billy assured me that the video would be "tasteful."

So my buddy Fetzer and I drove to Raleigh on the appointed evening. We found his reverence outside the cavernous nightclub where the filming was to take place, eating fried chicken and turnip greens off a Styrofoam plate and surrounded by his entourage, which that evening included four members of a motorcycle gang in full colors. *Ugly* boys.

While we were waiting for the "shoot" (as we show business folk call it), Fetzer and I slipped across the street to grab a sandwich, accompanied by a country-music singer named Pinky Wyoming, who was also there for a shot at glory. Pinky is a large woman, very large, with a long blond wig, a pink cowboy hat, and white boots. Fetzer had purchased his entire wardrobe that afternoon for $9.00 at the Abundant Life Thrift Shop: great pointy shoes. I'd come from work, so I was relatively staid in khakis and boots, although I was wearing an orange cap that said "Elvis—Memphis Loves You," with a picture of the King in profile.

"Are y'all in a play?" asked the State U. student working the counter.

"Whaddaya mean, 'play'?" Fetzer demanded. "Somethin' funny about the way I look?"

The poor kid apologized.

"Didja ask them Hell's Angels if they was in a play?" Fetzer grumbled, as he walked off with his sandwich.

The kid watched us warily, all the way out.

Back across the street, Billy introduced us to his costar, Diamond Lil, three feet of dynamite with a blond Mohawk haircut, and to her friend and mentor, the Fabulous Moolah. Moolah (whose real name is Lillian) is a personable, fiftyish blonde who was for many years World Champion and now runs a school for lady wrestlers in Columbia, South Carolina. We chatted for a while, then went inside where a makeshift ring had been set up.

The Los Angeles film crew, about a dozen of them, were making mysterious chalk marks on the floor and moving lights and cameras around, looking professionally blasé and ready to get back to the Sir Walter Inn and a few lines of coke or something. The scene they were filming that night was the wrestling match at which Billy first spies his ladylove. (The love scenes were filmed the next day at a trailer park in Apex, North Carolina.) My brief moment in the spotlight came when the reverend and the motorcycle guys and their women and a baby named—well, it sounded like "Redemption" and maybe it was—when these folks and Fetzer and Pinky and I and assorted other hangers-on watched Moolah and Lil go through some choreographed wrestling moves while we hollered "Kill her! Kill her!" and waved empty beer cups around.

Look for it on MTV. I'm the one in the orange Elvis cap, next to the baby. I almost hate to say it, but there's a sense in which that's what the South is all about in 1989. Whatever else it may be, it's not boring.

(July 1989)

IV. Hot Flashes

I see here where the police chief of Somersworth, New Hampshire, in unhappy possession of the remains of five infants (so far) apparently murdered sometime in the 1950s, told *Newsweek*, "It's almost too bizarre to be true. You don't think these things happen in our part of the country—maybe down South."

Why do we put up with this stuff? A possible answer comes from the student paper at West Texas State, which reports that when the university offered its students a seminar in assertiveness training, nobody showed up. An employee of the university counseling center grumbled that "the lack of interest in the seminar was indicative of the general attitude of this area." She said there was "no desire for motivation to do anything."

Maybe they were praying. Southerners just *will* do that. In Mobile, a schoolteacher who made her charges say grace before lunch was sued by the village atheist, one Ishmael Jaffree. Federal District Judge W. B. Hand struck a blow for sanity by ruling that such prayers are indeed constitutional—a proposition that wasn't in doubt for the first 90 percent of this nation's history—but he was quickly slapped down by a higher court. Mr. Jaffree's children will not have the burden of having to pray added to that of being named Jamael, Makeba, and Chioke.

Also on the church–state front, the Black Student Movement Gospel Choir at the University of North Carolina, Chapel Hill, was asked by the Central Committee of the Black Student Movement to add secular songs to its repertoire, lest BSM funding from the student government be jeopardized. At last report, choir members had refused.

And in Carrollton, Georgia, Keith Brand and Brentha Hager plighted their troth on the West Georgia Fairgrounds before a twenty-five-foot flaming cross. Bride and groom were both decked out in the dress uniform of the Ku Klux Klan, as were approximately one hundred of the spectators. Both told reporters that the Klan is a family affair. The new Mrs. Brand dispensed advice to others contemplating marriage: "There's a lot of ways to keep your marriage happy and together. This is one good way." (California has the Esalen Institute, we have this. OK, now: who got first choice?)

Incidentally, my agricultural correspondent tells me that the hog and wheat producers' associations have ladies' auxiliaries known, respectively, as the Porkettes and the Wheathearts. Looking for a regional angle, I tried without success to learn what the equivalent organizations for the wives of cotton and tobacco producers are called. Until someone tells me differently, I'd like to believe that tobacco growers' wives are called the Coughin' Nells.

In sports news, Matt Doherty, a Long Islander who plays basketball for the University of North Carolina, offered this explanation for the sorry behavior of Duke fans at ball games: "They're mostly just a bunch of northerners. As far as they're concerned, cursing and personal insults are a part of the game."

And it appears that Southerners really are more polite. Researchers at Chapel Hill left 399 stamped and addressed letters under the windshield wipers of cars parked at nearby colleges, each letter scuffed to make it look as if someone had found it on the ground and stuck it on the nearest car. What made the biggest difference in whether someone was willing to help an unknown soul by mailing his letter for him? The car's license tag, that's what. Sixty-one percent of letters left on North Carolina cars came back. Only 35 percent of those left on out-of-state—mostly Northern—cars did.

That's what social science is good for.

By the way, North Carolina's license plates used to say "First in Freedom," referring to the dubious but inspirational "fact" of the Mecklenberg Declaration of Independence. Now they say "First in Flight." This does not mean "First to Flee" (which would not be a happy construction at all, given the supposed etymology of "Tar Heel" as a reference to the valor of North Carolina troops); rather, it refers to the undoubted but boring fact that two Ohioans chose Kitty Hawk as the place to launch their flying machine.

I liked the old motto better. It was almost as good as New Hampshire's "Live Free or Die." (They may kill babies up yonder, but they have a way with words.) Nevertheless, North Carolina's new plates just took first place in a national license plate competition. (A national *license plate* competition?)

The *North Carolina Independent*, source of that news, also reported that North Carolina is first in pirated sound and video recordings. "Of the estimated $65 million of such materials seized in the country last year, more than $18 million worth was found in North Carolina." An unidentified U.S. attorney chalks it up to the state's "bootleg mentality."

Speaking of copies: when Bojangles opened a branch up yonder in Manhattan to tempt the jaded palates of New Yorkers with mass-market versions of fried chicken, Cajun beans, and dirty rice, its manager was quoted as saying: "We don't think of it as Southern food. We think of it as American food from another part of the country." Hard to say, isn't it, whether it's more offensive when they say it isn't Southern food or when they say it is.

Anyway, the question of ersatz Southern food has now even led to federal meddling. (Why am I not surprised?) This time the Department of Agriculture has really put its foot in it, though, by attempting to define barbecue, a piece of effrontery so outrageous that it even moved Tom Wicker to wit. I hesitate to step in where angels fear to tread and the agriculture department should have, but it sounds as if the feds have a point (and I'm not talking about the one Governor Wallace called attention to). At issue was whether Maurice Lee II of Boley, Oklahoma, can peddle a pressure-cooker-cum-smoker called the Smokaroma by saying that it produces barbecue. The USDA says no: it may taste like barbecue, look like barbecue, smell like barbecue, but it's not barbecue.

I agree; if it doesn't come out of a pit behind a cinder-block building with a sign that says BBQ, it's not the real thing. Nevertheless, in an imperfect world where Texans and Carolinians put up with each other's cooking the wrong animals, it seems to me that the thing to do is simply to avoid Mr. Lee's product. That's what states' rights is all about.

In other hog news, a Dallas newspaper reports that an eighty-two-year-old man in Jacksonville, Texas, has bred a strain of hogs that look and taste like the hogs that he remembers from his youth, before Poland China swine took over the market about 1915. They are leaner than modern hogs, and he calls them "red waddles" because—well, because their wattles waddle when the red waddles waddle. "The hogs speak for themselves," their master declared, but he nevertheless went on to add that "Hogs don't light up cigarettes and bring diseases upon themselves. Hogs will not chew tobacco. Hogs will not go and get sloppy drunk. A hog will not use dope and blow his mind until he becomes a homosexual."

Those good habits put them at least one-up on the young men of Atlanta. Dr. Steven Offenbacher of Emory University reported that a study of five hundred Atlanta boys, ages ten to sixteen, found that 20 percent used "smokeless tobacco" almost daily; 15 percent chewed and 11 percent dipped (some obviously did both). Another quarter had indulged, but weren't regulars. Many of the younger chewers mixed their Red Man with bubble gum.

The study found the young men were four times as likely to dip or chew as to smoke cigarettes, but if you think Dr. Offenbach is happy about that, guess again. He's a periodontist, and his studies show that going smokeless makes gums recede. (Q: How can you spot a good old boy? A: Look at his gums.)

Finally, strange things continue to happen in Dixie, and nowhere is stranger these days than Texas. In Houston, Chinese entrepreneurs are building no fewer than three competing China-towns, according to the *Wall Street Journal*. One, a Mr. Woo, has made his fortune with a Mexican restaurant named El Sombrero. Another Chinatown going up in a mall ten miles outside Houston will be called "Tang City Plaza" (too bad there's no Mr. Poon involved). At the groundbreaking, a high-school band played "The Yellow Rose of Texas."

Those who are skeptical about all this growth may have their suspicions reinforced by a multimedia presentation (what used to be known as a slide show, with taped commentary) called "Looking South: Prospects for the 80s." The Southern Growth Policies Board produced this piece of uplift, and accompanied it with a string-band rendition of "All of Me (Why Not Take All of Me)."

(1983-1984)

❧ Food for Thought ❧

Much of the news these days seems to be about food—or maybe it's just that I've been dieting, so I notice it more. Anyway, one of the dumber remarks of the 1984 presidential campaign (a campaign notable for dumb remarks) came from Joe Frank Harris, governor of Georgia. Asked if he approved of Geraldine Ferraro, he replied: "Yes. I asked her if she had eaten grits and liked them, and she said, 'Yes.'—and she passed the test." He should have asked if she knew what they were. Most politicians will eat anything for a vote.

Here in the South, we don't like our politicians red, but hotdogs are another matter. Hotdog trials at the *Chicago Tribune* put the ruby-red Rebel brand dead last, but a weenie expert told the paper that bright red varieties are popular throughout the South. Consumers in other regions prefer a dog with a brownish cast; on the West Coast they like a coarse grind and heavy smoke; Northeasterners like a soupçon of garlic.

The vogue for things Southern seems to have receded somewhat from its high-water mark in the first year of the Carter administration, but it can still be found here and there. A *Raleigh News and Observer* reporter discovered to her dismay a New York restaurant called Carolina where the "barbecue" was grilled on mesquite and served on a bed of leaf lettuce with Dijon mustard. A side order of slaw cost $2.25. The owner, a native New Yorker who concocted his recipes himself, said the restaurant's name came to him in a dream. Maybe he should have tried red hotdogs.

Male bourbon-drinkers beware! In the worst news for Southern taste since the discovery that snuff-dipping causes gums to recede, a researcher at the University of Pittsburgh has reported that your julep contains betasitosterol, biochanin A, and genistein. What (you might well ask) are those? Well, they are phytoestrogens—estrogens derived from plants. Men with healthy livers probably have nothing to worry about, but if you have cirrhosis, these chemicals may produce the same unfortunate effects as animal (or steroidal) estrogen, to wit: your voice may change, your beard may thin, and your figure may become more . . . voluptuous. (And you thought white wine did it, didn't you?) Of course, if you have cirrhosis, you have more important things to worry about.

Speaking of food, the *Norfolk Ledger-Star* reports that Southside Virginia tobacco growers, in a move about two hundred years overdue, are diversifying into crops like broccoli and cantaloupe. Richmond households have been paying premium prices for California cantaloupes that average two and a half pounds and are grown with thick rinds to protect them in transit. Now that they can buy thinner-skinned, six-pound, locally grown melons

we must hope they haven't forgotten what cantaloupes are supposed to be like.

In other agricultural news, a UPI dispatch reported that the
twenty-one-thousand-pound satellite carried into orbit by Challenger in April 1984 contained (among other things) kudzu seeds
from the Park Seed Company. The seeds were to be picked up and
returned to earth in February 1985. I have scanned my usual
sources diligently for news of their return and some hint of how
they liked it up there, but I have seen nary a word. *Why is this
being kept from the American people?*

Kudzu in space—and rhesus monkeys in Florida. The New York
Times News Service reports that, like walking catfish, leprous
armadillos, giant South American toads, wild parrots, lovebugs,
and retired Canadians, monkeys have come to Florida, liked it,
and stayed. Some three hundred troublesome specimens, apparently descended from eight escapees from the set of a 1939 Tarzan
movie, started attacking citizens and otherwise making a nui-
sance of themselves in the wilds around Silver Springs. The
hard-pressed officers of the Florida Game and Freshwater Fish
Commission ordered Silver Springs to do something, and found
themselves labeled "savages" and "Gestapo scumbags" when
Silver Springs began to trap the monkeys and sell them to a
Pennsylvania medical research supply house. At last word, the
trapping had stopped, and 140 or so monkeys were being left
undisturbed—but no doubt there are more now.

Speaking of violence against animals, I've just come across a
grand story from the *Memphis Commercial Appeal* for June 17, 1884.
"There is a bold gang of robbers and housebreakers working this
city now," it says,

> and it behooves every citizen to keep a well-loaded shotgun near at
> hand and ask no questions of unseasonable visitors, and crack away
> at every unusual noise. Better kill a cat or two through mistake than
> be robbed of all your worldly possessions, and perhaps get a broken
> head for interfering.

This Southern tradition of self-reliance persists, as everyone
knows, and a few mistakes are still reckoned a small price to pay.
In Houston, according to the Associated Press, a Baptist preacher,
the Reverend Larkin Power, was leaving his Rotary meeting at the

Holiday Inn when he encountered his wife being led away in handcuffs by the police. In his righteous anger he hit a sheriff's deputy "right where it hurts." Unfortunately, Mrs. Power had been duly arrested, at a "party" arranged by the vice squad. She was charged with prostitution, he with aggravated assault. Joe Bob Briggs, the inimitable former drive-in movie critic of the *Dallas Times-Herald,* commented: "I'm sure [Mrs. Power] was just in there witnessing to some sinners, and matter of fact, I wish she'd come up here and witness to me."

Despite what you see on "The Dukes of Hazzard," hell-for-leather driving is not a universal Southern pastime. In fact, according to the Federal Highway Administration, the five states with the highest rates of compliance with the 55 mph speed limit include West Virginia, South Carolina, Arkansas, and Georgia. (The worst are Nevada and Massachusetts.) I mention this because it appears that it's dangerous to rush Southerners. Or so the *New York Times* implied. An article on Texas warned visitors not to honk at other drivers: "It's considered rude. You could get shot."

The *Times* sniffed that "people from other parts of the country take the view that shooting people is a bit rude itself." But of course people get assaulted in New York for *no reason at all.* And one of the most interesting things to emerge from the Bernard Goetz affair was a list of who is licensed to carry handguns in New York: it included the publisher of the *New York Times.*

Most Southerners take the view that self-defense is not just for the publishers of elite newspapers. The contrast between Southern and Northern attitudes was illustrated a while back by the case of Mrs. Roberta Leonard, a sixty-five-year-old visitor to the Big Apple from Sylacauga, Alabama. Shortly after arriving at the Port Authority Bus Terminal, Mrs. Leonard used her cane and a .32 she happened to be packing to stand off a welcoming committee of young New Yorkers who wanted her pocketbook. When the police arrived, they arrested nine people. One of them was Mrs. Leonard, charged with carrying a pistol without a permit.

Still on the subject of violence, the Preston Brooks Society has proposed that we observe September 20 as a South-wide day of mourning and self-examination. It was on that date in 1975 that Ray Burgess cashed his chips. The Honorable and Reverend Ray was a lay preacher and Alabama state legislator who was in the habit of bringing his pistol onto the floor of the Alabama House of Representatives. When some of his brother legislators took exception to his practice and threatened a resolution to forbid it, he agreed to stop. But he vowed to carry his sidearm elsewhere and announced that he had armed his entire family. His life, he said, was "a gift of God, and God gave me the ingenuity to protect that gift."

After his death, his colleagues eulogized him as a man who "contributed immeasurably to the enrichment of our cultural, economic, and everyday lives." Mr. Burgess was shot in the head by his wife during a quarrel.

(November–December 1985)

∾ Science and Religion ∾

I gather that the Texas Board of Education has done something commendable, but I don't know exactly what because the *Washington Post* (my source) was too busy deploring it to describe it. I assume it was something great because it reduced the *Post* to stammering incoherence. "Unbelievable" was only the beginning; "worse than silly . . . dishonest, futile and stupid" were among the high points.

Apparently the board adopted some sort of "regulations allowing youngsters to graduate from high school without ever having heard of Charles Darwin or the theory of evolution." But it seems to me if that's all they don't know they'll be better off than most high-school graduates in any state I'm familiar with. Wonder how many D.C. high schoolers could identify Darwin or give an accurate précis of his theory?

The *Post*'s editors ought to explain why this particular lacuna is so distressing. Would they be equally upset by a ruling that graduates need not "have heard" of Jesus and His theory of redemption?

Someone needs to point out, first, that we don't have a national educational system; second, that if states and localities are going to support public schools in the first place, they should decide what is to be taught in those schools; third, that they should have the right to make even foolish decisions.

On the same subject (more or less), there's good news from MIT for creation scientists. Dr. Hyman Hartman, a meteorologist, has suggested that there are some problems with the theory of the origin of life supported by most of his colleagues—that life originated from organic compounds formed by the action of lightning on an ammonia-methane atmosphere. Hartman believes that the earth's atmosphere was nitrogen, water, and carbon dioxide (like that of Mars today); if so, lightning wouldn't do the trick. He thinks the crucial reaction was between carbon dioxide and a substance called montmorillonite, in the presence of ultraviolet light.

What is montmorillonite? Well, it's a kind of . . . Well, you see, it's . . . What it is, is clay.

And while we're talking about religion, it's cheering to see that American ingenuity still contrives to frustrate federal meddlers. The non-Communist public continues to pray more or less at will, out of school or in it.

Since most non-Communist Americans seem to be in the South, or moving to it, the school-prayer issue necessarily has a regional tinge. All the examples of defiance reported in a recent *Wall Street Journal* article came from Dixie. In Liberty, Kentucky, for instance, a school forbidden to post the Ten Commandments in classrooms posted instead a page from the *Congressional Record*—on which were found the Ten Commandments. In North Carolina, a survey estimates that 18 percent of all public schools simply ignore the Supreme Court's usurpation and offer daily prayer anyway.

When prayers are outlawed, only outlaws will say prayers. Didn't we learn anything from Prohibition?

Bootleg prayer seems to be pretty much a Southern phenomenon, but some other folks don't like being pushed around either. In Winnipeg, where a new law requires all restaurants that seat more than thirty people to provide a nonsmoking section, restaurateur Tony Rambone has designated his front veranda as the nonsmoking section—not unaware of the fact that temperatures there are often well below freezing.

In this country, of course, antismoking laws have been pioneered by San Francisco, home of Sister Boom-Boom and the 1984 Democratic Convention. Leave it to the modern Democratic party to meet in a city that regards smoking—and little else—as a crime against nature. Mama always said you don't have to drink and smoke to have a good time, but I don't think San Francisco is what she had in mind.

When my wife ventured out to Marin County recently, she came back with a copy of the local newspaper, *The Sun*. All I know is what I read in the paper: the Church of the Healing Hands advertises a Friday-night hot-tub liturgy, while the Institute of Colonic Hygiene announces that it has changed its name to the Inner Beauty Institute and offers something called "full body facials."

Southern California seems only marginally less weird. Dr. Robert Franklyn, a Los Angeles plastic surgeon who, in 1952, pioneered augmentation mammaplasty (b**b jobs, as they're known in these parts), claims that "We're 10 to 15 years ahead of the East Coast." Dr. Michael Hogan, an NYU plastic doc, agrees. His West Coast colleagues routinely use implants three times larger than the ones common in the East. Where's Ralph Nader when you need him?

Look. If we can't secede, can we kick them out?

(January 1986)

❧ Odds and Ends from Here and There ❧

The last couple of years have been busy ones here in the South. Mississippi finally ratified the Nineteenth Amendment to the U.S. Constitution, giving women the vote. At Billy Bob's, in Fort Worth, Merle Haggard stood all 5,095 customers to drinks. And in Hardwick, Georgia, Daniel Sargent, twenty-seven, a one-legged, diabetic, and legally blind armed robber, escaped from a state prison by climbing over a twelve-foot fence. (He was captured, according to newspaper reports, "within yards" of the institution.)

In the course of a single trip, an Amtrak Miami–to–New York train hit and killed a woman running on the tracks in Georgia, smashed a pickup truck in South Carolina, and plowed into a flatbed truck in North Carolina. Maybe we Southerners ought to move a little faster.

North Carolina is celebrating its four-hundredth anniversary and Princess Anne came to help. A local paper described the plans for her visit and announced that, "In addition, a flotilla of sailing ships from Elizabeth City led by Walter Cronkite will sail into Manteo Harbor that weekend." Nearby, at New Bern, freshwater fishermen landed a 240-pound bull shark. Some thought the eight-foot-long person-eater had been lured up the Neuse River by increasing salinity; others speculated that he was fleeing Walter Cronkite.

In Dallas, meanwhile, the Gay and Lesbian Student Support Organization at Southern Methodist University applied three times for formal recognition to the SMU student senate. Three times, the student senate said no. After the third turndown, the president of SMU was finally heard from: "Organizational recognition," he said, "is inconsistent with the goals, purpose, philosophy, and religious heritage of a Methodist university." Does that mean it's wrong?

Who'd have thought students would be the ones to uphold standards in institutions of higher education? But it's so. At Washington and Lee, the student government requested that the faculty require students to wear coats and ties to class. (C'mon guys: make it a "non-negotiable demand." Didn't you learn anything from the sixties?) And in Charlottesville, Mr. Jefferson's university, not to be outdone by W&L in the standard-upholding department, removed the Muzak from its telephone system. Formerly, callers put on hold were subjected to the earwash that we have grown all too accustomed to in public places. A faculty resolution prompted by embarrassment at the thought of long-distance callers being treated to a hundred violins playing "Feelings" did the trick. The assistant vice-president in charge of this sort of thing said some people told him the music was "the most grievous problem to confront the university in 200 years."

Elsewhere in the Atlantic Coast Conference, Clemson got a new basketball coach. When Cliff Ellis left the University of South Alabama, the *Tampa Tribune*'s headline was "ELLIS TO LEAVE USA FOR CLEMSON." Another land-grant school, at the other end of the South, found a new use for cow manure. According to an article in the *Daily Texan*, while restoring an old building at Texas A&M the Aggies contrived to make new bricks look old by smearing them with the stuff, a process called (the story says) "organic patination."

As sociologists, street cops, and political bosses know, only carefully controlled lawlessness can keep a system of unworkable laws working. Federal controls on diesel fuel made even less sense in Louisiana than a 55 mph speed limit in Nevada. When they began to be rigidly enforced after some years of looking the other way, even good Americans were driven to seek federal aid. Mr. Tee John Mialjevich of Delcambre, president of the Concerned Shrimpers of Louisiana, appeared before the House Subcommittee on Merchant Marine and Fisheries to say: "We need help, now that we can't buy hot fuel anymore." A typically out-of-touch congressman asked him about "hot fuel": "Is that a special mixture for fishing boats?"

In other political news, 1984 North Carolina gubernatorial candidate Lauch Faircloth said of his hometown of Clinton that it has the only McDonald's in the country that serves McChitlins. About the same time, Fritz Hollings, whose sense of humor doesn't entirely make up for the disreputable company he keeps, suggested that Southerners aren't excited by the issues that apparently vex other Americans. When a reporter for the Yankee press asked him how his stand on a nuclear freeze would go down in Alabama, the senator allowed as how most Alabamians thought a nuclear freeze was a popsicle. And the authentic voice of the South was heard once again from Billy Carter's filling station. Eddy Rogers of the local seed and feed store told the *Wall Street Journal* that he was going to vote for Gary Hart in the primary because "he's the only candidate I never heard of until February."

(February 1986)

ᴥ Raw Bits ᴥ

From California comes word that the Stanford Research Institute has developed a typology of Americans based on their (excuse the expression) life-styles. Of course the types aren't distributed uniformly across the U.S.; three in particular are geographically concentrated. "Achievers" are more likely than others to be wealthy, middle-aged suburbanites in Southern California and the Midwest.

(George Babbitt lives.) Also financially well-off are the "Socially Conscious": younger, well-educated folk who pile up in New England and on the West Coast. "Belongers" make up 37 percent of the U.S. population; they are patriotic, family oriented, politically conservative, and tend to live—guess where.

Meanwhile, the Roper Poll has been asking Americans how they see regional differences in the U.S. Over all, the West is seen as the "most exciting" and prettiest region, and the best place to vacation. The Wild Northeast is seen as most dangerous, as well as most cosmopolitan and most expensive. It is also believed to be where "most of the people who run things" live, which is probably true enough. The Middle West comes out middling, neither best nor worst, in most respects; it does get rated "least exciting," though, something that sounds more and more attractive the older I get. The South gets credit for the best weather (although the summer before the survey we just about dried up and blew away), and our people are seen as the friendliest and most religious. Although it would be news to, say, Louisianans, Roper also found that most Americans believe the South has the best job opportunities. Look out, Yankee, Sunbelt's gonna get yo' mama.

Which may have something to do with mini-course 2062: How to Speak Southern, offered recently by MIT's Laboratory for Nuclear Science. Make of that what y'all will.

Meanwhile, up the road from MIT in Lincoln, Massachusetts, a little drama answered the perennial question, can any good thing come from Arkansas? According to the *Anglican Digest*, when a Filipino Sister of St. Anne took her cheap but treasured wristwatch to a Lincoln jeweler for repairs, he told her that "Only an Arkansas tinkerer could repair this." So she sent it to the parents of a student from Arkansas, and it came back good as new.

Speaking of the South's friendly and religious people: I don't plan to vote for any TV evangelist for president, but I do admire some of them and defend them occasionally from ignorant criticism. But a few Gantryesque specimens make it all too easy for critics of the breed to score. Consider, for example, the allegedly Reverend Jim Whittington of Greenville, North Carolina. Mrs. Mozelle Ussery of La Grange, Georgia, sick with leukemia, wrote him some time ago, after watching his syndicated television program. According to the AP, he subsequently sent her roughly thirty computer-generated letters. One letter said, "The Lord spoke to me to have you prove yourself by sending an offering of $15 (Malachi 3:10)," and the last one read: "My dear friend Mozelle, you can get in trouble with God and miss your blessing by not being obedient. . . . I don't want your blood on my hands at the Judgment, Mozelle." Mrs. Ussery was unresponsive because she had died seven months before. Her husband was sufficiently annoyed by the last letter to send copies to several newspapers. Preacher Whittington commented: "I only asked the man for $15, and he's giving me thousands in free advertising."

Far be it from me to urge federal regulation. Instead, let us pray—for whatever may be appropriate.

In other First Amendment news from North Carolina, a state legislator introduced a bill to ban the sale of *TV Guide* in the state if the magazine did not apologize for insulting the sweet potato in one of its advertisements. The honorable gentleman pointed out that a town in his district, Tuber—er, Tabor—City, has an annual yam festival, whereas nobody has a *TV Guide* festival. (Listen, it keeps them out of trouble.)

Despite such stories, let us not forget that state legislatures are our first line of defense against federal tyranny. And not just in the South. Out in John Wayne country, some state politicos have been aiding and abetting their constituents' contumacy. Last I heard, for instance, legislation was pending in Wyoming, Nevada, and Montana to reduce the fine for speeding (up to 75 mph) to $1.00, thus technically complying with the federales' silly speed limits while ensuring that no one will be seriously inconvenienced by them.

Unfortunately, it probably won't work. The feds are making it plain that they intend to cut off highway funds to states that post limits and ignore them. When Florida got threatened with some proviso about the percentage of drivers who must comply, the Sunshine State meekly started arresting folks.

To me, this bespeaks a serious failure of the imagination. I'm not hog-wild about highways in the first place, but even if we accept the need for them, there are alternatives to the federal dole (better: make that Dole, after the ex–Tar Heel secretary of transportation). Back in the bad old days of regional antagonism (about 1968), for instance, Floridians' neighbors in Georgia outlawed studded snow tires. The penalty for this insult to Georgia highways was a $1,000 fine. Most miscreants paid readily enough, since the alternative was a year spent at repairing the damage and doing other forms of road work under armed supervision.

Of course the law was just an exaggeration of Georgia's ancient speed-trap tradition, directed at New Yorkers passing through en route to Florida; few Georgians felt the need for snow tires, studded or otherwise. (Since the last Yankee who made it through Georgia without being stopped was General Sherman, you can understand why Georgians have taken such exquisite care to see that it didn't happen again.) But the law not only pandered to unworthy xenophobic impulses, it was also a potentially nice little money-maker. I never did hear how much it raised in fines and unreimbursed services, but Florida might want to consider something similar, if the Department of Transportation wants to get nasty about it.

The problem with this approach, of course, is that the quarrel isn't with hapless Northern tourists. But I have an alternative to suggest. Ask yourself: how do the federal boys determine how fast Florida drivers are going? Floridians ought to think about making it illegal for anyone but the state police to operate radar equipment. A few DOT highway engineers on Florida chain gangs would be an edifying spectacle. Even if their fines didn't make up for the federal money cut off, it might be worth it. Sic semper tyrannis.

(February 1987)

～ Covering Dixie Like the Dew ～

Time for another roundup of Southern news you may not have seen. Let's start off slow, with this item from the *Chapel Hill* (N.C.) *Newspaper*:

> Arnold D. Rollins of Rt. 5 Box 372, Chapel Hill, reported a hit-and-run accident on Columbia St. and Rosemary St. at 11:30.
> According to police reports, a pedestrian ran into the corner of Rollins' tow truck. Rollins says he was heading north on Rosemary at

about 20-25 mph when a boy jumped out of a car stopped at the intersection and ran into the fender of his truck.

Rollins said that the victim did not stop, but spun around, fell, and then hopped away from the accident.

No damage or injuries was [*sic*] reported.

(I told you we do things differently down here.)

How about this tidbit, from the Marseilles of the South: The jury that acquitted Governor Edwards of Louisiana on fraud and racketeering charges stayed at the Avenue Plaza Hotel in New Orleans. When they checked out, according to the hotel's owner, they took twenty-four towels, valued at $200, with them.

Next door in Mississippi, during archery season (which runs for about a month before the start of gun season) even the use of crossbows is forbidden. But last year 4'3" Kenneth Hodge pointed out that the law has its, ah, drawbacks. Hodge's arms are too short to draw a twenty-eight-inch arrow. Mississippi has, shall we say, seldom been on the cutting edge of equal-opportunity legislation, but state representative Will Green Poindexter responded to Hodge's complaint with a bill that would have allowed dwarves to use crossbows. I don't know if it passed or not, but I think it's a great idea, and while they're at it they ought to ask them to wear little green suits.

And speaking of wildlife: the floods of 1986 in Jefferson County, Arkansas, were not without their silver lining. According to the *Arkansas Times*, one man whose home was submerged for a weekend strung a trotline across his front yard and caught more than three hundred fish.

The same journal reported that a filling station near Sheridan, when chided about a sign that read "Mechnic on Duty," changed it for one that said "Mechanick on Duty." When told by a passing busybody that was wrong, too, the proprietor replaced it with one that read: "Broke Cars Fixed."

A Mississippi correspondent has sent me a marvelous advertisement for South Central Bell. "KEEP UP A SOUTHERN TRADITION," the ad suggests. "VISIT WITH YOUR FOLKS THIS SATURDAY." "Visiting is a favorite pastime in the South. Southerners love to talk." Announcing cheap weekend rates for in-state calls, it goes on: "This Saturday, swap stories. Share a secret. Visit with your folks. It's a custom worth keeping."

Amen to that, I say, but my man in Mississippi spells out the irony: "Who would have dreamed that the phone company—corporate America, technology itself—would become an institution keeping alive the Southern identity?"

But I don't know—can the South survive this? The *Charlotte Observer* reports that households in Orange County, North Carolina, home of your servant and the University of North Carolina, are more likely to subscribe to the *New Yorker* than are households in New York City.

Of course the big news of the past year down here has been the Jim and Tammy Faye Bakker imbroglio, which brought in Jerry Falwell toward the end, then yielded place to the Last Temptation of Jimmy Swaggert—all of which gave rise to a good deal of humor, most of it unprintable. It shouldn't be surprising that the best jokes, like their reverend subjects, came from our neck of the woods. To have sacrilege you first need orthodoxy, and anticlericalism is found in priest-ridden societies, not secular ones. A certain irreverence—or at least skepticism about institutional religion—is a Southern tradition as well established as evangelical Protestantism itself. In "Long-Haired Country Boy," for example, Nashville's Charlie Daniels makes it plain that he doesn't doubt the literal truth of the Bible, but he quite explicitly doubts the bona fides of the TV preacher who "Wants me to send a donation / 'Cause he's worried about my soul." And Ray Stevens swears that his song "Would Jesus Wear a Rolex on His Television Show?" was written by Chet Atkins *before* the PTL scandal broke.

Combine Southerners' inherited distrust of prelacy with trickle-down Aquarianism from the sixties, and you get some truly bizarre results—like the local boogie-woogie man who bills himself as "the Reverend Billy C. Wirtz, High Prophet of Polyester, Director of the First House of Polyester Worship and Horizontal Throbbing Teenage Desire and Our First Lady of the White Go-Go Boots Worldwide Love Ministries, Inc." Would anybody from Scarsdale have the slightest idea what *that* is all about?

Every time I start to wonder if the South is blanding out, I run across something like that—or like this splendid story, sent my way by a friend in Nashville.

Seems there was something of a parking problem recently in Estill Springs, Tennessee, caused by several thousand people who came to see the face of Jesus revealed on the side of a General Electric deep freeze located on the front deck of Luther and Arlene Gardner's mobile home. What local journalists took to calling "Jesus-on-a-freezer" appeared each night when the Gardners' neighbor turned on his porch light, until said neighbor tired of devotees dropping film wrappers in his yard and removed the light. At last report, the Gardners were thinking about moving their home and their freezer to a new location and setting up their own light. (And people thought Flannery O'Connor made this stuff up.)

The Estill Springs apparition naturally occasioned jeers from secular humanists, of which even Middle Tennessee has a few. According to the *Nashville Tennessean*, one Audrey Campbell performed her song "Porch Light Jesus" to laughter and applause at the Unitarian Universalist First Church of Nashville. "Some people get the Shroud of Turin and some get a freezer," she explained. "You make do with what you've got." Ms. Campbell reportedly hoped to sign a recording contract.

Tennessean news editor Dolph Honicker poked fun, too. He claimed the face was that of either Willie Nelson or the Ayatollah Khomeini, and said he could also make out a large, slanted capital-letter N and the letters $v\ r\ y$ or $v\ k\ y$—in either case, he admitted, a message that was Greek to him.

But Honicker had the grace to observe that the Gardners were behaving admirably. At a time when everybody from Jim Bakker to a Unitarian folksinger is figuring how to make a buck off simple faith, all the Gardners wanted was to share freely what they believed they had been given. No parking fees, or lemonade stand, or T-shirts—just an invitation to come and marvel at this marvelous thing.

And, as my Nashville friend wrote, "There is an awful sincerity about the lady who owns the freezer that makes it seem sinful to ridicule this small claim to fame, perhaps the nearest thing to achievement she's ever had. We Bible Belters—and I do not use the phrase pejoratively—have a certain zaniness that goes with the territory. She's nearer to me religiously than a whole heap of seminarians wining and cheesing up there at [the Episcopal seminary at] Sewanee."

Luther Gardner, told of Ms. Campbell's song about his freezer, said simply: "This is something from God. It's not something for people to make fun of. I'm sorry. It's just not the right thing to do." He's right, of course—at least about our snottiness.

And just think: if God really did manifest Himself on a major appliance—well, let's just say that He has a puckish sense of humor I hadn't suspected, and He isn't making it easy for us smart alecks.

(December 1987)

∼ Talkin' Freedom Blues ∽

I've been sitting here listening to the University of North Carolina's student radio station play "Hotrod to Hell," a cut from Elvis Hitler's new album *Disgraceland* (you think I could make that up?), and somehow the time seemed right for another roundup of Southern news that they've probably been keeping from you.

Speaking of the higher learning, for example, I'll bet you didn't see the note in the *Chronicle of Higher Education* about the faculty-staff directory at the University of Tennessee in Knoxville which listed under "Education, College of," an entry for the "Readin Center."

The lower learning made the news, too. The *Jackson Clarion-Ledger* reported that Mississippi ranks second only to Arkansas in public-school paddlings. In a recent year nearly fifty thousand Mississippi students (one in eight) heard the tune of the hickory stick. For what it's worth, the Magnolia State also had the lowest percentage of "seriously emotionally disturbed" children in its schools. Spare the rod and—? No, surely not.

In other news from Southern education, back here in the Southern Part of Heaven (as Chapel Hill's boosters sometimes call it) one of our students recently reported the theft of his license plate. No, not his car, his license plate: a vanity number that read "POONTANG." Some innocent in the state motor vehicle department must have let that one by, or maybe it's protected by the First Amendment. But the First Amendment cuts both ways when it comes to license plates. I read that ACLU types in Maryland have objected to plates with messages like "GOD IS." At last report, the state was going to recall plates with religious messages. You figure it out.

Not long ago, on US 15-501 near Durham (what used to be called the Jefferson Davis Highway—and whatever happened to the signs?) I saw an evil-looking young man with a black goatee driving a car with license number "MB 666." If we're going to interfere with religious messages, let's start with that one, OK?

This religion business does keep coming up when people talk about the South. For instance, in *Channels*, a trade magazine for broadcasters, a writer of the television program "Designing Women" spoke about an episode in which one of the Southern women of the title wanted to become a Baptist preacher but was turned down because she's female. The writer, a Southerner herself, said that even though the show was critical of Baptist traditionalism, it drew "negative comments within the industry" because "some people assumed that we were trying to do a Jerry Falwell thing!"

Poor Jerry. Another cheap shot. But the woman has an interesting point. Apparently treating evangelical Protestantism *at all* is viewed with suspicion. Certainly it's unusual. "You would have thought we'd done a show about the leprechauns or something," she said. "No one has ever in the history of prime time television done a sitcom about Baptists. . . ."

By the way, in the National Organization of Women's *State-by-State Guide to Women's Legal Rights*, ranking the states according to how well they comply with the liberal view of what women need, the three "best" are Washington, Massachusetts, and New York. Of the five "worst" only Nevada is outside Dixie; the other four are Mississippi, Alabama, South Carolina, and Georgia—setting for "Designing Women" and Charlene's thwarted vocation.

Ah, Georgia. Did you notice how many of the news stories filed from the 1988 Democratic Convention mentioned Atlanta's "table-dancing" establishments? It's surprising how many reporters found time to check out this traditional Atlanta art form. Andy Young's municipal government, anticipating exactly the sort of stories that were written, tried to close these places, but failed. It's that ol' debbil First Amendment again. (Freedom of expression? Of worship?) Yankees have always said that Southern men put women on pedestals, but I don't think this is what they meant.

Incidentally, I don't know why people haven't done sitcoms about Baptists. Lord knows they can be funny. Listen to the Reverend Joseph Chambers, for example. According to the *Charlotte Observer*, he told a meeting on AIDS that "Prayer always works. Condoms work only 80 percent of the time."

Pardon my free-associating, but that reminds me of a new champagne I read about in the *New York Times*. Are you ready for Marquis de Sade Private Reserve Grand Cru, vintage 1981, about $45 the bottle F.O.B. Paris? Its marketing director said: "I don't think it will be a huge success in the Bible Belt." But, he added, "it will do very well in New York, Beverly Hills, and San Francisco." Yes, indeed.

Tell you what, we'd leave them alone if they'd leave us alone. But here comes a Washington lawyer—two words that should terrify and nauseate honest folk everywhere—to sue the state of North Carolina, challenging a law that exempts the Bible from state sales tax. The smarty-pants former Duke student is suing on behalf of a Jew, two Hindus, and two members of the ACLU who want Bible buyers to render unto Caesar.

For my part, I find it charming that North Carolina doesn't tax Holy Writ but (unlike most states) does tax the sale of food. That eloquently bespeaks a conviction that (all together now) man does not live by bread alone. Maybe you read that somewhere?

Incidentally, the *Charlotte Observer* also reports that a marketing survey ranking the top hundred markets according to the percentage of households in which the Bible is read regularly put Charlotte fourteenth, with 28 percent compared to a national average of 18 percent. I guess cheap Bibles could be one reason.

In a probably unrelated development, the AP reported that Charlotte leads the nation in per capita ketchup consumption. (Three of the top five cities were Southern: Atlanta and Memphis were the other two, with Minneapolis and Omaha tagging along.) Rick Carter of the Hickory House in Charlotte said folks put the red goop on "just about everything." "It's just like beer—they suck it down." Between services.

Speaking of things that pinko secular-humanist liberal hermaphrodites don't want us to do, remember the old joke about the teacher who sees some kids kneeling in the hall ("What are you all doing?" "Shooting dice." "Oh, that's all right—I thought you were praying.")? Well, three children in Marion, North Carolina, were suspended from grade school not for praying but for preaching. Matthew and Duffey Strode were witnessing outside school one morning before class, when the principal bade them desist and come inside.

Ten-year-old Duffey replied: "Woe unto you, scribes and pharisees."

Not to be outdone, five-year-old Matthew observed: "Marriage is honorable in all, and the bed undefiled. But whoremongers and adulterers God will judge."

Six-year-old sister Pepper kept the silence enjoined upon her sex, but the principal suspended all three anyway.

Meanwhile, some other Tar Heel schools faced a different sort of First Amendment issue. Down the road in Durham, a junior-high principal confiscated a student's denim jacket because it had a rebel flag on the sleeve, and a number of other high-school and junior-high students were suspended when they defied orders not to wear such patches. One administrator defended his actions by saying that displays of the flag "might cause trouble." A local commentator rightly observed that on that basis Ole Miss was right to refuse admission to James Meredith.

Excuse me if I exit editorializing, would you? This annoys me right smart.

Look, we're not talking here about including the rebel emblem in a state flag the way Mississippi and Georgia do. We're not talking about flying it over the statehouse, like Alabama, or including it as part of policemen's uniforms, like Franklin, Tennessee. We're not talking about selling Confederate-flag license plates in state-run agencies, as in North Carolina. In each of these cases, maybe there is something to be said for getting government out of the act. Maybe.

But in Durham all we had were some teenage Hank Williams, Jr., fans, proud to be Southern boys. They weren't Hitler Youth; the kid whose jacket was taken said in an interview that he thinks "the Klan's a bunch of jerks." You might ask why schools that long ago abandoned dress codes get to make up new ones on the spot. Since every Satanist and table-dancer in the South seems to be protected by the First Amendment, why not these lads?

Of course, students' rights have never been a big number down here. Recall those paddling statistics. But there is a wonderful irony in the fact that one of the teachers enforcing these improvised rules was reportedly wearing a "Black By Popular Demand" T-shirt.

(May 1989)

∽ The Last Round-up ∾

As I write, 1989 is drawing to a close, ending a decade that, all things considered, could have been worse for the Republic. But lest we wax too smug about the success of voodoo economics and Star Wars diplomacy, let's consider some recent, revolting developments on the cultural front.

The big news in the art world last year was the attempt by my state's senior senator to impose fascistic thought control. This was the sort of language generally used to describe Senator Helms's proposal, inspired by a couple of particularly raunchy examples, that taxpayers' money not be used to support obscene art. As it happens, I was in Washington while Mr. Mapplethorpe's notorious photographs were on exhibit, and snuck off to have a look.

To tell you the truth, I wish I hadn't. When Jimmy Walker said that no girl was ever ruined by a book he revealed his contempt for books, if not for girls. And a picture's worth a thousand words. Even I picked up a few images that will be with me for a while; those photographs could bend an impressionable young mind completely out of shape.

In fact, I think my senator wimped out on this one. Jesse just wanted to deny federal funds to this exhibit; me, I'd shut it down and put an armed guard on the door. Why not? Thirty years ago these photographs couldn't have been publicly displayed in any American community, and I don't think our country's a better place now because they can be.

When it comes to state support for sadomasochistic homosexual art, give me Georgia state representative Billy Randall's bill to make Little Richard's "Tutti Frutti" the official rock and roll song of Georgia. (Representative Randall is forty-five, a dangerous age.) Last I heard, the bill—one clause of which reads, "WHEREAS, a wop bop a loo bop ba lop bam boom"—had stalled, which is a shame. Georgia ought somehow to honor the best poet from Macon since Sidney Lanier.

The other big First Amendment news last year, of course, was the decision by the Eleventh Circuit Court of Appeals that pregame prayers at Douglas County (Georgia) High School football games violated the separation of church and state. *Time* reported that fans in Sylacauga, Alabama, responded with mass chanting of the Lord's Prayer at the start of their team's first three games (which the team won). In Escambia County, Florida, preachers with bullhorns led the crowd in prayer. And in Chatsworth, Georgia, fans turned their radios to full volume as the local station broadcast a prayer. "There's more than one way to skin a cat," the station manager told *Time*.

In Montgomery, pregame prayers at the municipal stadium were led by the Honorable Emory Folmar himself. Mr. Folmar, mayor of Montgomery, is a colorful character known to many of his subjects as "the Mayortollah." About his habit of traveling armed, I once heard this joke:

Q: Why does Emory carry a nickel-plated revolver?

A: So it won't rust in the shower.

Down the road at Tuscaloosa, campus police at 'Bama are also ready for whatever comes along—for now. A study commission has concluded, however, that their purchase of automatic shotguns and semiautomatic pistols was "unnecessary and unwarranted." According to the student newspaper, the *Crimson White*, the report also criticized the campus police for setting up a S.W.A.T. unit. This kind of negativity would never have been tolerated when the Bear was running things.

But that's the Second Amendment. Getting back to the First, maybe we can forgive the ACLU a few excesses for its defense of the right of junior-high students in Durham, North Carolina, to wear rebel flag patches on their jackets. Such patches had been banned by administrative edict as "likely to cause trouble," but after a successful suit in district court the flags were readmitted to the classroom. So far they've caused no trouble.

That can't be said for what the makers of *Shag* did with the flag in that teen movie (starring Bridget Fonda). Their desecrations elicited spirited protest from at least one member of the Sons of Confederate Veterans. Personally, I thought the bikini was rather fetching.

If we have to do something about Confederate flag bikinis, though, I have an idea. I see where a Tennessee legislator has introduced a bill that would levy a fine of $1.00 on anyone convicted of assaulting someone who's burning an American flag. Well, let's punish ripping off a rebel-flag bikini with about the same severity. (Incidentally, these Tennesseans take the flag-burning threat seriously. Servpro Industries, of Gallatin, offers to fireproof your flag to 3,000 degrees.)

In any case, Bridget Fonda's indiscretions are nothing compared to her Aunt Jane's. Some folks down here are still not ready to forgive old Jane her trip to Hanoi. The catalog of D&G, a Columbus, Georgia, dealer in "militaria," offers bumper stickers that read "Boycott Jane Fonda, American Traitor Bitch" and—I'm sorry, folks, but this was America in 1989—something called "Hanoi Jane urinal targets." Reminds me of the Mapplethorpe exhibit.

Here in Chapel Hill, buffalo-rights advocates struck a blow against speciesism. Calling Buffalo Bill a "butcher," they got a sculpture of his head and those of three buffalo removed from the lobby of the post office. The work was on loan from a local sculptor in connection with the issue of a new fifteen-cent buffalo stamp. Had the artist been receiving federal funds, perhaps someone would have spoken out for her First Amendment rights.

I hope you don't get the impression, incidentally, that Chapel Hill trendinistas are the only Southerners who care about animal rights. I mean, you can't top a clipping from the *Jackson Clarion-Ledger* that recently trickled in, headlined "Insult to Dog Linked to Slaying." That's *concern*. It seems that Mr. Jerry Wade, twenty-eight, of Calhoun City, Mississippi, made rude remarks about a dog belonging to Mr. David Powell of Derma—specifically, Wade said he "could get a [expletive deleted] off the street to whup [Powell's] dog"—whereupon Mr. Powell shot Mr. Wade once (but that was enough) with a .38 he happened to have at hand.

And lower down the evolutionary scale, in Matthews, North Carolina— No, let me start that over. In Matthews, North Carolina, crustacean rights were vindicated when a man who had paid $270 for a 21.4 pound Maine lobster, estimated to be 147 years old, freed the critter. According to the AP, when television coverage evoked a flood of phone calls asking for clemency the buyer said, "Oh, to heck with it." "Lobzilla," as the Large One had come to be called, was shipped back to Maine at the expense of a Washington-based animal-rights group, there to enjoy his old age back in the deep.

Returning to the civil liberties of putatively human beings, the Invisible Empire Knights of the Ku Klux Klan may be taking the North Carolina Department of Transportation to court. See, North Carolina has what is called an "Adopt-a-Highway" program. If your club or company agrees to clean up litter from a stretch of roadside, a sign goes up attesting to your public spirit. More than forty-five hundred groups now clean up about ten thousand miles of road, but the Department of Transportation drew the line when the KKK applied. One reason the Knights were not allowed to be points of light, it was said, was that people would deliberately throw trash on the highway to make work for them. (As far as I know, no one suggested that the Invisible Empire could have an invisible sign.) To show the Kluxers that there was nothing personal about its decision, the Transportation Department also turned down applications from a Chapel Hill rock band called the Sex Police and a Raleigh lingerie shop called the Bra Patch. (Maybe the pun only works if you have a Southern accent.) This one's probably headed for the courts.

Speaking of things that shouldn't burden our legal system, an associate professor of education at our university surveyed female graduate students on their experience with "sexual harassment" and found what she interpreted as appalling levels of ignorance. According to the newspaper account, fewer than 3 percent of these women thought they had been sexually harassed, even though 30 percent had been "subjected to suggestive stories told in their presence" and 26 percent had heard "sexist remarks regarding either their behavior or their career options." Apparently these women simply didn't realize that this stuff is sexual harassment, not just boorish, ill-bred behavior. For that matter, neither did I.

Nor did residents of a women's dormitory at Western Kentucky University, it seems. Male students offered them a "tuck-in" service that included milk and cookies and a bedtime story—in fact, a choice of stories, traditional or "hot" (clipped from *Penthouse Forum*)—and what do you think they chose? Yep, every single one.

Meanwhile, back in Chapel Hill, the "Lewis Streak," in which young men from Lewis dormitory once a year strut their stuff for the residents of several nearby women's dorms, came under fire. According to the *Daily Tar Heel*, "University officials fear it undermines efforts to stop date rape and sexual harassment on campus." The dean of students was quoted as saying this particular act of self-expression "is no longer acceptable in this campus community," and that it presents "much potential for personal injury as well as for the infliction of emotional distress."

OK, guys, here's my plan. You take photographs, see, and blow them up to life-size. Then you, like, *carry* them past the dorms, and if anybody objects, it's art.

(April 1990)

❧ Funny Business ❧

Cleaning out my drawers, I find regional news items (some newer than others) from the worlds of religion and business, with some miscellaneous statistics for garnish. Beginning with religion, of a sort:

In Tupelo, Mississippi (where Elvis was born in 1935), two brothers went on trial for attempting to murder Judge Tommy Gardner, by hexing him. Leroy and John Henry Ivy hired a hoodoo hit man from Jamaica to do the job, and all was going well until the judge's wife got suspicious. Seems the Ivy boys called her to ask for a photograph of her husband and some of his hair.

Apparently this sort of thing is big business in North Mississippi. The *Wall Street Journal*, ever alert to the commercial implications, reported that the mojo department of A. Schwab Department Store in Memphis sells about twenty-one tons of hoodoo supplies a year.

But if you think weird occult practices appeal only to poor ignorant rural black folk, think again. Last year a Floridian dying from a brain tumor advertised his services as a messenger to the dead. For twenty dollars Ken McAvoy promised to deliver your message to anyone on the other side, and he offered a written guarantee.

And then there's Sherri Cash, a well-off ignorant urban white woman, alias Venus Moonbaby. Ms. Moonbaby tests auras and sells healing crystals at a New Age pharmacy in Atlanta. "There's a theory," she told *America* magazine, "that Atlanta is a reincarnation of the continent of Atlantis and that a lot of people who were in Atlantis together have been pulled back to Atlanta."

Maybe that explains why somebody there thinks farmers' market employees need California-style human potential training. Eight employees of the DeKalb Farmers' Market claimed in an Atlanta court that they were fired or mistreated after they refused to take part in self-actualization sessions developed by Werner Erhard. Erhard, you may recall, is the Californian who invented "est," in which people pay large sums to be locked in hotel ballrooms with strangers and denied access to toilet facilities. Personally, I prefer mojos and goofer dust.

I've said before that the only reason to care what Californians do is that we often seem to wind up imitating them. That said, here's another enormity to watch out for: the Sausalito City Council has established a "cholesterol-free zone," by requiring restaurants to offer no-cholesterol food to patrons. Any decent barbecue joint would go out of business first.

Wonder what Sausalito would make of this sign from Sharp's Stop & Shop, spotted by the *Arkansas Times*:

FROZEN
YOGURT
NIGHTCRAWLERS

Actually, that might sound good to folks who like raw fish.

Speaking of raw fish, after Ben Jones, the actor who played Cooter on "The Dukes of Hazzard," got elected to Congress, he told the Washington press: "You think I don't have culture just because I'm from down in Georgia. Believe me, we got culture there. We've always had sushi. We just used to call it 'bait.'"

Jones isn't your usual blow-dried pretty-boy Southern pol. Not to put too fine a point on it, he went through a few wives and a lot of whiskey before (as he told the reporters) "I awoke naked in a tattoo parlor in Talladega, Alabama. I knew it was time to change my lifestyle. So I went into politics."

Maybe old Cooter could moonlight explaining Southern culture to Californians at Berkeley, where a professor of business has suggested that courses on the cultures of "such subgroups as Mormons, Armenians, and white Southerners" should be required. Actually, according to the *Chicago Tribune,* Professor David Vogel was making fun of a proposal to require a course on the cultures of black, Asian, Hispanic, and "native" Americans, but it sounds good to me. If anyone needs a consultant I'm available at my usual rates.

One Southern difference from Californians that needs explaining was revealed when Compton Advertising Inc. asked 1,007 adults how old they felt, compared to their actual age. College graduates, the financially well-off, divorcées, and Californians (not mutually exclusive groups, obviously) are likely to feel spryer than they should. Southerners are more likely to act their age: only 59 percent feel younger than they are, compared to 70 percent of Westerners. This may help to explain another difference, reported recently in the *Wall Street Journal*: a marketing director at the company that makes Northern-brand toilet paper says that "Californians go for more sheets," and thus for thinner paper, while Southerners like it thick.

Or then, again, maybe Southerners are just wiping up stuff. Another *Journal* story reported that when Monsanto asked a sample of American women who in their households is most likely to spill and stain things, most pointed the finger at children under twelve. But not in the South Atlantic states, where 38 percent indicated that their husbands were the main household slobs. Elsewhere only 10 to 18 percent picked the old man.

In other marketing news from the *Journal,* the makers of Mountain Dew announced a campaign to "reposition" that soft drink. Apparently its core market now comprises what a former product manager calls "the pickup truck and construction set," folks who "had their glory days in high school"; for them, Mountain Dew is "a nostalgic vehicle back to those glory days." (Shoot, and here I thought we just liked the way it tastes.) Movie star Patrick Swayze—a Southerner, but a polished one—was to be featured in ads designed to appeal to city slickers. Mr. Swayze achieved stardom in *Dirty Dancing,* but he's better known to us right-wing extremists for his role in the anti-Communist classic *Red Dawn* (Wolverines!).

Still saving your Confederate money? The London *Times* reported the sale at Sotheby's of five thousand Confederate bonds, held all this time by British and other European investors. They brought £352,000 at auction, nearly twice the £180,000 estimate. That's still pretty far from their original $60,000,000 value, but they're coming back.

More business news: *USA Today* reported in the fall of 1989 that the fifty-six-foot chicken which had long been the most interesting feature of the Atlanta suburb of Marietta would soon be gone with the wind. It was supposedly not in keeping with the new image of the restaurant it has graced for the last twenty-six years.

Despite Georgians' attempts to disguise their essentially down-home nature, though, they're still too country for the cosmopolitan management of RJR Nabisco—or so I surmise from the fact that the cigarette and cookie company is moving its headquarters again, this time to New York. Not long ago RJR moved to Atlanta from Winston-Salem, leaving the Camel City, the company's new president explained, because it is too "bucolic." A writer for the *North Carolina Independent* reported that "when we heard that, half the town scrambled to whip his ass and the other half scrambled for their dictionaries." (This may have been the first time in history, he suggested, that the educated class was first to fight.)

Wonder what they've done with that chicken? I say give the bird to RJR.

It is true that we have a rather old-fashioned business climate in much of the South. A newsletter called *Credit Card Bankruptcies*, for instance, reports that the seven states where Chapter 13 bankruptcies make up the highest percentage of all filings are North Carolina (62%), Tennessee (60%), Alabama (56%), South Carolina (55%), Georgia (50%), Arkansas (46%), and Mississippi (40%). In New York and Massachusetts, by comparison, the percentages are 17 and 16, respectively. If I understand this correctly, Chapter 13 simply involves a stretched-out repayment plan, not outright welshing. It is, in other words, the honorable way to deal with financial embarrassment.

It may be relevant that North and South Carolina have the lowest ratios of lawyers to regular folk in the country (1:694 and 1:654), while New York and Massachusetts have the highest (1:234 and 1:212). It is also interesting that the IRS reports that Southerners (along with Westerners) are below the national average in "voluntary taxpayer compliance"—which suggests an underlying principle that I'll let you figure out.

The Japanese know a good thing, even if RJR doesn't. They're coming in droves, and *Tennessee Illustrated* has given a new dimension to Southern hospitality by publishing a list of handy phrases for its readers. *"Haguki to hoppeta no aidani hitotsumami irenasai,"* for example, means "Put a pinch between your cheek and gum." *"Vorusu wa sugoine"* translates as "How 'bout them Vols?"

But making things easy for newcomers can be carried too far. In a completely revolting development, the dulcet Southern tones of Ginny Moss have been replaced by the crisp Yankeefied accent of another woman on the public-address system of the Memphis airport. The *Commercial Appeal* quoted an airport spokesman who said that Ms. Moss was originally chosen because her accent was "a voice that was typical of this area, something that said: This is the South, this is Memphis." Unfortunately, Yankees and foreigners claimed to have trouble understanding her.

That, in my view, ought to be their problem. *Our* problem, though, is that some Memphians complained that her voice was too Southern, "that this was a sound the airport should not promote." They should take a cue from the seismologist right there at their own Memphis State University who told the *Wall Street Journal* that "Massachusetts and Texas are inching toward each other, and that's bad news." He was talking about the prospects for a major East Coast earthquake, but the proposition is true in general.

(May 1990)

≈ Another Country ≈

A lot of news lately has had to do, one way or another, with country music. In a roundabout way, a story out of South Carolina in the fall of 1989 got me thinking about that particular contribution of the South to world civilization.

It seems the dean of student affairs at the University of South Carolina asked the band to stop playing "Louie, Louie" at Gamecock football games. The spontaneous dancing the song provoked threatened the structural integrity of the university's football stadium.

Now, "Louie Louie" is a grand period piece, a classic of the early 1960s, as the makers of *Animal House* recognized. It's got a great beat, you can dance to it, and obviously people do. But "Louie Louie" is about as far removed from country music as an American popular song can be. A remarkable aspect of that song, almost its essence, is that you can't understand the words. Moreover, *it doesn't matter.*

With country music, if you can't understand the words there's no point to it. The best of it is just good Southern talk, set to what are usually some pretty banal tunes. Just listen to George Jones, or to Hank Williams, Jr., or to Loretta Lynn. Two examples, off the top of my head, of the power of words in country music: If the story in Dolly Parton's "Coat of Many Colors" doesn't make you cry, you have a heart of stone. And next time some judge is too scrupulous about defendants' rights, you'll find that Charlie Daniels's "Simple Man" articulates your feelings so well that you may want to reconsider them; it is, in fact, a stirring invitation to lynch law.

The point is that country music is almost always *about* something—not just about feeling romantic or lustful, either—and it recounts its stories with attention to the telling detail and the just-right phrase. Remarkably, this is more true now than even a decade ago. After some years of wandering in the lush wilderness of "the Nashville sound," a number of young singers have shown that you *can* turn back the clock. Among these neotraditionalists, my favorite (and apparently everybody else's) is North Carolina's Randy Travis, who rivals the great George Jones when it comes to tearjerkers. Kentucky-bred Californian Dwight Yoakum is also worth a listen, although he has become a little too mannered for my taste.

Even more interesting in some ways are a few young musicians who have not simply reverted to the classic style. Lyle Lovett, for instance, can do traditional country as well as anyone, and does it to startling effect on his version of Tammy Wynette's hit "Stand by Your Man." As that example indicates, he doesn't hesitate to do the unexpected: one side of the album *Lyle Lovett's Large Band*, for example, isn't country at all, but big-band swing. My point here, though, is that Lovett turns a phrase and tells a story with the best of the traditionalists.

So does another Texas singer-songwriter, Steve Earle. He, too, is no traditionalist; for one thing, he writes memorable tunes. His politics are probably unsound (though not his contempt for politicians). But his lyrics present a far more vivid and sympathetic picture of the frustrations of small-town and blue-collar American life than anything you'll hear from Bruce Springsteen. He sings about his "Sweet Little '66," oil-burning and gas-guzzling, but "made by union labor on American soil." (This is not your generic Beach Boys car song.) He sings about the life of a traveling musician with "a three-pack habit and a motel tan." And one of the all-time best lines in country music comes from "Week of Living Dangerously," a song about a family man's impulsive Mexican fling: "I threw the car-seat in the dumpster and I headed out into the night."

Country music often presents little dramas, and sometimes they're grotesque—like life. Let me record a few recent news items that could easily be the stuff of country music. (OK, a transparently flimsy transition. I know.)

Consider the story of an infant put out for adoption who grows up and inadvertently marries his own mother. Sort of a classic theme, wouldn't you say? As it happens, that's the real-life predicament of a Tennessean named Danny James Bass. Mr. Bass has now filed for divorce, and he's trying to sell rights to his story to the producers of "Dallas." But I say it's a natural-born country song.

Or how about the saga of Mary Sue and Junior Davis? Last year a circuit court judge in Tennessee ruled that the dozen children of the recently divorced Davises were entitled to the protection of the state, notwithstanding that the offspring in question were embryos resident on petri dishes in a hospital freezer. Apparently Junior wanted to massacre the innocents to avoid having to pay child support, while Mary Sue wanted to keep the little chaps alive, whether out of maternal feeling or spite was not stipulated. (Incidentally, the same folks who explained to me why only the mother's wishes should be consulted were mightily displeased when those wishes prevailed, in a ruling based not on her rights but on those of the children.) Science and law march on, and I know there's a ballad in there somewhere.

You think we may not be ready for songs about incest and infanticide (or whatever)? Well, maybe not, but we already have a bunch about adultery and domestic violence, and at least one each about statutory rape (Hank Williams, Jr.: "Knoxville Court-house Blues"), homophobic violence (Charlie Daniels: "New Uneasy Rider"), and castration (Bobby Bare: "Big Dupree"). If you don't know country music, incidentally, maybe I should point out that the last two of these songs are funny.

Country music can also be downright weepy, of course, especially after a few drinks. And it seems that listening to the "wailing, lonesome, self-pitying" variety of country music encourages drinking. After a ten-year study of a bar in Missoula and less intensive study of sixty-five other taverns in the Minneapolis area, James Schaefer told the American Anthropological Association that slower music means faster drinking, and he has the numbers to prove it. "I don't think this warrants a surgeon general's warning or anything," Schaefer told the AP. "But people should be aware that they are more likely to lose their control and self-restraint in a country and western bar than anywhere else."

It was not reported whether Leonard Ray Lee was listening to country music but he certainly had been drinking when he lost his self-restraint last August and led police on a chase through Wilson County, North Carolina, that covered fifty miles in half an hour. (That's an *average* of 100 mph, for those of you who are computationally challenged.) The chase ended after a cross-country run through a number of fences and a police car. An image worthy of "The Dukes of Hazzard": when Lee's El Camino got stuck in a ditch it was knocked free by a police car that struck it from behind.

Lee told Trooper Cecil Mercer that he'd always wondered what a high-speed chase was like, had enjoyed himself, and had no regrets. I'll be disappointed if nobody's immortalizing Leonard Ray in song right now; the outlaw ballad is a standard genre, after all.

Incidentally, I don't know that there's a country song in the arrest some time back in South Carolina of James Brown (Lee Atwater's friend) for a spree almost as spectacular as Mr. Lee's— Mr. Please Please Please may be the wrong color—but I love the fact that he tried to claim diplomatic immunity, as "the Ambassador of Soul." (It seems that Rep. D. Douglas Barnard said once that "James is indeed our number-one ambassador.") Nice try, James. His Excellency is now doing six years in prison. The Reverend Al Sharpton (Tawana Brawley's friend) observed that "The world would not have done this to Bach, Beethoven, or Brahms." Could be, but those dudes never tried to run down police officers with their pickup trucks while jacked up on PCP.

Speaking of desperadoes, the *Roanoke* (Virginia) *Times* reported the arrest of five of them for catching bass with dynamite in Smith Mountain Lake. The arrests reportedly came after a "two-year undercover investigation." This led columnist Dave Barry to wonder how an undercover agent penetrates a fish dynamiting ring. "Does he just show up at the lake one day, poke through his tackle box for a while, and then announce in a loud voice: 'Darn! I forgot my dynamite!'?" If Jerry Reed can sing a courtroom song about alimony ("You Got the Gold Mine, I Got the Shaft"), surely someone can do something with a fish dynamiting trial.

By the way, don't get the idea that the drama in country music is all in the lyrics. Consider Grand Ole Opry star Little Jimmy Dickens, who was having his breakfast one morning last year when his wife read him an article in the *Nashville Tennessean* about Lydia Roberts. Ms. Roberts had been in jail for ninety-nine days because she had no money to post $2,500 bail on a bad-check charge. Jimmy turned to his wife and delivered this great line in iambic tetrameter: "Go get that woman out of jail." She did.

In yet another Nashville court last year, bluegrass music legend Bill Monroe, seventy-seven, stood accused of hitting Ms. Wanda Huff, fifty-one, in the mouth with a Bible and trying to kill her with firewood. (That's all the newspaper said.) Mr. Monroe countercharged that Ms. Huff had harassed him by letter and telephone, made numerous threats, thrown her glasses on the roof of his house, and let his dogs out of the kennel. Charges against Mr. Monroe were dismissed when Ms. Huff was found to have brought a loaded pistol to court.

While we're on the subject of guns, and potential country-music lyrics, the *North Carolina Independent* claims to have overheard this one at the Dixie Gun and Knife Show in Raleigh: "I only aimed a gun at one human being, and then I married her."

Enough odds and ends. The point is just that, to coin a phrase, life imitates art, and country songwriters have a lot of raw material to work with—without even leaving Nashville, for that matter.

Country music still has a special relation to the American South, of course, but (no doubt thanks in part to U.S. Armed Forces Radio) it now has fans around the world, and increasingly performers, too. I have never personally heard the music at an establishment in Manila called the Hobbit House, where all the staff are midgets (my informant caught a show that featured a midget Elvis impersonator), but I have heard Buck Owens as rendered by a Filipino band at the Intercontinental Hotel in Jakarta.

More interesting than slavish imitation of American singers singing American songs, though, are what seem to be emerging indigenous country music traditions. Some unlikely places are assimilating country music and making it their own. Let me close by telling you about the Thai Country Music Hall of Fame.

A notice in the "Outlook" section of the *Bangkok Post* for September 15, 1989, announced that "the biggest event ever in Thai music history" was to take place the next day. Over a hundred singers and composers were gathering for a festival to celebrate "Half a Century of Thai Country Music" and to name fifty of the all-time greatest songs to the newly established Hall of Fame.

Now, I had no idea that there was such a thing as Thai country music, much less that it had been around for fifty years. But the very first Thai country song, *"O Chao Sao Chao Rai"* ("The Farm Girl"—I'll just give the translated titles from now on), was sung in 1939 by Kamron Samboonnanond (whose gilded guitar was to be displayed at the festival). Obviously, "The Farm Girl" was one of the songs destined for the Hall of Fame.

Choosing the other forty-nine was harder. Not only did a song have to have staying power, but both its tune and its singer's style had to be original, which ruled out a number of well-known songs, including the ever-popular "Love Faded at Bangpakong." The Thai Cultural Commission also required that the language of Hall of Fame songs be "in good taste," and so (I quote from the *Post*) "Lop Burirat's *'Diew Kor Mum Sia Rok'* (I'll Eat You Now), though very popular, failed in this category." Similarly, numbers not "in tune with the morale and culture of society" were excluded. Given that Bangkok is world-renowned for what is sometimes called its "sex tourism industry," that might seem to leave a good deal of latitude, but a number called "Still Looking Good at Thirty" was excluded on those grounds.

This festival was a government undertaking, sponsored by the minister of education, a fact that would have caused problems in the U.S., but if you're going to have government patronage of the arts there's a lot to be said for monarchy. No Thai Civil Liberties Union stepped forward to argue about the commission's right to impose these criteria or the selection committee's interpretation of them. At least a Thai Mapplethorpe or Serrano will get no recognition or support from his government.

To judge from their titles, Thai country songs deal with pretty much the same themes as American ones. "Still Looking Good at Thirty," for instance, could be put up against Jerry Lee Lewis's "Thirty-nine and Holding." But one of the Hall of Fame titles shows that the East can still be mysterious, and that maybe Kipling was right about when the twain would meet. Among seven songs "chosen to be specially honoured," and presumably thoroughly "in tune with the morale and culture of society," was one whose title the *Post* translated as "The Odour of Mud and Buffalo."

(June 1990)

V. Public Life and Public Policy

~ Ole Ted ~

I generally try to write about such timeless themes as Yankee perfidy, leaving others to comment on the ephemera of American politics, but sometimes current events cry out so forcefully for attention that I must yield. Such is the case with Senator Kennedy's efforts to win the 1980 Democratic nomination for president.

As I write, the man's campaign is running out of gas (like the rest of us). Folks seem to have rallied 'round the incumbent—which, if nothing else, gives some of us a reason to be grateful to the Ayatollah Khomeini. Every cloud has a silver lining, as they say, although hard-core Kennedy-haters probably won't sleep well at night until the senator is reposing somewhere with a stake through his heart.

For my part, I rather like the fellow. He's certainly the closest thing to a good old boy Massachusetts will ever produce—which isn't to say he ought to be president, merely that I think he'd make a pretty good drinking buddy, as long as somebody else did the driving.

I recognize, though, that my appreciation of Kennedy's good qualities is a minority view in these parts. Even in the fall of 1979, when the pollsters were telling us that he had won the hearts and minds of the American people, they had to make an exception for the South. It looked for a while as if our beloved region would once again be playing immovable object opposite an irresistible force sweeping down from the North. I began to wonder if we had some sort of hereditary predisposition to lost causes.

It wasn't just that the loser saving Kennedy's seat for him was our loser. Until the mullahs put it to us, there wasn't much support around here for Carter. But there was even less for the challenger. And that needs some explaining.

Someone is bound to say that the reason Southerners never have liked Kennedy is his religion, but that won't wash. True, Al Smith lost a lot of votes, and John Kennedy lost a few, on that score. But Southerners no longer have anything against Yankee Romanists, as such. JFK demonstrated to everyone's satisfaction that his religion had nothing to do with his conduct in office—or anywhere else. Clearly the same would be true of Ted. It's significant, I think, that in all the anti-Kennedy fulminations I've listened to in the past few years, no one has mentioned the man's

165

religion except a couple of feminists who suspected that, deep down, he might be unsound on abortion.

Nor has Kennedy been victimized by Southern puritanism, as some dimwit suggested in the *New York Times*. Sure, he didn't behave like a gentleman on one well-known watery occasion, but not many folks down here would hold his bad habits against him. Shoot, we're talking about the region that bred Big Jim Folsom. Kissin' Jim, you'll recall, was the governor who supposedly left Alabama littered with his illegitimate children—and his weakness for spirits was legendary, too.

No, I think what Southerners dislike about Kennedy isn't so much that he backslides from time to time. We all do that. But he goes about it in such a mealymouthed way. The approved Southern style is to 'fess up. Carter did, and in *Playboy* at that. He didn't have much to confess, but give him credit for making the most of what he had. And Folsom—well, the story is that the governor once told a campaign crowd: "You know what my opponents are gonna do. They're gonna get some good-looking blonde woman, and they're gonna dress her up real fine and they're gonna walk her past. And, friends"—a sigh, and a rueful shake of the head— "they're gonna catch Big Jim every time."

If I were Senator Kennedy's adviser on the Southern vote, I'd have put him on regional television—right after an Alabama football game would have been dandy—and told him to come clean. Can't you hear it? "Friends, they're gonna catch Big Ted every time."

Southerners would love him for it. We'd pray over him. We might even vote for him to make him feel better.

(June 1980)

❧ Taxing Matters ❧

In a North Carolina newspaper a while back—yes, a *North Carolina* newspaper—I actually read an editorial urging Tar Heel legislators to raise the state tax on cigarettes. What is this world coming to?

The state's present tax is apparently the lowest in the nation, and you might think North Carolinians would join in praising their politicians' restraint, in this one matter at least. But, no, here was a newspaper editor urging that the tax be increased from two cents a pack to a nickel or even a dime—that is, by 300, 400, or even 500 percent.

He argued that the state needed the money. But of course if people quit smoking, there would go the anticipated revenue—poof! up in smoke. So the editorial pointed out that a ten-cent tax introduced in Norfolk did not affect consumption at all.

In other words, there isn't even a public health rationale for it; it's gouging, pure and simple. Tobacco growers needn't worry. Smokers, already accustomed to abuse in public places, guilty and half-apologetic and probably not well, will meekly and quietly ante up whatever is required of them.

Now the newspaper in which I read this proposal is proud of its liberalism. Surely its editorialist has merely overlooked the fundamental truth that cigarettes don't pay taxes, people do. (That ought to be a bumper sticker, if it isn't already.) The burden of a cigarette tax wouldn't fall on the yuppies of the Research Triangle—no, it would hit poor high-school dropouts, folks for whom tobacco offers one of the few consolations in an otherwise pretty dreary life. This newspaper vigorously opposes the sales tax on food (or did until a Republican governor proposed to repeal it). Well, the cigarette tax would be like that food tax: regressive, only more so.

If taxing people for doing something that's bad for them won't make them stop, and if it's not an equitable way to raise revenue, there's only one reason to do it.

Vengeance. Nonsmokers suspect and ex-smokers know that smokers enjoy it, and some resent that. This sort of puritanism isn't a worthy basis for public policy. Anyway, the surgeon general keeps telling us that smokers will pay for their pleasure soon enough. Some of them are sick already. Does this newspaper want to impoverish the sick? Surely not.

I have a better idea. How about a tax on Volvos? That would be a relatively benign, progressive tax. Hardly anybody but M.D.s can afford the things anyway, and they could easily cough up another thousand dollars or so per vehicle. Just another couple of appendectomies for them. Shoot, it would even add to the exclusivity of the thing.

After all, nobody has to drive a Volvo. I know, because I went cold turkey after sixteen years. It's just a matter of will power.

But (I hear someone say) Volvos aren't bad for you the way cigarettes are. Well, I don't know, has that been proved? I know they pose a hazard to the *spiritual* health of others in the vicinity, because I violate the Tenth Commandment every time I see one.

Besides, buying a Volvo is detrimental to our balance of payments. This might not be so bad if the money were going to some deserving country that would otherwise be a candidate for foreign aid, but money spent on Volvos goes directly to one of the most obnoxious nations in the world, an overdeveloped country with a busybody government that tells its citizens how to raise their children and its international betters how to run their foreign policies. If I didn't feel sorry for the Norwegians, I'd say let the Russians have Sweden. But I'm getting off the subject.

There's one other argument for taxing cigarettes, so specious that it's barely heard at all in North Carolina, but those from other states may have encountered it. North Carolina's present tax is said to be so much lower than other states'—New York's, in particular—that various unsavory characters find it profitable to smuggle North Carolina cigarettes into New York. Raising Carolina's taxes, it's said, would cut off this trade.

Well, sure, but why should Southern smokers pay for the avarice of Yankee politicians? Why should our legislators protect New York's from the consequences of their greed? Let them pay to enforce their own silly laws. I would love to see customs stations on the George Washington Bridge. Maybe we could set some up down here, while we're at it. There are some New York products I'd like to keep out.

Alternatively, New Yorkers could reduce their cigarette taxes to a reasonable rate and make up the difference with their own tax on Volvos. Volvos are harder to smuggle than cigarettes, too.

(August 1985)

❧ Birthday Thoughts ❧

Some folks in these parts—maybe in yours, too—were dismayed when the Congress whooped through a national holiday on Martin Luther King's birthday. That one of Dr. King's close associates was in all likelihood a card-carrying Commie had just been documented in a book by David Garrow (who somehow contrived to view that fact as a criticism of the FBI). My senior senator, Mr. Helms, didn't like that one damn bit, and argued that the reverend doctor was not the sort of American who ought to be honored with a holiday.

This kind of thing is why some of us find our senator endearing: he always stands up for his principles without considering political advantage, good taste, or even common sense.

"There is a higher truth, beyond the merely empirical." I wrote that once, and nobody wanted to argue about it at the time. For Senator Helms to put the historical facts on the record did no harm, of course: later generations may wish to consider them. At least in the short run, though, those facts were rather beside the point, which was to welcome black Americans into full citizenship by giving them what Columbus Day has become for Italian-Americans, or St. Patrick's Day for Hibernians.

Nobody likes a party pooper. From his experience as a critic of Abraham Lincoln, our mutual friend Mel Bradford could have told Jesse that. Whatever the amalgam of good and bad, wise and foolish, in Martin King's actual, empirical character, he was a great leader of his people. Like Lincoln, he has become a symbol of the cause he led; criticism of him is now taken to mean opposition to his cause—and often rightly.

In any case, those who disapprove of his holiday will have their revenge soon enough. It can't be long now until the same people who have trivialized George Washington's birthday get to work on Dr. King's:

"Stock up on sheets during the MLK Birthday White Sale."

"Free at last? Not quite, but greatly reduced."

"I have a dream: 20 percent off all items in the store."

That sort of thing. When it happens, it should surprise no one. It will be entirely in keeping with ads that show little George with his hatchet going around cutting prices.

Anyone who feels there is a false analogy here—that some intrinsic difference between George Washington and Martin Luther King will protect the latter's memory—should consider what our culture has done to yet another winter birthday, the one we celebrate on December 25. The festival of conspicuous consumption that Christmas has become is enough to bring out the Puritan in even a lackadaisical Anglican like me.

There's no point in whining about "greed." Although the sheer effrontery of our commercial civilization has driven many sensitive but weak-minded souls into the arms of antidemocratic movements of both Left and Right, the alternatives, without exception, have proved to be worse. We simply have to accept the fact that the manifold blessings of freedom come at a price. Fish got to swim, birds got to fly—and merchants got to sell things.

And don't get me wrong: when I want to buy something, I'm glad they're there. If sometimes they get carried away—well, they wouldn't do it if it didn't pay. The appropriate response to commercial excess is not to outlaw it, but, if possible, to make it unprofitable; failing that, to ignore it.

There is something to be said against the public observance of Martin Luther King's birthday, and the same could be said about Washington's birthday, or Our Lord's: the worth of these exemplary figures doesn't depend on Caesar's recognition, and their commemoration shouldn't depend on his favor.

That's too rigorist for me, though. If Caesar wants to recognize these holidays, I say let him. But those who want to honor Martin Luther King or George Washington—a fortiori, those who want to worship Jesus of Nazareth—shouldn't allow their mode of commemoration to be established by political fiat or commercial interest. They should teach their children why these men are worth honoring, and nurture their devotion privately (which is not to say individualistically), in their households, in their churches, with their friends. If these holidays become nothing more than excuses for a day off from work, or for storewide sales, then I'm with the abolitionists.

(March 1986)

❧ Potomac Fever ❧

After William J. Bennett was appointed to be secretary of education, *National Review* ran an appreciative essay on the appreciable Mr. Bennett in which *NR*'s Washington inside-dopester, John

McLaughlin, concluded that "with a bit of grooming, up-front experience, and continued exposure to Potomac fever [Bennett] may have the making of a politician." "There are," he added, "worse corruptions."

Oh? Name one.

My acquaintance with corruptions, such as it is, teaches me that many are essentially self-destructive ("victimless," in the current jargon), and that most of the rest involve abusing others one at a time or in small groups at most. The characteristic corruption of politicians, however, is that they enjoy, or come to enjoy, pushing people around, and these days politicians push people around in very large numbers indeed. Our suspicious Founders were on the right track when they tried to bind the power-hungry with the chains of the Constitution. Too bad they've slipped those chains.

The problem—and it's one I gather the Reagan administration faced in its early days—is that, while big-government ideologues take to politics like ducks to water, most principled anti-Federalists have things they'd rather do than go to Washington and push people around. They have products to manufacture, fields to harvest, books to write, sick people to heal—and if they don't have something better to do, they'll find something. They tend to think that politics are not important (mistaking ideal for fact), or at least not worthy. In any case, few have enough sense of duty to overcome their distaste for Washingtonians, or the instincts to flourish among them if they do. What this means is that a conservative administration has to fill many of its positions either with the incompetent, who need the work, or with slimy politicos of the sort that run college student governments.

But the saddest spectacle of all is when good people do go to Washington and succumb to Potomac fever. John McLaughlin is a case in point. No column of his would be complete without at least one lip-smacking reference to "insiders"—pals of his who have told him something or other. The man clearly enjoys his job more than he should. Similarly, several folks I knew years back as wholesome, anti-statist lads and lasses went to D.C. as members of the Reagan team. They now live and breathe politics, read the *Washington Post* unapologetically, and speak in reverent tones of "the President," "the Secretary," or "the Senator." That this feeds their own self-importance is sad, but relatively harmless. Far worse is that it feeds the self-importance of their bosses, who should be incessantly reminded that their jobs rest on something very like extortion.

Washington attracts unpleasant characters in the first place, and something in the atmosphere turns even apparently decent people into toadies, bullies, sycophants, *Post* readers. If the *American Spectator* can survive its move to Washington from Indiana with its irreverence intact, it will be some kind of first. It has moved, after all, to a town that thinks Mark Russell is funny.

Real Americans don't like Washington. We'll go, ride the subway, take in the museums—what the hell, we've paid for it. But some of us feel unclean after we've been there a while. My wife and I were driving home once through Virginia, after a weekend spent with an assortment of policy analysts, Legal Services lawyers, consumer advocates, congressional staffers, and the like. When a long line of army vehicles passed us, headed north, my wife (God bless her) turned and yelled, "Go get 'em, boys!"

Well, anybody who's had anything to do with the military knows that's not the answer, but there's no denying that the old boil-lancing impulse surfaces whenever my nose gets rubbed in how America's substance is splashed around and taken for granted. (I guess it could be worse, though. As one of my more down-home friends says, thank God we don't get all the government we pay for.)

In my own line of work, I see a lot of colleges and universities. I've concluded that you can generally tell how good a university is by the architectural prominence of its administration building. The relationship is inverse. At Oxford, for example, the administrative offices of the university are tucked away on a side street— very difficult to find without directions. Oxford is a great university. One of its officers told me once that he looks in the mirror every morning and says to himself: "I know I'm an evil, but am I a *necessary* evil?"

Bill Bennett may well do the same. If so, I hope he keeps it up. We'd be better off if all of John McLaughlin's friends did it. Maybe Reagan—excuse me, the President—could suggest it in his next speech. But I can't imagine Ted Kennedy, or Joe Biden, or Lowell Weicker going along. The sad thing is that too many one-time conservatives wouldn't buy it either.

                                                            (April 1986)

Why do agencies of the U.S. government make such heavy use of Federal Express?

No, that's not a riddle. It's a serious question. I have been dealing of late with a number of federal bureaucrats (never mind why), and it seems that almost invariably they communicate by Federal Express. Next-day service, too, not the cheaper forty-eight-hour rate.

Has anyone else noticed this? Hands up—yes, I thought so.

I think I have figured it out, and it's not just that the U.S. Postal Service, like Savings Bonds, is for the rubes, who don't know any better. It all comes back to the strategic failure of the Reagan administration.

Ronald Reagan has surprised me twice, so far. If anyone had told me while I watched him give The Speech for Barry Goldwater back in '64 that he would someday be president, I'd have scoffed. But I'd have been wrong. If anyone had told me back in 1980 that well into his second term there'd have been nothing much in the way of structural change in our bloated, officious, smothering government, I'd have sneered again. And been wrong again.

Let's face it: the Reagan administration may be a public relations success, but it has been a substantive flop.

I should have seen the signs right after the election. I was dealing with one of the many federal agencies that gives away money to the undeserving and/or well-to-do (OK, like me: go ahead and say it). An acquaintance on the staff confided to me that he and his coworkers were very worried. "They're talking about cutting our budget in half," he told me. "They say we may have to take a 10 percent cut in staff."

We were on the telephone, so he couldn't see my expression. Fifty percent budget cut = 10 percent staff reduction. There you have in a nutshell the argument for abolishing programs rather than simply cutting them back. There was one brief shining moment in the winter of 1980–1981 when inside-the-Beltway types feared the worst from this Hollywood madman. Nothing he could have done would have surprised them. They saw him as a berserk right-wing loony who had unaccountably been elected in a landslide, and who was certainly going to shake things up beyond recognition. And he blew it.

Now, the agency I've been dealing with lately is one of the least necessary of the hundreds of federal bureaus, commissions, and agencies. It doesn't do a great deal of harm only because it doesn't do a great deal of anything; certainly it's one of the ones most Reagan voters would miss least. If I'd thought about it at all back in 1981, I'd have assumed it was destined to disappear in the Great Shake-Up.

But of course that didn't happen. Instead, this agency is one of the many that the Reagan administration has more or less hobbled, without inflicting any permanent or serious injury. At the top, Reaganites come and (if they're halfway competent) go. They put in their stretch in this bureaucratic Siberia, try to keep it from getting in the papers any more than necessary, spend the budget that Congress insists this enterprise deserves, and are eventually rewarded by better jobs in agencies that the administration obviously cares more about. While they're in place, the permanent staff regard them with undisguised hostility, as interlopers who will be replaced after the next Democratic victory.

These people, administrators and staff, are the ones who keep sending me missives by Federal Express. At first I thought it was outrageous that this grotesquely expensive form of communication was used to transmit the trivial stuff that I was getting, but I have come to realize that spending money is the *point*. The political appointees at the top are happy to see the agency's money spent on mailing unimportant messages around the country; at least it does no harm. The permanent staff people are content to hunker down and wait out the Reaganites, but in classic bureaucratic fashion they want to spend everything allotted to them so that no one will propose to cut their budget for next year.

Does anyone have a better explanation? It's a hypothesis, anyway, and if I'm right, there's a nice play in Federal Express stock for anyone who can predict the outcome of the 1988 election. Remember: you read it here first.

(August 1986)

❧ Why Don't We Do It in the Road? ❧

A pathologist who recently moved from Vermont to North Carolina has written an article in the *Journal of Forensic Science* about the old Southern custom of lying in the road. The good doctor was apparently unacquainted with this practice, and he was upset to discover that every couple of weeks, on the average, some Tar Heel gets run over and killed while engaged in it. Driven by the Yankee passion to explain things, this fellow argues that most of the fatalities are drunks looking for a warm place to sleep it off, who have the misfortune to choose poorly lighted country roads. They don't do this sort of thing in Vermont, he concludes, because the roads aren't warm enough.

Speaking of alcohol, my state, like many others, has now raised its drinking age to twenty-one. That strikes me as a singularly silly thing to do, but let's give the other side a fair hearing. Why would a reasonable person believe that raising the drinking age is a good idea?

As I understand it, the argument has something to do with the specter of drunken teenagers driving around killing people, and, God knows, that's a sobering thought. Nobody—not even I for the sake of argument—thinks drunk teenage drivers are a Good Thing. Let's get that straight, to begin with.

But I'd as soon be hit by a drunk teenager as by a drunk octogenarian. And isn't the question really that of when people become adults, responsible for their own behavior? Obviously it depends on the individual, but if we must have a universal, agreed-upon fiction, shouldn't it be something less than twenty-one? I read somewhere that there used to be seventeen-year-old clipper-ship captains. If we treat twenty-year-olds like children can we reasonably expect them to behave like grown-ups? Are we going to extend adolescence until it meets middle age?

Think about it. At eighteen you can join the armed forces without parental consent. I've never bought the argument that "if they're old enough to fight they're old enough to vote." Dogs fight. But if they're old enough to fight, surely they're old enough to drink. Are you telling me all those jarheads from Camp Lejeune are supposed to sit around drinking root beer?

And certainly if they're old enough to *vote* they're old enough to drink. The eighteen-year-old vote now enshrined in our Constitution means we trust these beardless youths and gentle maidens to decide between Democrats and Republicans. Why can't we trust them to decide whether to face the world drunk or sober? (And given some of the alternatives our politics produce these days, a few belts might help with that choice, too.)

But there is the statistical argument. Apparently eighteen-, nineteen-, and twenty-year-olds tend more often than their elders to get drunk and run their cars into stationary objects and their fellow citizens. I'd be curious to see the statistics on sixteen- and seventeen-year-olds. I'll bet that they kill themselves and others pretty often, too, with or without the assistance of liquor. This suggests an alternative solution, one more consistent and, to me at least, more philosophically satisfying. Raise the driving age. At eighteen, let people drink, drive, vote, enlist, get married, go to the gas chamber—pretend, that is, that they're grown-up human beings.

My real objection to North Carolina's raising its drinking age, though, has to do with why we've done it. We did not do it for the good indigenous reason that a lot of our citizens think liquor is the Devil's brew. Our legislators ignored that sentiment readily enough when they approved local option on liquor-by-the-drink to appeal to tourists and conventioneers too dumb to figure out how brown-bagging works. No, our drinking age was raised because our federal highway funds would have been cut if it weren't.

This was done by the same legislators who recently passed a law requiring the use of seat belts in automobiles—not because they were convinced that the previous absence of such a requirement was a mistake, but because some unelected bureaucrats in Ronald Reagan's Department of Transportation threatened to put exploding bags in the front seats of our cars if they didn't. Roughly the same federales decided some years ago that North Carolina's schoolbuses were the wrong color. When they threatened to cut off our welfare if we didn't repaint them, our state officials rolled over for that one, too.

This craven capitulation to federal displeasure is getting out of hand, and I think the drinking age is as good a place as any to draw the line. Yes, I know the Yankees have the Bomb now, but what the heck—let's make them use it. Where is the patriot to tell Washington to take its highway money and go to hell? Where is the Patrick Henry to say we've already got too damn many highways? If we build more, folks will just lie in them.

(October 1986)

∼ Does Anyone Feel a Draft? ∽

I grew up in the Volunteer State of Tennessee, so called because of its citizens' enthusiastic response to the First Mexican War. Maybe growing up there colors my view that wars ought to be fought by folks who want to fight them, and it certainly increases my estimate of the number of young men who enjoy that sort of thing. So I start with a prejudice against conscription, anchored in a belief that it wouldn't be necessary in a healthy society.

That's why I viewed with suspicion a recent report from the Ford Foundation called *National Service, What Would It Mean?* I thought it was going to make a case for reinstituting the draft. But in fact it's something far worse.

The report is hot for the idea of Americans' serving the public good at public expense. By the public good, it doesn't mean just the armed forces, and by Americans it doesn't mean just late teenagers; the writers think such a program could well enlist the retired, victims of midlife crisis, displaced homemakers, and others of the idle, unskilled, or directionless. They worry about the negative effects on some—teenage mothers, for example—but by and large they like the idea of Americans' donating a year or two of their lives to the State, involuntarily if it comes to that.

The report examines just four possible plans. One would leave service voluntary, just greatly expand the Peace Corps and VISTA and stuff like that. Provide more alternatives, you understand. Since it's a little pricey—say, $2.6 billion, in round numbers—and since it hasn't escaped the authors' notice that the Great Society is on the back burner for the duration, their other three plans involve a little coercion, to bring in community service at below-market prices.

The simplest and probably the cheapest would require high-school seniors to do 240 hours of unpaid community service to receive a diploma. The authors say this enterprise would cost a mere $20 million or so, for administration. (Reaganomics means austerity, remember?) But they believe that even with this bare-bones approach, "opportunities for personal growth would be substantial."

The next plan would reinstitute the draft, make it universal, and offer a choice of two years' active military service, five years in the reserves, or one year of civilian service. (Do these guys live in the same world I do? One year of picking up litter in the national parks equals two years of active service in the military? Maybe the press release got the numbers switched.) The report writers worry that this might violate the Thirteenth Amendment's prohibition of involuntary servitude, although why the draft never did that before eludes me.

The last brilliant idea, and the authors' fave rave, is a "universal" program requiring one year of national service from every eighteen-year-old, or the payment of a 5 percent income tax surcharge in perpetuity. This would "develop more public services than could be offered through any other program," but the authors admit that they don't have a clue how much it would cost. If everyone takes the 5 percent buy-out option it looks like it could be a real money-maker. Of course, we're trying right now to take poor folks off the tax rolls altogether, which would remove their incentive to enlist, so we might wind up with a National Service Corps composed exclusively of young people who expect to make a lot of money some day.

Nobody asked me, but let's start over. Did the Ford Foundation's report writers ever consider the philosophical objections to compulsory service as anything other than a possible source of "non-cooperation"? Maybe they did, and the summary I read just didn't find it worth mentioning. Anyway, for starters, may we take it as axiomatic that we shouldn't force people to donate a substantial part of their lives to the state without compelling reason? That clearly follows from my—and, I would insist, America's—default libertarian assumption that free men and women shouldn't be forced to do *anything* without a damn good reason.

The question then becomes, what is a "compelling" reason? National defense is such a reason—and maybe the only one. Repairing rusty bridges or running inner-city youth programs won't do. And God knows the point of a compulsory program isn't to provide "opportunities for personal growth" (although that might happen). Still with me?

So if a draft is necessary to defend the nation, it's a sad day for the nation, but let's draft, by all means. If it's not necessary for that reason, though, then, a fortiori, there's no case for compulsory national service of any sort.

Now, I recognize that the social consequences of our present, all-volunteer force are probably unfortunate. Another Vietnam war would be fought by roughly the same blue-collar boys who fought the last one, with even fewer young urban professionals than before. True, the fact that our soldiery would all be volunteers might buy us peace, if only in the sense of peace and quiet. As soon as the draft was abolished, recall, Vietnam protest backed off from a rolling boil to a simmer. And today's students would undoubtedly be noisier about American involvement in Central America if they believed they might actually have to go there. But whether this is a reason to favor an all-volunteer force or to oppose it isn't entirely clear.

And, anyway, it's a side issue. We're concerned here with whether a draft is necessary for our defense, not whether it would better serve social justice or foreign policy.

I've asked this question of a lot of people who know a lot more about this than I do (which isn't hard). Many say that the expense of our volunteer armed forces is exorbitant, but there we're all entitled to an opinion, and I beg to differ. We ought to be willing to pay what it takes to defend ourselves. No, the question is whether we are paying enough—whether we can pay enough—to do that.

What are the military consequences of relying on volunteers? Can they fight in modern warfare? Will they? Here, unfortunately, opinions differ. The Pentagon line seems to be: no problem. That it's an official line doesn't mean it's wrong, but there are plenty of junior officers and civilian students of the military who disagree. And among them, there's a good deal of talk about reviving the draft, in some form or other.

One arrangement to be avoided at almost any cost, everyone agrees, is the old system, under which young men who were rich enough or smart enough to stay in school until age twenty-six didn't have to go to Vietnam. The upshot is that we now have a generation of ministers and tenured academics whose calling was, in many cases, faint. As well as a lot of justifiably ticked-off veterans.

Most advocates of a reinstated draft favor some system of universal service, on grounds of both justice and political good sense. And the idea doesn't outrage public opinion (although that in itself is no reason to do it): 65 percent of adults favor compulsory one-year service; even 58 percent of those eighteen to twenty-four do so.

But if we have to have a military draft, let's do it frankly. Forget the Ford Foundation's plan to smuggle it back in as an alternative to forestry work. If it has to be done, let's have universal military training. If we're going to draft eighteen-year-olds, let's put them all in uniform and let them work out with bayonets. (Yes, women, too. The Israeli model isn't a bad one.)

After basic training, if we don't need all those soldiers (and assuredly we don't), then let them do "public service" work, but they should do it in uniform, as soldiers. Nobody says soldiers can't repair roads, teach people to read, assist in public-health clinics. (Alternatively, we could station one every twenty feet along our southern border to interdict drugs and illegal immigrants. We could call it "Hands Across South Texas.")

What about that teenage mother the Ford Foundation is worried about? And my wife reminds me that there are other people—ballet dancers, for instance—who really can't spare a year at age eighteen. That's easy. They can get deferments. But they'll be *deferments*. And for each year they put their service off, they'll serve an extra month. So if they don't get around to it until they're thirty, when their fifteen-year-old daughters have children of their own or their ballet careers are over or whatever, they'll serve a year longer than an eighteen-year-old.

But even those thirty-year-old grandmothers and retired dancers should be in uniform. So should draftees with hernias, and flat feet, and unusual sexual preferences. Universal would mean *universal*, and putting conscripts in uniform would tell them, in effect, we wouldn't do this to you if it weren't important.

(March 1987)

≈ Monumental Folly ≈

The other day I got a "Dear Friend" letter from Malcolm Forbes asking for a contribution to the Reagan Presidential Library. It raises all sorts of questions. For instance, does Malcolm Forbes really think of me as a friend? Where has he been all this time? A friend in need is a friend indeed, Mr. Forbes, and I've got two daughters to send to college. How about if I contribute to your foundation and you kick in to mine? Shall we say 5 percent of annual income?

But leave aside the fact that my new friend could build this edifice from his pocket change if he really thinks we need it. Let's ask a fundamental question that the letter doesn't really address: Why in heaven's name should there be a Reagan Presidential Library?

Well (I hear you say), Kennedy has a library, Johnson has one, and Nixon, even Carter. True, all true. If Reagan had no library, he would not be in the company of these worthies; he would be libraryless with the likes of Washington, Jefferson, and Lincoln, men to whom the idea of a presidential library somehow didn't occur. (Can you imagine John Adams's pals hustling funds by direct mail?)

Ah, but (as Forbes's letter puts it) "Think what rich repositories for history and sources of perspective we'd have if there had been libraries for our earliest Presidents! They would be treasuries valuable beyond measure." Yeah. Think what prodigies of scholarship we would witness at the Martin Van Buren Presidential Library, the Millard Fillmore Presidential Library, the William Henry Harrison Presidential Library, the—well, you get the idea.

There are many reasons to oppose this well-meant but ill-considered enterprise. There is, in the first place, the libertarian argument—obvious (as usual), but overlooked (also as usual). The $45 million to buy the land and build the building is to be raised from private contributions, more or less voluntary, but that's just the beginning. The annual budget to operate this show is bound to be well up in seven figures, probably eight—not chicken feed, outside the Beltway—and that money will come from the public coffers. From you and me, that is. Like it or not. Forever.

Why are presidential libraries thought to be an appropriate use of public monies and open space? They serve no useful scholarly purpose. What could possibly be in an Andrew Johnson Presidential Library in Greeneville, Tennessee, that is not more conveniently available somewhere else under the present dispensation? Future historians studying our times will already have to check in at presidential libraries in Boston, Austin, San Clemente, Atlanta, and—where is the Ford Library, anyway? Grand Rapids? Aspen? (I guess I could look it up. If there isn't one, I'll take back every mean thing I've ever said about the man.) Adding one more to the list wouldn't hurt much—just another few hundred bucks on the historian's NEH grant. But it wouldn't help either.

Of course, we shouldn't think of these libraries as simple repositories. They are, above all, monuments to presidential ego. And that is disturbing. Maybe our presidents have always thought of themselves as demigods entitled to pyramids maintained at public expense, but, if so, they kept their opinions on this matter to themselves for the Republic's first century and a half. A healthy public opinion would have hooted them down. Where did we go wrong? Whatever happened to republican simplicity?

There is also the otherwise delightful fact that presidents come and go every four years, or eight. If each president gets a library, and the nation survives, in a couple of hundred years the countryside will be littered with these structures, each with its complement of chantry priests and lay brothers. And the whole creaking, groaning apparatus will be supported by levies on the toil of an urban peasantry too ignorant to reflect that the system swept away at the Reformation only took 10 percent.

Moreover, it's obvious that not every president will deserve a monument. In fifty years, our grandchildren will wonder why we bothered to memorialize some of those we already have. We shouldn't rush into these things, as any graduate of Warren G. Harding High School could tell you. I like Teddy Roosevelt, but he does look a little silly on Mount Rushmore, and *Cape Kennedy* was quietly dropped when it became indelicate to refer to the Kennedys and water in the same breath.

I don't mean to pick on Ronald Reagan. In this, he's just acting like a typical modern president. But he disappoints me when he acts that way, because sometimes I've almost believed that he wasn't one. I would rejoice—many Americans would rejoice—if he would drop Malcolm Forbes a note. "Dear Friend," he could say: "Thank you for your efforts to build a library to house my papers, but I've decided to put them in the National Archives, where related materials will be more conveniently available. A businessman like you will recognize the significant economies of scale in putting them there, too, and I like to cut the costs of government when I can. I know the library was meant to be a monument as well, but that's not an appropriate use of tax money. Why don't you take what you've raised and buy some small arms for the Contras?"

I say Ronald Reagan ought to write this letter. Do you think he will?

(August 1987)

∾ The Judgment of History ∾

Satire is a difficult form these days. Reality keeps calling, and raising. Let me tell a story that illustrates the difficulty.

Back at the time of the Iran-Contra flap, when it looked as if President Reagan's Teflon was wearing thin, pundits began to write about how his "place in history" was in jeopardy. My buddy Tim, a historian, casually suggested that a president really needs professional historians on call to warn him about how history will judge his actions. I thought that was a funny idea. Tim and I started goofing on it, and we wound up writing a proposal to establish a Council of Historical Advisers.

We argued that such a body would answer a real need. After all, every politician above the state-legislator level wants to be regarded with favor by history, and presidents in their final years in office, especially, seem to worry about it a lot. They're not running for anything, and posterity doesn't even have a PAC, but they just can't kick the habit: they start to suck up to the electorate of Yet-to-be.

But history takes time (as Gertrude Stein remarked), and that makes them nervous. Since we can't poll the Great Unborn, obviously, we have to rely on speculation, and Tim and I argued that the judgment of history is too important to be left to the speculation of well-meaning amateurs. We suggested that a panel of historians could be engaged to deliver official preliminary verdicts of history. If nothing else, that would free presidents to worry about the things they're hired to worry about.

We were rolling. We proposed a body like the Council of Economic Advisers, a group of experts to make the close calls and hard decisions, to tell presidents how they'll stand in the past of the future. We suggested a setup like the Supreme Court's: a fixed number of members, nominated by the president and approved by the Senate, serving for life, contingent on good behavior. (Sure, the criteria for good behavior might be hard to establish, but those for life aren't self-evident either.) We wanted to guard against "council-packing" by presidents tempted to believe that adverse judgments were the work of small-minded pedants trying to deny them their historical due.

We suggested that the council could make itself useful day-to-day by finding historical precedents for administration proposals or by making sure that policies said to be unprecedented really were. It could also remind busy presidents and other top-level administration figures of the historical facts commemorated by holidays like Thanksgiving, Columbus Day, the Fourth of July, and Christmas. Speechwriters could call with questions about the current state of historiography: "William Bradford in Plymouth—still an important player?" "Any Hispanics sign the Declaration of Independence?" "Remind me: what happened at Munich?" With answers in hand, writers could use phrases like "history tells us" or "the lessons of history" in full confidence that, in a pinch, they could buck responsibility to the council.

But the historical advisers would really earn their keep in times of crisis. A president could call in the council's chairman and say "I want to invade" or "I want to cut a deal." Then: "What will be the judgment of history? Will it threaten my place in history?" The chairman would summon the advisers. (Robes of office—perhaps tweed—might be appropriate.) The council would solemnly deliberate and by formal vote determine history's verdict. Like economic forecasts, of course, it could be subsequently adjusted.

Well, it turned out that proposals of this sort had come up before, but had never gotten anywhere. When Fritz Hollings was running for president in 1984, for instance, he promised he'd shoot all the economists in government and replace them with historians. But this shameless pitch for historians' votes wasn't enough to get him the nomination. Believe it or not, eight years earlier, in 1976, a group of historians had actually, seriously, urged President-elect Carter to set up a formal body like the one we were proposing. Historians, however, were one special-interest group to which Carter didn't pander.

Anyway, we concluded that this could be a bold initiative, one President Reagan could use to put his mark on the closing years of his administration. We predicted confidently that history would applaud. We wrote our proposal up as an op-ed piece and fired it off to a number of your high-class dailies.

All of them turned us down. Every last one of them.

Now, I can understand the conservative ones' doing that. At the time everything but the stock market seemed to be falling apart, and they weren't in the mood for satire. But I must say that it was a bit of a puzzle when the *New York Times* didn't want it. I'd never before seen the *Times* pass up the chance to kick a conservative when he was down, and I thought anything that poked even mild fun at the Reagan administration would be a shoo-in. Tim and I began to think maybe the idea wasn't as amusing as we thought it was.

Then, lo, nearly two months after we'd sent our piece to the *Times*, that paper's op-ed page carried a piece by Stuart E. Eizenstat, whom some may recall as a supporting player in the forlorn Carter White House. Eizenstat called for the creation of a "White House secretariat . . . charged with providing the political appointees on the National Security Council and domestic policy staff with historical analogues, thereby helping keep Presidents out of trouble." Such an "institutionalized memory," he argued, would "reduce the likelihood that past mistakes would be repeated." Sound familiar?

Now, I certainly don't mean to suggest that the *Times* pilfered our idea and farmed it out. Great ideas often occur to many people more or less simultaneously. Anyway, as I said, the idea was not a new one. But I do conclude from this episode that the *Times* appreciates flaky ideas only when people aren't facetious about them. Keep that in mind the next time you read our nation's most influential newspaper.

(October 1987)

∾ Goetzing Down in the Gunfire State ∾

On October 1, 1987, Florida's new handgun law went into effect and the talking hairdos on the evening news had an arched-eye-brow contest. As you may have heard, law-abiding Floridians, tired of being an unarmed minority in the Sunshine State, rared back and passed a law that allows any Floridian with no police record, $145, and two hours to spare for token instruction to get a permit to carry a concealed weapon. Moreover, for a while at least, thanks to a loophole in the law that no one seemed to be rushing to repeal, it appeared that anyone would be allowed to pack a pistol in plain view.

Florida, of all places. Who'd have thought it? The least Southern of the Southern states. But I guess a full-page ad in *Southern Living* magazine some time ago should have told us something like this was coming. It was for the National Rifle Association, and it showed a Cuban-American Florida state legislator fondling his pistol and saying he wouldn't give it up without a fight because he knows what it's like to live under Communist tyranny. This isn't the image *Southern Living* usually tries to project, but it does look a lot like life, at least as far as Florida's concerned. Those of us who still think of Miami as a retirement home for old Trotskyite garment workers from the lower East Side are at least twenty years out of date. South Florida has more Cubans and Nicaraguans than retired New Yorkers these days, and some of those guys are real Americans.

Now, I should say that my Second Amendment fundamentalist friends find me squishy-soft on the subject of handguns. I tend to believe that we compromised the constitutional principle when we gave up the right to carry automatic weapons, bazookas, and flame-throwers, and I've always thought that anything legal you can do with a pistol, you can do as well or better with a long gun. You can shoot varmints with a .22, protect your home with a shotgun, resist tyranny with a deer rifle. About the only thing a .38 is better for is knocking over liquor stores, and it would be all right with me if we outlawed handguns altogether. (That is, if my state did—your state can do what it pleases. That's what federalism is all about.)

But I must say the right people are upset by Florida's new law.

Maybe it's worth a try. A friend of mine who drives a tow truck told me recently about going out at night to pull a car out of a ditch. "There was two of them when I got there, but there must have been ten after I got it out. They said they wasn't going to pay me—no way. So I reached back and got my shotgun and told them: 'I'm taking this car in, and you all can get it back when you bring the money.'"

Did they pay up?

"They come in the next day."

Did he always take his gun along?

"I don't leave home without it. You know, people are so *mean* these days."

Robert Heinlein has observed that an armed society is a polite society, and Lord knows Florida can use all the civility it can muster. But plainly the guardians of our civic morality are less scandalized by how mean people are these days than by what Floridians are doing about it. So keep your eye on how this experiment is evaluated by the media.

No fair saying that Miami has the highest murder rate in the U.S., if not the Western Hemisphere. It had that already.

No fair, either, saying that more murders are now committed with handguns. That may be so, if only because people don't have to use sloppy, slow, unreliable methods like knifing, strangling, or bludgeoning. The state-by-state statistics suggest that tough gun laws mean mostly that crimes of passion get committed with other weapons; where there's a will, there's a way.

No, the statistic to look at is total homicides, however committed, excluding those in self-defense. Why exclude those? Because that's the point: Floridians apparently intend for some different folks to die now. Folks that deserve it. I don't know if it's working that way or not, but would it be a bad thing if it were?

The fact of the matter is that Floridians don't display much in the way of enlightened liberal concern for the lives of scum. It was in Florida, after all, that an oft-burglarized storekeeper was acquitted recently for rigging a booby trap that electrocuted a young share-the-wealth activist. Florida is right up there with Texas in legal executions, too; you might say that its new gun law just extended the definition and, ah, privatized the process.

Some other statistics we might check out are those for robbery, burglary, and rape. When the law went into effect, the network news shows all carried interviews with young women on firing ranges saying things like "If somebody tries to rape me I'm going to blow him away." I wouldn't be surprised if some rapists have moved to New York. As drive-in movie critic Joe Bob Briggs observes: "There's something about a woman in a bikini with a machine gun strapped across her chest that says, 'Hey, women are people too.'" Maybe pocketbooks that might hold Smith & Wessons can get the same message across. The old Colt .45 wasn't called "the Equalizer" for nothing.

A book you probably haven't seen reviewed in the mainstream press presents some evidence to back me up. In *Armed and Considered Dangerous*, James Wright and Peter Rossi report the results of interviews with nearly two thousand felons, doing time in the prisons of ten states. A majority of these experts agreed that criminals avoid potential victims they believe to be armed, and two out of five had themselves decided in the past not to commit a crime for that reason. Three-quarters agreed that burglars avoid occupied houses for fear of being shot, and over a third had actually been scared off, shot at, or captured by an armed victim. (These gentlemen, by the way, had had no difficulty obtaining weapons, even under restrictive laws, but over 80 percent of those who had used guns to commit crimes said that if they couldn't get handguns they'd switch to more deadly sawed-off rifles or shotguns.)

So, as I said, Florida's experiment is worth a try. I do have one suggestion, though. It's a mushy, liberal, Great Society kind of proposal, probably just a reflex left over from the bad company I kept in the sixties, but I can't help it.

Look here: the price of a good pistol, plus $145 for a permit, plus two hours of lessons—that's a lot to ask from poor folks. They're probably the ones who need protection the most, too. They've got no perimeter alarms, no chain-link fences, no Dobermans between them and the predators. Do we want them driven to bootleg dealers, to back-alley armorers? To Saturday night specials that blow up in your hand? Of course not. Come on, Florida—how about gun subsidies for the poor?

I say if we can put a man on the moon we can put a decent weapon in every glove compartment.

(January 1988)

It hasn't escaped attention down here that it's a presidential election year. My buddy Eugene, who cares about these things more than is good for him, explained to me the other day why George Bush is going to be our next president.

"Well," he said, "first we had Jimmy doing his Woodrow Wilson impression, right? Upright Christian soul, square dealing among the nations, all that B.S. Now we've got a Harding clone—less filling, tastes great, back to normalcy with handsome Mr. Feel-Good. Except it seems like we got him for the whole eight years, so the way I figure it we're overdue for Coolidge. Now ask yourself: who does the best Coolidge going?"

"Paul Simon?" I suggested.

"Forget him. *Revenge of the Nerds: The Final Chapter.* Half the voters think he's the one that makes records with Zulus, anyway. Be serious. What real candidate would look stupidest in an Indian warbonnet?"

Well, I had to admit that he had George Bush there. That's the kind of oblique angle that usually makes Eugene worth listening to. He's the one who told me why there's still some life in the bull market, despite the little correction in 1987. "Seven fat years, then seven lean years," he said, taking a pull on his Pabst Blue Ribbon. "It's in the Bible. You can look it up."

This was supposed to be an interesting election for Southerners. When our Democratic politicos set up the Super Tuesday primary, some hoped it would help a homeboy like Chuck Robb or Sam Nunn get the nomination. But the leading homeboys apparently took one look at what they'd have to kiss and eat to get the nomination (and I'm not talking about babies and bagels) and decided that if being senator or governor was good enough for Richard Russell and Harry Byrd it was good enough for them. Now it seems the principal effect of Super Tuesday was a boost for the embarrassing campaign of Jesse Jackson—a homeboy sure enough, but not exactly what our solons had in mind.

What has happened? Is returning the party of Jefferson and (Andrew) Jackson to something like their principles really a lost cause? For that matter, what's wrong with lost causes? We used to be attached to them down here. Where are the old-time rebel-yell attack-and-die Southern Democrats?

There used to be two political styles in the South: on the one hand, boring conservative penny-pinchers who ran good minimalist state governments; on the other, grotesque, extravagant creatures from the depths—expensive, but entertaining. Politics in most Southern states cycled from one style to the other. But penny-pinching is out of style, and Edwin Edwards may have been the last of the great rogue governors from hell. Now we're getting the worst of both styles: boring big spenders. You might say we've traded blowhards for blow-dries. Even Louisiana is filling up with Carteresque pinstripes who talk like James Moffett, head of the Louisiana Council for Fiscal Reform, quoted as saying, "A modern era of politics is fixing to evolve."

Among the Democratic presidential candidates, only Jesse Jackson has anything to offer someone nostalgic for the old tradition of demagoguery and hypocrisy, but I guess you can't expect nostalgic traditionalists to cotton to Jesse. Aside from Jackson, young Al Gore is the only Democrat who can claim any Southern connection, but he's very much in this new mold. Between tokes, Tipper's husband did put in some time in the state his daddy represented in the Senate, but (as even the *Wall Street Journal* has noticed) Gore is less a Southern candidate than a Washington political consultant's idea of a Southern candidate. Frankly, he's a Southerner like George Romney was a Mexican, and if folks down here buy him as a favorite son, it will be a triumph of political marketing.

Meanwhile, all the Republicans have to offer is Pat Robertson. (Yes, I know George Bush claims he's a Texan, but he owns a funeral plot in Kennebunkport, Maine. Need I say more?) What about the reverend?

Well, I heard a story once about this gospel quartet that was singing a gig at a church back up some hollow in East Tennessee. Midway through the service, the deacons start hauling in cages, and it becomes clear that some snakes are going to be handled. The baritone turns to the lead tenor and whispers, "Where's the back door?"

"I don't see one," the tenor whispers back.

The baritone casts a glance at the back wall. "Where do you reckon they want one?"

A lot of people feel that way about Robertson. In many circles, as Jesse Jackson might put it, he's respected but he won't get elected.

So it looks as if we don't get a Southern candidate this year. Maybe after the last one, some folks think that's just as well. At least the conventions are going to be in Atlanta and New Orleans, so some of our people are going to make some money off this deal.

One of the remaining good things about America is that we don't have to watch politicians if we don't want to. Not long ago the twenty-five hundred good Americans of Mountain City, Tennessee, rose in righteous and near-unanimous wrath when the local cable company replaced the game shows and reruns of the USA Network with something called C-SPAN, which offers gripping stuff like live coverage of congressional committees.

A letter writer in the weekly *Tomahawk* put her finger on the basic problem with C-SPAN: it's "boring," she said. Other irate mountaineers wrote to say that they resented having a "government channel" thrust into their living rooms, but that's not fair. Believe it or not, C-SPAN is actually not a government channel. Apparently somewhere there are private citizens willing to pay to watch the preening of politicians. But not in Mountain City.

We're not crazy about it here in Chapel Hill, either. Last September our twenty-one-thousand-seat gymnasium, often used for rock concerts, was the site of an alleged debate among the Democratic presidential candidates. When it was announced that the seven dwarves were coming, the university news bureau got calls asking what kind of music the Presidential Candidates played. When our people realized the horrible truth, they stayed away in droves. David Bowie had filled the place earlier in the week at twenty dollars a head, but only a quarter of the seats were occupied as the candidates shared their predictable views on education and kicked Bill Bennett around for a while.

The proceedings were supposed to be televised, but a technical snafu blacked out the first twenty minutes, which our local educational station filled with a documentary on Finland. They got some telephoned complaints—when the glitch was corrected. Folks wanted to see the rest of the program on Finland.

Nothing personal, Democrats. About the same time, down in

South Carolina, they had trouble filling a stadium for the Pope. Aside from some mutterings out of Bob Jones University and one grumpy "My Holy Father is in Heaven, not Rome" bumper sticker, I didn't detect any anti-Catholicism around here. But neither was there any rush to go see the leader of somebody else's religion. Catholicism for the Catholics seemed to be the dominant view, which made it difficult for the visit's sponsors since there were probably more seats in the stadium than Catholics in South Carolina. I gather they wound up busing the Pope's co-religionists from Pennsylvania and points north.

But enough about politics and religion. Let's talk about something serious, like why hotdogs come in packages of ten when buns come in packages of eight or twelve. The *North Carolina Independent* (from which I also got the Mountain City story) reports that two researchers at an obscure land-grant school in Raleigh answered that question in an article in the *Journal of Business.* The discrepancy exists because people want it that way, that's why. "If in fact customers wanted to have hot dogs and buns in equal packages," these scholars wrote, "someone would have already done it."

Your tax dollars at work. Next question?

(March 1988)

～ Jesse, I Hardly Knew Ye ～

Some of us down here took exception a while back when freelance smart-mouth John Aldridge referred to Jimmy Carter as "a redneck peanut farmer from Georgia." We felt it was a gross libel on rednecks.

Of course, Aldridge didn't mean to be complimentary. Calling our former president that was about as malicious, as offensive, and as beside the point as calling Jesse Jackson a nigger preacher from Chicago. Call Carter naive; call him ineffectual; call him, even, a wimp. Call Jackson manipulative; call him hypocritical; call him, even, a knave. But let's stick to name-calling that has something to do with character, ability, or performance.

What prompts me to bring this up is the apparently quadrennial newsworthiness of the Reverend Mr. Jackson. Here he is back again, like a bad penny. It's tempting to say that he's the Democrats' problem—and it is fun to watch them tiptoe around him as if he were a land mine. But he's not just an accident waiting to happen to somebody else's party, he's a problem for the rest of us, too.

Not that he's going to be president, or even the Democratic nominee. Even the Democrats aren't that suicidal. But it's regrettable that he has been allowed to become the de facto spokesman for black Americans. If he's accommodated by the political system, it will be disastrous. But if he isn't, many blacks will apparently feel rebuked and scorned, still again. They don't need that, and the nation doesn't either.

How can we account for the extent of his support among blacks? Surely many of them know better. Surely their defense of this indefensible man is reflexive, knee-jerk, much the same as what I felt when John Aldridge made me momentarily regret that I hadn't voted for Jimmy Carter. They must suspect that white folks dislike Jackson for the wrong reasons, the way I know some people disliked Carter for the wrong reasons. Some of Jackson's supporters even imply from time to time that it's only because he's black that he won't be nominated.

Friends, that's rubbish. The fact of the matter is that if he weren't black, you never would have heard of him. His politics wouldn't get him to first base in this country. He is, basically, a black Jim Hightower.

Jim who? (That's my point. Jim Hightower is a Texas populist whose political career has probably topped out at agriculture commissioner.)

Personally, I regret that the right reasons that sensible people, black and white, should dislike Jackson—or at least dislike the idea of entrusting him with any responsibility—are so compelling. I started out with a warm spot in my heart for him. Of course, I briefly had high hopes for Jimmy Carter, too.

Still, Jackson did go to North Carolina A&T in Greensboro, and he has been a loyal alumnus. And the mother of a friend of mine knew his mother, back in South Carolina, and said she was a fine woman. (The South is still like that.) Besides, like many Southerners, I'm a pushover for the traditional black-preacher rhetorical style, and give Jackson credit: he spews rhetoric like a Ted Sorensen in meltdown. Much of it is baby talk, but you can pan in that stream and find real gold. How about this, from the summer of 1987: "I'd rather run to the special interests than run from the special prosecutor." Not bad—not bad at all. Hard to imagine Walter Mondale coming up with that.

Besides, Jackson used to say some good things. My memory isn't what it used to be, but I sure do remember his addressing a convocation in Chapel Hill back in the early seventies. He was preceded on the program by an economics professor who droned on through a paper on (as I recall) "human capital development." Our black students had turned out in force to hear Jackson, and their impatience became manifest in conversations less and less sotto voce. When it came Jackson's turn to speak, he began by chewing them out. He said their manners were abominable, and their mamas would be ashamed of them. Besides, he said, the professor was saying things they ought to pay attention to. How were they ever going to amount to anything if they didn't shut up and listen to people who knew more than they did? (Incidentally, the professor was Ray Marshall, who later became secretary of labor.)

That's the Jesse Jackson some of us used to admire. He was an impressive figure, preaching self-reliance and self-respect to people who seemed ready to hear that message. It's hard to imagine that Jesse Jackson even thinking "Hymietown," much less saying it—and he didn't pick that up in the South, by the way.

So, how did a black preacher with Southern manners and all-American values become a virtual Sandinista in little more than a decade? Was it an act all along, just opportunism, recognizing that becoming the favorite civil rights leader of people like me would pay off in money for PUSH and influence for Jackson? Did it just stop paying?

Or has Jackson really changed? Did influence and celebrity go to his head? Did he fall in with bad companions? (He certainly has some now, not just minor-league bigmouths like Louis Farrakhan, but the real McCoy: Fidel and Arafat and Daniel "Specs" Ortega.)

If the old Jesse was a charlatan, he sure fooled me. But I almost hope he was. Because if he wasn't—if he was the leader I thought he might be—what has become of him is tragic.

(July 1988)

❧ Bringing It Home ❧

I once described Jesse Jackson's politics as those of a black Jim Hightower, meaning that if he were white his politics would guarantee him obscurity. As a matter of fact, though, if it's a flaming lefty you want, Hightower is a much more interesting proposition than Jackson. You're unlikely ever to get the chance to vote for him unless you live in Texas, where he's commissioner of agriculture. But you might enjoy knowing he's around.

He's an old-fashioned, traditional Texas populist, for better and for worse. You just have to ignore his puerile soak-the-rich rhetoric. He's a chronic offender against the Tenth Commandment. And I suspect the only reason he doesn't go in for jejune Third Worldism is that state agriculture commissioners don't get asked their foreign policy views much. But he's not just another pretty face.

I started out skeptical about Hightower. For one thing, he's the darling of some of our local trust-fund Marxists, who find his ritualistic Reagan-bashing congenial and his personality—well, just deliciously authentic. So when he spoke in our town and some of these folks asked if I was going to hear him, I allowed that personally I wouldn't cross the street to hear the paranoid ravings of some down-home redistributionist.

So I didn't go. But I wish I had, now that I've come across an article by Hightower (obviously once a speech) in the Southern Regional Council's magazine *Southern Changes*. Lord, *listen* to the man.

Sure, you'll hear an occasional Jacksonism, like: "Our program will work if we base the nation's growth not on the Rockefellers, but on the little fellers. It will work because it taps genius instead of greed." But when Hightower turns to policy, he calls for "developing our own enterprises" and "localizing our economy." He comes on, in short, like the Nashville Agrarians, authors of *I'll Take My Stand*.

He invites us to ponder the story of the Texas watermelon farmers who were losing 60 percent of their crop for lack of a market. While the Kroger supermarket chain was importing melons from Florida, Texas melons were rotting in the field. "What little they did sell was out of a pickup truck on the side of the road, getting a penny a pound for it." A marketing co-op now means they sell Kroger half a million pounds of watermelon—at seven and a quarter cents a pound. Melon farmers' income has more than doubled, and consumers, instead of paying $3.50 for Florida melons, "got that sweet Walker County melon for $1.98."

Hightower has other examples of successful agricultural co-ops. Low-income Mexican-American farmers in the Rio Grande valley, for instance, now sell squash and peppers directly to the Pathmark chain for four times what they used to get from wholesalers. This isn't charity, or affirmative action; Pathmark sets the specifications for quality, and still buys cheaper than it used to.

Hightower claims that something called the Mexico-Texas Exchange Commission has successfully organized various international trade projects and joint ventures, and that similar ties are being forged with Israel and with Italy. "We're finding markets around the world directly from our state." He acknowledges that Texas has some things going for it, including "an awfully good-looking agriculture commissioner." But he insists that other states can do it, too, individually or on a regional basis. "There's no reason the South and individual states can't form their own foreign relations. You don't have to go through the State Department for this."

From time out of mind, Southern agricultural reformers have called for diversification, and Hightower is a traditionalist in that respect at least. Why has his department been encouraging blueberry production? Because a small farmer "can make a living on forty acres of blueberries in our state," that's why. "In fact if you diversify your acreage and set aside maybe four acres for blueberries you'll make enough on that four to subsidize the cow and wheat operation that you're running on the other four hundred acres that you might have." Have West Texas farmers with square miles of wheat been going broke? "Now they are producing sprouts on an area about the size of a kitchen table"—and making money.

The old diagnosis attributed the South's economic ills to its semicolonial economy, producing raw materials, importing finished goods, and losing money on the exchange. Henry Grady used to tell about a Georgia funeral, pointing out where the casket was made, where the Bible was printed, where the shroud was woven, and so forth—and concluding that all Georgia provided was the body and the hole in the ground. Hightower argues that this is still too much the case when it comes to foodstuffs. Forget the Sunbelt: "We have grown the raw commodities and shipped them to Chicago and Philadelphia and Los Angeles where they chop it up, put it in a box, freeze it, and sell it back to us at a hundred times what we sold it to them."

Just so, until recently Texas wheat farmers sold their wheat to mills in Kansas for a nickel a pound. "In Kansas they were making Texas wheat into plain old white flour in barrels and selling it back to hotels and bakers in Amarillo for twenty-eight cents a pound." What could be done? Get Texans into the milling business, obviously. Now the first flour milled in the panhandle in a generation is produced in Dawn, Texas—"300,000 pounds of flour a day. That'll make a pretty good biscuit."

Just a drop in the bucket, you say? "We're not talking about a science-fair project; this is a real enterprise that will put $10 million a year into Dawn and in its first year of operation will create fourteen jobs right there. Now that doesn't solve Texas's unemployment problem but it takes care of it in Dawn pretty well." You say this is an old-fashioned, band-aid approach to economic distress? Well, what's wrong with that? "Instead of worrying about the global situation, let's worry about where our people live. A little bit here and a little bit there will add up."

Consider the crawfish industry. Gulf Coast rice farmers have begun to raise those little suckers because "all you do is put a little bad hay out there in that rice paddy and throw some crawfish in and come back later with some nets." They sell them to Louisiana packing plants at 75 cents a pound. Good deal, right? But wait a minute: the packing plants have been selling deheaded, deveined frozen crawfish to Houston restaurants at $7.50 a pound, wholesale. Here's Hightower: "Now maybe we're not too bright in Texas, but we can dehead crawfish. We're about to be in the crawfish processing business in Port Arthur."

The man says so many good things. For instance: "You aren't putting people in business to fail. You have to work on the market development so what they produce actually has a market, preferably one that is already established and signed for before you build a processing facility."

He sums up his basic strategy: "if you have lemons, make lemonade." And he waxes evangelical about extending this principle beyond agriculture. "We can have a decentralized economy that's environmentally sound, that generates wealth at a local level, that has not only jobs but good-paying jobs that are upwardly mobile, that allows a local, diversified, abundant management opportunity for little people to be involved. It doesn't have to be owned by some conglomerate. We can do this ourselves and our people can be the managers and the owners."

You don't have to be a left-winger to like the sound of that. In fact, many left-wingers wouldn't. This message plainly isn't for doctrinaire socialists, or for the crypto-socialists who want Washington to rare back and impose a national industrial policy. But it sounds good to me. I can't say whether Hightower's program makes economic sense or not, but these are the kind of themes that can get people excited, and they appeal to wholesome impulses, native and fine. I'm not floating a Hightower-for-president trial balloon—Texas commissioner of agriculture sounds just about right—but I'm glad he's talking.

If you're suspicious (and you probably should be), you might note that Hightower isn't entirely clear about the role of government in all this. He says only that the state should be a "catalyst," one that "work[s] with local folks to create a pool of capital so they have the financing to do what they are wanting to do in an enterprise that makes economic sense."

Now, if that means subsidizing marginal enterprises with government grants or below-market loans, to hell with it. We've already got an example of how that works, in the Farmers' Home Administration. But if it means working with entrepreneurs to develop business plans, helping them through bureaucratic red tape, and putting them in touch with hardheaded and beady-eyed investors—well, then it seems to me that only rigorous libertarians or Wall Street lackeys could object.

"Wall Street lackeys." Read enough of this stuff and you start talking that way, too. But, of course, so did the authors of *I'll Take My Stand*.

(August 1988)

≈ Under the (Smoking) Gun ≈

In his *Wall Street Journal* column, Mr. Alexander Cockburn—whose regular presence in the premier organ of capitalist opinion, by the way, nicely illustrates Marx's maxim about rope—argued that the current antismoking hysteria is a capitalist plot. The loathsome Cockburn adduced an article in an obscure publication of the Sparticist League which maintained that antismoking campaigns are intended to control workers more closely, to increase productivity without increasing wages, and to reduce corporate ventilation costs. Cockburn also observed that an early, and rabid, antismoker was Adolf Hitler.

All of this was delivered deadpan, and it is no more ludicrous or farfetched than Cockburn's other opinions, so he may even believe it. But he was purveying disinformation (maybe not for the first time): it is well known here in North Carolina that antismokers are serving the international Communist conspiracy.

I offer in evidence the copies of *Pravda* that Philip Morris sent to several hundred newspaper editors and the like a while back, with a note observing that "*Pravda* does not carry cigarette advertising, or indeed any advertising." That may seem a little silly, but get a load of the lefty response: according to the *New York Times*, Democratic Congressman Mike Synar accused Philip Morris of "red-baiting" and called the mailing an "embarrassing throwback to the dark days of McCarthyism."

Synar ought to look at *Tobacco Culture*, by T. H. Breen, a serious historical monograph that attributes American independence to the irritation of Virginia tobacco growers at being jerked around by English merchants. No smoking, no U.S.—get it, Synar?

The attitude of those planters was a lot like my buddy Eugene's. When Northwest Airlines announced a smoking ban on all its flights, Eugene announced that he was going to boycott the company. Since Northwest doesn't go anywhere Eugene wants to go, I recognized this as a statement of principle. Besides, Eugene doesn't smoke. When I asked him why a nonsmoker would object to a no-smoking policy, he said: "I might decide to start." Don't tread on Eugene. He doesn't like being told he can't do things.

Given tobacco's association with the cause of freedom, I don't think the present climate of epidemical fanaticism (Burke's phrase) augurs well for the Republic. So I'm on the smokers' side.

Besides, I like smokers. I like to be with them when they're smoking, because passive smoking is the only kind I allow myself these days, and when they're not, because they tend to be good company. Didn't you ever notice that people in the smoking sections of airplanes were having more fun than the people up front? Laughing and joking and talking with one another? Getting acquainted, not just staring glumly at their newspapers and avoiding eye contact? Smokers are sociable folks. That's why most of them started smoking in the first place. I wish airlines would set aside special sections for smokers, even if they won't let people smoke. I'd ride there.

Pipe-smokers, especially, tend to be pleasant folks. My favorite example of a self-evident truth is Mike Royko's observation that no one was ever mugged by a pipe-smoker. (Child-molesting, maybe, but not mugging.) Some time ago the *Lutheran Standard* ran a photograph of a man with a pipe, and some churlish Mrs. Grundy wrote to complain. Another reader, a pipe man, wrote wistfully about "the little song that Johann Sebastian Bach wrote for Anna Magdalene, *Erbauliche Gedanken eines Tabakrauchers,*" with its happy reflection on the spiritual meaning of pipe smoking—"the smoke that rises like incense, the fire that reminds one of hell, and so forth." He translated the refrain thus: "And so on land, on sea, at home, abroad, / I'll smoke my pipe and worship God." Lutherans, he wrote, should resist "the further Methodistization of what was once the church of the Bible, Bach, and beer." Amen to that, says this disaffected Anglican.

Yes, I like smokers for their good nature. I also like their humility. Smokers are acquainted with human weakness and frailty. They know that people are a pretty sorry lot. They don't have great hopes of changing human nature. Few are into social reform in a big way. Hell, they can't even quit smoking.

Many smokers would agree with Robert Rosner of the (anti-smoking) Smoking Policy Institute who said this to the *Wall Street Journal*: "Smoking—the very fact of a cigarette dangling from one's mouth—is viewed as a breakdown in someone's self-discipline." But they would go on to ask whether self-discipline is the highest of virtues. Higher than charity? Compassion? Humility? Not all of us admire the ostentatiously self-disciplined. But someone like Rosner (who makes his living "help[ing] companies to establish smoking restrictions"—and what kind of job is *that*?) couldn't be expected to understand.

So I like smokers, and I feel sorry for them, even more than for other abused and downtrodden minorities. As the habit wanes, I also feel sorry for the tobacco farmers and cigarette factory workers whose taxes pay my salary, and for Garland, my longtime tobacconist and friend.

But I must say I'm damned if I feel sorry for the tobacco companies. Like rats leaving a sinking ship, they're diversifying out of the cigarette business as fast as they can. I see where RJR Nabisco even developed a "smokeless cigarette"—about the sort of limp-wristed accommodationism you'd expect from a cookie company, isn't it? That's the act of a company that doesn't believe in its product.

I don't like cigarette companies that imply that there's something wrong with smoke. Smoke is their business and they ought to *like* it. I do. One of my early memories is of my grandfather's smoking Camels at a high-school football game: a crisp November evening, and that marvelous fragrance. Sneer if you will, but if people can wax lyrical about wood smoke on the New England air or burning leaves in the small-town Midwest, I reserve the right to my own smelly nostalgia. I smoked for thirty years, and quit for my health, not because I didn't like smoke.

So I'd have more respect for RJR if they'd taken a lead from the success of Jolt Cola ("All the sugar, twice the caffeine"). That Jolt is selling out in U.S. college towns tells me that college kids are sick of being told what's good for them by middle-aged health-and-safety fascists. If RJR really wanted to *sell cigarettes*, they wouldn't dink around with gimmicky smokeless cigarette-type nicotine delivery devices. They'd bring out something like "Death" cigarettes: "All the nicotine, twice the tar." They'd put a skull and crossbones on the pack, print the surgeon general's warning twice the required size, and sell them with slogans like "What the hell!" and "Do you want to live forever?"

If they smelled like those Camels did back in 1950, who could resist?

(March 1989)

～ The Heartbreak of Satyriasis ～

I started writing this when David Garrow's biography of Martin Luther King appeared, with its revelations about Dr. King's sexual habits, just in time for Christmas 1986. I put it aside because I wasn't happy with it. In the summer of 1987, the Hart and Bakker scandals made me dust it off and try again. I still didn't like it. Spring of 1988, and Jimmy Swaggart prompted me to have still another try, also unsatisfactory. In 1989 we heard about John Tower's "gamy" behavior (*Time*'s adjective) and about the love life of the prime minister of Australia. Even old Ted Kennedy was back in the news, although with Ted it's hardly news. Here I am, trying again, and this time, for better or for worse, I'm going to plow through to some sort of conclusion.

Ponder this story. At a dinner party held by a foreign head of state to honor a visiting American politician, the guest of honor "fumbled Mrs A., kissed the shrieking Miss B., pinched the plump Mrs C. black and blue, and ran at Miss D. with intent to ravish her." After reportedly behaving like a "must elephant," our countryman was carried by six sailors "by main force" back to his ship, where his wife awaited him in the public saloon cabin. Then—but let his host tell it:

> This remarkable man satiated there and then his baffled lust on the unresisting body of his legitimate spouse and copiously vomited during the operation. If you have seen Mrs —— you will not think this incredible.

OK, who is this great American? Lots of possibilities, aren't there? This particular lecher, however, was none other than our former president and my fellow Republican U. S. Grant, whose straight-ahead amatory style seems to have had much in common with his military one. His host was the viceroy of India, Earl Lytton.

This story may be as new to you as it was to me when I encountered it in Paul Johnson's collection of political anecdotes. But any reader of history will know that rutting politicians are not a new thing. The twentieth century has witnessed many revolting innovations, but this isn't one of them. Politics seems always to have attracted alpha males. Venery almost goes with the territory, and Gary Hart was a traditionalist in this respect, if no other. The Kennedy brothers, Nelson Rockefeller, Lyndon Johnson, Wilbur Mills, Wayne Hays—the list goes on and on. My fellow Tar Heel Elizabeth Ray never published her appointment book, but Washington gossip says that it was something of a *Who's Who*. My source says the only surprise is how many of these old goats were willing to pay for it. But at least they weren't molesting congressional pages.

Obviously many public figures have disgraceful private lives. So, of course, do many private figures. So what? My question for today is: When is this sort of thing any of our business?

In 1987 there was a lot of discussion about whether the *Miami Herald* had a right to investigate Gary Hart's sex life. The general conclusion seemed to be yes, if only because Hart had virtually dared the press to do it. But a substantial minority opinion said no, that it was an unjustifiable invasion of Hart's privacy. (Oddly, or maybe not, I didn't hear anyone say that Jim Bakker's shenanigans were none of our business. Think about that.)

Now, I'd insist that trying to cover up one's misbehavior is itself relatively petty misbehavior. Some of us may prefer unapologetic sinners like, say, former governor Edwin Edwards of Louisiana (who once claimed that he could survive anything short of being caught in bed with a dead girl or a live boy), but that's an aesthetic judgment, not a moral one. As La Rochefoucauld observed, hypocrisy is the tribute vice pays to virtue. Gary Hart was less culpable for lying than for what he did that needed lying about. Jim Bakker's sin was adultery, not paying hush money (unless the money wasn't his).

As for the public's rights, surely we're not entitled to know whatever anyone can dig up about anybody at all. Private citizens have a right to privacy. Even many "public figures" within the meaning of our pitiable libel laws have that right. But there are whole categories of people whose sexual and financial affairs ought to be fair game for investigative reporters and inquisitive biographers. Foremost among them are our public officials and those who seek to be public officials. We ought to be informed of their peccadilloes, even if we don't really want to know. We need to be told what kinds of people are seeking the license to speak on our behalf and to push us around. And politicians ought to be harassed anyway, on general principles. The *Herald* did right (although I hate to see the press get sanctimonious).

We're also entitled to know—indeed, obliged to inform ourselves—of shabby behavior by those who aspire to positions of moral leadership. People, that is, like Jim Bakker and Jimmy Swaggart. Obviously, marital fidelity and financial integrity are not immaterial to judgments of character, and those who seek the public's confidence, and contributions, should expect the public's scrutiny.

But if the case for disclosure is made on that reasoning alone, don't we lose our right to know about the private lives of politicians who can't hurt us any more or preachers who no longer want our money? What possible right do we have to scurrilous stories about U. S. Grant? How can we be entitled to know about Ike's girlfriend, or Eleanor Roosevelt's?

Let's consider the case that got me started on these reflections, that of Martin Luther King, as revealed in David Garrow's book. For the record, Garrow is a former colleague and friend of mine, although we have hardly an opinion in common. One opinion we do share, though, is that King did all of us down here a service by his part in getting the segregation monkey off our backs, and by going about it in the way that he did. King was a brave man and a world-historical figure. But Garrow's research in the FBI files makes it obvious that he was also a compulsive philanderer.

Maybe King felt bad about it. (Garrow didn't say, but Taylor Branch's subsequent book suggests that he did.) Nevertheless, King continued to misbehave even after it was perfectly plain that the walls had ears.

I don't believe we have a "right to know" about these activities. But—follow this closely, now—I don't agree with those who argue that Garrow shouldn't have reported them. He had no right to suppress what he learned. Like the courts, good, truth-telling scholarship and journalism require the truth, the whole truth, and nothing but the truth. Scholars and journalists should not withhold facts that are part of the story that they are telling (as Jack Kennedy's hagiographers presumably did).

And certainly not from fear of the consequences. Shortly after Garrow's book appeared a historian worried in my presence about "what happens when the rednecks get hold of this." Well, brother (I told him), I've got news for you: the rednecks already knew about this. They were telling me about it a quarter-century ago. In my youthful Freudian wisdom I thought they were "projecting," and they may have been, but even a blind hog gets an acorn sometimes. What's more, all of my friends with even the remotest connection to "the movement" now assure me that, of course, they knew all about this, too. If Garrow's revelations haven't had much in the way of political consequences, it may be because I'm the only American who didn't already know that King was a womanizer.

But even if those revelations had somehow discredited the movement as well as its leader, I think Garrow was obliged to report them. When biographers learn something that sheds light on their subjects' characters, or when journalists learn something newsworthy about figures in the public eye, the canons of their professions rightly require that they tell us. In other words, once Garrow learned of King's sexual habits, he could tell us about them or drop his project altogether, but he had no right to present a distorted picture.

I know an anthropologist who disagrees. Basically, like the historian, she feared that Garrow's account would give aid and comfort to the bad guys. It's not surprising that this same woman once wrote a book that didn't mention the economic base of the community she studied—which was burglary. She felt that it would put the community in an unfavorable light; people, she said, "wouldn't understand." But public relations be damned: her job as an anthropologist was to make us understand, to tell us about that community. And she didn't do it. She should have helped us to see what that activity looks like from inside—where, I'm sure, it looks different.

Just so, Garrow would have been wrong not to tell us what he learned about King. He was writing scholarly biography, not a brief for canonization. If I have a quarrel with him, it's that he doesn't begin to explain what he found—indeed, doesn't seem to recognize that anything needs explaining.

On the other hand, it seems to me that the FBI had not only the right but the obligation to suppress that information. Their job isn't biography; in fact, they ought to be in the business of keeping secrets. It's appalling that they had those motel-room tapes in the first place. Bugging King's room was a gross violation of an American citizen's rights, hard to justify even by the well-founded suspicion that one of his pals was a Communist. But releasing the tapes or transcripts to people like Dave Garrow compounds the offense. And the fact that the Bureau had no choice under the Freedom of Information Act strikes me as still another reason that law needs rethinking. Where does this stop? Can I take those FBI tapes and make an LP?

I'm unhappy to learn about this aspect of Dr. King's life. I don't think the world is a better place because we know about it, and it may be worse. But I'm not sore at Garrow for doing his job. I'm sore at the FBI for eavesdropping in the first place, and for releasing this material in the second.

As for Martin Luther King—well, I find I'm becoming more tolerant in large matters, less so in small. (People can't always keep their marriage vows, but they can turn their damn radios down.) Still, I'm sore at Dr. King for his unwillingness or inability to keep his pants on. There would have been nothing to tape, nothing to release, nothing to publish, nothing to explain, if King had behaved as a clergyman—hell, as a husband—ought. There is a cruel irony in the fact that this man, who made such a powerful appeal to conscience, should himself have had a conscience in this respect so manifestly inadequate.

Political and moral leaders ought to behave themselves for the same reasons as the rest of us, and for one more reason, peculiar to themselves: misbehavior by a leader betrays his cause. Religious broadcasting will be a long time recovering from the blows that Jim Bakker and Jimmy Swaggart dealt it. The political allies of Gary Hart and John Tower aren't likely to forgive them any time soon. Martin Luther King endangered not only his own good name, but the movement he led.

(August 1989)

VI. Views from the Lower Right

❦ The World According to NPR ❧

The other morning National Public Radio offered its listeners an interview with a Texas mass murderer to go with their cornflakes. This monster, who had confessed to 250 or so murders, told the reporter that some of them were "sacrifices to Satan." Aghast, the reporter asked, "You don't really believe in Satan, do you?" (He did.)

In the world according to NPR, it seems, mass murder gets more respect than religious belief, orthodox or perverse.

In actual fact, the *N* in NPR should probably stand for Northeastern. (And my buddy Tom says the *P* should stand for People's—or Pink.) Sure, the network drags in a lot of Californians to comment on this and that, and serves up a few domesticated Southerners and other regional and ethnic specimens, but for the most part the NPR sensibility is Yankee yuppie secular humanism, if you'll excuse the expression.

Take this Devil business. The reporter seemed surprised that anybody, even a mass murderer, believed in Old Nick. Well, the last figures I saw on that (in an article in the autumn 1974 issue of *Listening*) put the percentage of Southerners who were absolutely certain that Satan exists at 72 percent—up from 53 percent nine years earlier. By comparison, only 29 percent of Northeasterners believed in him, and that figure had decreased from 33 percent in 1964. Overall, 50 percent of Americans believed unreservedly and another 21 percent said it was "probably true" that the Devil exists. And belief was increasing everywhere except in the Northeast.

Who's out of touch here?

Another example. When a movie reviewer on "All Things Considered" discussed a movie that hinged on whether the two main characters—who were (as the country song puts it) married, but not to each other—would or wouldn't, the NPR anchorwoman professed disbelief that two adults, these days, would hesitate. Well, I don't have the numbers on it, but I can testify that there are lots of folks out here in the provinces and even some in the Northeast, if you look for them, who try, sometimes successfully, to keep the Commandments, even the Seventh.

The fact is that religion is still a force to be reckoned with in American life. But you wouldn't know it to listen to NPR—or, as Benjamin Stein has observed, to watch prime-time television.

Leave aside the fact that it is pernicious to have "opinion leaders"
so out of touch with the country that supports them; I suggest
that it's actually dangerous. Look at what happened to the Shah.

(May 1985)

∽ Dr. Bob's Unusual University ∽

Bob Jones University. Isn't that that segregationist place down in
South Carolina someplace?

Well, yes and no; or, rather, no and yes. BJU is in Greenville,
South Carolina. And it did lose its tax exemption a while back
because its administration—which means the Reverend Dr. Bob
Jones, Jr., son of the founder—forbids interracial dating on what
it/he believes to be biblical grounds. But if Bob Jones is racist, in
the strict sense of that much misused word, it is hardly segregationist: it has a number of black students, and yellow ones, and
probably red ones, too. In an odd way, Bob Jones is a very cosmopolitan place.

Perhaps you never heard anything good about it, but there are
circles, worldwide, in which it's regarded as not just a reputable
school, but an outstanding one. Among those who share its brand
of orthodoxy, it has an international reputation and international
connections. Ian Paisley was an honored guest for a World Congress of Fundamentalists, and its students come from all over for
what it, almost uniquely, offers.

Bob Jones is, first and last, an institution dedicated to its founder's
version of fundamentalist Protestant Christianity. It offers pretty
much the usual range of postsecondary instruction, but within that
framework. In one recruiting ad, for instance, a young graduate
reports that her business degree and the Lord's blessing secured
her a post with the largest bank in northeastern Alabama. Its
education school seems to train teachers primarily for fundamentalist private academies, and its university press publishes an exten-
sive line of textbooks for such schools. BJU also trains preachers of
the Gospel, as understood by Dr. Bob, and it trains them well, by
its own lights, offering courses even in "missionary aviation."
BJU-trained missionaries—flying and earthbound—have extended

the school's reputation to some of the least hospitable corners of the globe.

Bob Jones calls itself the "World's Most Unusual University" (its radio station is WMUU), and it may be right. Although it has a very Southern flavor to it, the school has little to do with the middle-sized Southern city in which it is located, and one gathers that both BJU and Greenville prefer it that way. Visitors are welcome, although they must pass a guardhouse at the entrance to campus. Smoking is forbidden, obviously. A discreet sign on the museum states that modest dress is required. (Fair enough: I've seen similar signs in Orthodox Jewish neighborhoods.)

When I visited Bob Jones one winter afternoon, it was like stepping through a time warp, back to a 1957 that never really was. Although as a matter of fact I was in the company of an interracial couple (Caucasian-Oriental), I don't think we drew any disapproving glances on that score. But I was self-conscious for the first time in years about my modest beard and moustache.

The dominant first impression of BJU students is one of healthy vigor: for boys, the muscular Christian mode; for girls, the perky style I always associate with cheerleaders. Closer examination reveals a pretty full complement of tubby late adolescents and pimply ectomorphs, but these actual physical facts are effectively disguised by a stern dress code. Young men wear coats and ties, often suits. Young women wear over-the-knee skirts that look weirdly sexy to anyone who was a teenage boy thirty years ago. I'm told—I hope it's true—that Bob Jones women were forbidden to wear makeup until that became a mark of the counterculture, whereupon they were required to wear it. I do know that BJU now offers instruction in "cosmetology."

All students of both sexes are earnest in appearance and restrained in demeanor. Many look like the kind who would tell you that they have nothing against good, clean fun. They look ready, even eager, to help the visitor with directions, physical or spiritual, or to explain why Billy Graham is a renegade. Surely some students are there grumpily, because their parents thought it would be good for them, but they cannot be detected on sight—and probably a good thing for them, too.

The school's campus is modern, much of it in yellow brick, late art deco. It is intensively landscaped, and largely maintained by students. Boys are allowed to wear blue jeans while gardening, although it looked to me as if few chose to do so.

The university is justly proud of its museum of religious art, twenty-odd rooms of it. Some of it is very fine indeed: we're not talking about Last Supper bedspreads here. All of the art is old and European, which is to say Papist. Some of the martyrs depicted look even less comfortable than usual, which I attribute to their incongruous setting. Ian Paisley must have been almost as pained himself at all the reliquaries and portraits of bishops.

The bookstore, nearby, offers the usual assortment of T-shirts, mugs (coffee, not beer), pennants, and souvenirs, as well as some Most Unusual books. One examines Satanism in rock music. Another, called *A Church Built on Sand*, condemns the liberalism of the Southern Baptist Convention. The cover shows a church, with a more than incidental similarity to the Southern Baptist church across the road from the BJU guardhouse, sinking into quicksand.

Across from the bookstore is another large building, with an enormous room on the second floor filled with dozens of sofas. It is used for "dating," which means sitting and conversing, under supervision. When I was there, a handwritten sign announced "No Dating Friday Afternoon." The room was empty.

In the same building is a state-of-the-art multimedia center (excuse the expression), which offers daily presentations for prospective students and donors. My friends and I were neither, but went anyway. The production, by the BJU media department, is impressive, flashy, well thought-out. Like the aviation courses, it reminded me that BJU's attitude toward the modern age is not simply adversarial. Bob Jones people are not rigid traditionalists like the Amish. Indeed, it may be a mistake to think of them as traditionalists at all. It takes a lot of money to run a show like this, for instance, and BJU obviously has it, even after taxes. A loyal constituency helps, of course, but so do modern management and the whole apparatus of modern marketing, direct mail and all the rest. Old wine, perhaps, but very new bottles.

No, the school admits modernity, but wants it selectively, and on its own terms. It does seem to regard the outside world with considerable suspicion, and vice versa. Not surprisingly, there's something of a fortress atmosphere about BJU; for whatever reason, many outsiders profess to find the place somewhat fright-ening. The multimedia presentation has an odd emphasis on how efficient campus security is; across town, at (Southern Baptist) Furman University, the folklore among liberal faculty members has it that BJU is stockpiling arms.

I gather that the school did apply, unsuccessfully, for permis-sion to arm its campus police with automatic weapons, and a conspiracy theorist might speculate about the connection be-tween this alleged passion for weaponry and the school's links to the Protestants of Ulster.

It seems to me, though, that those who find BJU scary tend to be liberal Protestants, perhaps especially Baptists, who fear that they see in it the dark side of their own tradition. An outsider like me can look at it with a good deal more equanimity, and, from a distance, I find it an interesting and colorful tile in the American mosaic. Up close, it is, at worst, unpleasant—and no more so than any other exclusivist sectarian community. Bob Jones poses no clear and present danger to constitutional government or civil order. Among its supporters, at least the rank and file are utterly sincere in their beliefs, and give up a great deal in consequence. These are a stiff-necked people, and a peculiar one, but admirable in some ways.

I don't think they have the answer. But they're not the problem.

(May 1986)

≈ Death of a Communist ≈

Don't look to this essay for amusement. I'm not feeling light-hearted right now. This is a reflection on the life of a man who was once my friend, a man whose life and work demonstrate that meaning well is not enough.

Al and I were graduate students at Columbia in the sixties. For a short time we worked together in an informal study group preparing for comprehensive examinations. But our politics (con-struing that word broadly) made us poor harness-mates. Al was ferociously bright, very well read, and extraordinarily hardwork-ing, but we just had too little in common even to study together.

If Communists still carry cards, surely Al carried one. He was, by his own description, an orthodox Marxist-Leninist. I would say that his politics were more important to him than his academic work, except that he saw no distinction between the two: his "socialist" politics were his life. He was always dashing off to civil-rights demonstrations in Mississippi, or to support striking miners in Harlan County. In ordinary, nonpolitical discourse, he was a good-natured, sensitive soul, but such discourse with Al was rare. He took politics very seriously indeed, and when the subject came up (far too often for my taste) he displayed a blinkered sort of humorlessness. For him, revolution was no laughing matter. When a mutual friend spent a research year in Romania and came back a fervent anti-Communist, Al told him, "You're a good man, Dan. Too bad we'll have to shoot you." Dan swears to this day that Al meant it.

My usual defense against left-wingers is to tease them, but that didn't work with Al. He either didn't know he was being teased, or he responded with flat scorn. Either way, it wasn't any fun. On one occasion, though, I couldn't resist. Al and some of his comrades had started a magazine called *Ripsaw*, reviving the title of a long-defunct journal of hairy-chested radicalism. When their posters went up on bulletin boards around Columbia, I pointed out to Al that a real proletarian would know that the saw teeth on the magazine's logo were those of a crosscut saw, not a ripsaw. He looked at me suspiciously and stalked off, but I'll bet he looked it up, because the next day all of the posters were gone.

In an atmosphere vibrant with the enthusiasms of the New Left, Al was a constant, stern reminder of the old. During Columbia's troubles in 1968, he was in the thick of things, rushing from one meeting to another, drafting statements, addressing caucuses, posting placards. He had deep misgivings about what he saw as the amateur revolutionaries around us, and phrases like "infantile leftism" came easily to him. But when push came to shove, he and I wound up on opposite sides of the picket lines. I never had an easy conversation with him after that, probably as much my fault as his, but I regret it.

We went our separate ways, geographically as well as politically. Al took a college teaching position in the Northwest, where he belonged to the "editorial collective" of a journal called the *Insurgent Sociologist*. From time to time I saw him at conventions, peddling the journal. We barely spoke on these occasions, if we spoke at all; the last time, I wouldn't swear he recognized me.

Occasionally I ran across one of Al's dreary, unreadable, party-line books—attacking Solidarity, praising the USSR's human rights record, that sort of thing. I gathered from mutual friends that he had achieved a modest fame: the man to call when you wanted a specimen Stalinist to spice up your program. Someone told me that he vacationed at Soviet resorts in the Crimea; my informant may have been having me on, but it would have been perfectly in character.

I heard, too, that Al had campaigned unsuccessfully for the chairmanship of his department. Academic etiquette says you're not supposed to campaign for such a job (you should at least pretend that you have more important things to do), but Al never gave a damn for etiquette, academic or otherwise. He reportedly campaigned as "Big Al, the People's Pal," and I smiled at what I saw as evidence that middle age was mellowing him, giving him finally a sense of humor and perspective.

Then one day, at the age of forty-three, he took a gun and blew his brains out. According to the *Insurgent Sociologist*, his final words on a last note were "The working class will prevail. Carry on."

Al defended and worked for—well, damn it, for an evil empire. Yet he was an intelligent man, and a decent one, selfless and sincere in his devotion to what he believed was human welfare. To compare Al to the folks I know at Bob Jones University would have annoyed him, and them, too, but while Al's answer appeals to me far less even than Bob Jones's—indeed, Al's answer is part of our problem in a way that Bob Jones's is not—there is no denying that true believers of both sorts share some of the same admirable qualities.

It bears repeating that all of the hellish ideologies of our time appeal to good impulses as well as bad ones. It is comforting to think that evildoers are always evil people, but we deceive and to that extent disarm ourselves by believing that. Karl Marx himself insisted on the distinction between motives and objective consequences; he was right to make that distinction, and we can start by applying it to Marxists. Our collectivist adversaries' actions may have ghastly, Satanic consequences—may lead inexorably to the Gulag—but some of them are driven by something very like Christian charity. If we judge on motivation alone, Al was the people's pal.

And he used to be mine. When we were students together, he saw life as incessant struggle, and he relished both the life and the struggle. But he had become depressed, I'm told, and tired—so much so that he sought oblivion in death. I hope he has found rest. And mercy, too. I know what they say about good intentions, but surely—in that next world Marxists don't believe in—they count for something.

(June 1986)

~ Why I Am an Episcopalian ~

A friend of mine was having a theological discussion with his cleaning lady one day (people do that sort of thing in the South), and the subject of the End of Time came up. They agreed that the signs are all in place, and that it must be coming soon, if the Bible is to be believed.

"You know, Mr. F———," she said, "I believe that. I really do. But if you think about it too much, it will drive you crazy."

Some of us feel that way about religion in general, but from time to time we think about it anyway. This is one of those times.

My buddy Tim lives in Chicago. Now in his forties, he recently felt the stirrings of a long-dormant religious impulse. Raised in a Scotch-Irish household of stern Presbyterian persuasion, he naturally sought out the nearest franchise of that denomination. When its minister suggested that perhaps a refresher course would be in order after a twenty-five-year absence, Tim enrolled in a program for prospective new members.

After several meetings, Tim grew increasingly restive, and finally asked the question that was on his mind: What about sin? he said—You haven't mentioned sin. The minister hemmed and hawed, Tim reports, and replied, in effect, that modern churchmen don't believe in that any more.

Now, when it comes to sin, Tim is like the man who was asked if he believed in infant baptism: he not only believes in it, he's seen it with his own eyes. So he decided that the church of his childhood was no longer for him, and he was recently confirmed as an Episcopalian. He says Episcopalians will let you believe in anything you want to. Even sin.

Probably the best face that can be put on what's happening to the American Episcopal Church is to say that it's retracing its steps to the eighteenth-century Church of England from which it emerged. After Elizabeth I declined to put windows into men's souls, Anglicans could believe pretty much what they chose, so long as they maintained a decent regard for appearances. And once the Church of England got out of the religion business, it found all sorts of other interesting things to do. The American church seems to be doing the same.

For example, its bishops don't sit in the House of Lords, like those of its Established mother church, but they do their best to share in the task of government, if only by passing embarrassing resolutions on all sorts of matters beyond their competence. I have in my hand a pamphlet called *Policy for Action II: The Social Policies of the Episcopal Church*. Among the dozens of items, touching every aspect of foreign and domestic policy, probably the only ones that wouldn't make it through a conference of the non-aligned nations are calls for the USSR to allow greater emigration and to get out of Afghanistan. Since anti-Semitism seems to be increasingly a left-wing phenomenon these days—Daniel Ortega's record, for example, is none too good—maybe we can give the Episcopal Church a few points for coming down against that, too. But if Ortega could find anything else to disagree with, it's because Episcopalians have him outflanked on the left. (If he's following Fidel's lead in the matter of civil rights for homosexuals, for instance, he risks the disapproval of the American Episcopal Church.)

Now, when it comes to shameless capitulation to the Zeitgeist, we Episcopalians have a way to go to catch up with some other denominations (which shall remain nameless—I'm not knocking your religion). But we're moving up fast on the outside, proceeding to buy the whole mess of left-wing pottage served up by the *Nation*, and calling it "prophetic." But, then, state churches have always been notoriously worldly. And let's take it easy on the eighteenth-century Church of England. Without its shortcomings, would we have had the Wesleys and, later, the Oxford

Movement—or Trollope, for that matter? Any church that nurtured Samuel Johnson can't have been all bad.

Maybe in two hundred years people will find something equally good to say about the twentieth-century American Episcopal Church. But I doubt it. Acting like a state church only works if you *are* a state church. Post-disestablishment, you're just another voluntary organization, and the idea is widespread that members of a church ought to have some beliefs in common. Abandon orthodoxy—whatever your orthodoxy may be—and your disaffected members will defect to the competition, more or less quietly.

It's no accident that as the Episcopal Church has become more obviously concerned with the Third World than with the next world its downward spiral in orthodoxy has been tracked by a decline in membership. (Much the same could be said—and often has been—of the other liberal Protestant churches. But you can tell me about your church some other time.) The most visible ex-Episcopalians are found in the distressingly numerous breakaway Anglican bodies, but I know others who have turned to Greek and Russian Orthodoxy, Roman Catholicism, the Southern Baptist Convention, and tennis.

So why does my family hang on and grumble? Well, I can't speak for my wife and daughters, but in my case the reason is a mixture of two parts nostalgia, one part heterodoxy, and a dash of perversity.

There is, in the first place, the splendor of the ruined Anglican liturgy, sacked and burned by indigenous barbarians in our own time. The destruction is not yet complete; if I choose my time and place carefully, I can still find a sort of *Readers' Digest* Condensed Version of the liturgy that I, my parents, and about sixteen generations of Church of Ireland ancestors once found as natural and as necessary as air. One crime for which I could cheerfully send the Standing Liturgical Commission to share Cranmer's fate at the stake (which would at least give them something in common) is their severing of a link with past and future that once meant a great deal to me.

A second reason I don't jump ship, frankly, is that joining some other communion would make an implicit credal statement that I'm not ready to make. So would staying home on Sundays. Remaining where I was planted makes very little statement at all, and that suits me just fine. I'm not proud of this vegetable aspect of my affiliation. Quite the contrary. I just report it because I suspect a similar inertia is more widespread than is suspected by the clergy and clericized layfolk who run the Episcopal Church. Or maybe they do know about it. Maybe they're counting on it.

Anyway, and finally, I remain an Episcopalian because even if we are seeing the death throes of historic Anglicanism, those writhings afford the opportunity for a sort of grisly humor that I hate myself in the morning for enjoying. (Who was it that observed that even Dark Ages have their compensations?)

In what other nominally Christian church, for example, could you find a leader calling on his brethren to "realistically see how polygamy can be accommodated"? The Bishop of West Buganda did just that, at a recent consultation on "indigenization" held near Kampala. The accommodation of alternative life-styles is becoming something of an Anglican specialty, and one would think a church midwived by Henry VIII shouldn't have much trouble with that one. I can hardly wait.

Meanwhile, indigenization continues apace here at home. A few years ago the Bishop of New York broke new ground by ordaining an out-of-the-closet homosexual to the priesthood—a lesbian, as it happens, which added to the sensation, since women priests were a novelty at the time. (Bishop Moore always has been a show-off.) Since then other bishops have more or less knowingly ordained both male and female homosexuals, and for the time being it seems to be up to individual diocesans—a sort of ecclesiastical local option.

Now, I yield to no one in my admiration for states' rights, a principle that often makes for sensible politics (as I keep saying about abortion law). But it does duck the question of right and wrong. Governments duck that question all the time, and often should, but it's an awkward habit for churches to get into. Realizing this, perhaps, our presiding bishop has said that homosexuals should have "access to the ordination process," which may or may not mean—nobody seems to know—that they should be ordained.

Personally, I don't want to hear about *any* priest's sex life. In the nature of things, there have always been homosexual priests, but they haven't gone around forming caucuses and demanding to be heard—and heard, and heard. Will the love that won't shut up now come to figure as prominently in the politics of the Episcopal Church as in those of the Democratic party? How could I leave a church where that question remains unresolved?

(December 1986)

❧ Facing the Untoward in a ❧ Memphis Men's Room

I guess I should have known it would be an odd trip when the pilot told us as we were approaching Memphis that we could expect "a little choppiness, but nothing untoward." Untoward?

I was going to Oxford, Mississippi, to lecture at the University of Mississippi's Center for the Study of Southern Culture. I did that, and I made the usual calls. I pigged out on biscuits and gravy at Smitty's and catfish in Taylor. I stopped by Square Books, where Richard Howorth will shoot the breeze with you, if you want to do that, or leave you in peace to drink coffee, smoke your pipe, and read Fred Chappell's poems, if you'd rather do that. At a truck stop in Senatobia, I picked up a couple of cans of Sun-dried Mississippi Possum ("Killed by a truck on Highway 51 north of Nesbitt"). Back in Memphis, I swung by the Rendezvous for a mess of ribs, said howdy to the ducks at the Peabody Hotel, returned my rented car, and checked into an airport motel for an early Sunday morning flight.

Just a routine trip to North Mississippi. Nothing untoward.

But the next morning, in the airport men's room, I did run into something strange. I was minding my own business (believe me). A character with a gray flattop haircut and a pallid beer belly visible beneath the bottom of his tropical print shirt was shaving at the sink. He spoke.

"Worst trip I ever had in my life."

I was the only other person there, so he was obviously talking to me, but my mama always told me not to talk with strangers in public restrooms. So I tried my best to look sympathetic, without actually engaging him, you understand?

"Yeah, I could write a book."

Well, I had no choice, so I asked where he'd been.

"Been down to Costa Rica. Going back to Anchorage—Alaska? Got robbed down there. Whore took all my money. Five-fifty in cash and another fifteen hundred in travelers' checks. Left me twenty-seven dollars. Worst thing was, she took my return ticket. Had to buy a new one—pay full fare. Costing me five hundred more from Memphis to Anchorage than the deal on my old ticket. Had a great deal. . . . Weather was lousy, too. Heat wave. Hottest weather this time of year for twelve years. Some said thirty, but I think it's twelve. Sweat just running off me. Couldn't breathe. Come from the North like me, you're not used to that stuff."

"Be glad to get back home, huh?" He was between me and the door.

"Oh, yeah. But the trip was a success. Real success."

Now I was actually getting curious. "How's that?"

"Went down there to find a wife. Took an ad—you know, in the newspaper. 'Seeks companionship. Possibility of permanent arrangement in the U.S.' Sort of thing. Forty-one replies! Interviewed eight or nine of them. Meant to do more, but just too hot, you know? Women are desperate down there, get to the States. Beautiful women, too. All ages. Had 'em fifteen to forty-nine. Had one gal, twenty-five, spent three days with me. Bathed me three times a day. Kissed me and everything. Walked around with me, you know, holding hands. Her twenty-five! And me—" He shook his head. "That's the kind of wife a man needs, you know."

I asked if he'd found any keepers.

"Yeah. Gonna marry her. The oldest. She's forty-nine. I'm sixty-five, you know—we'll be more compatible."

What was she going to make of Alaska weather?

"Oh, we talked about it. I had a picture book, you know? Big color pictures of Alaska. I told her, she gets cold, put on more clothes. Down there, I get hot, what'm I gonna do—take off my skin? No, she'll be all right."

Another patron came into the men's room, which inhibited me, if not my new friend. Besides, I saw my way clear to the door. I told the man I was glad his trip hadn't been a total loss.

"Oh, it was a winner. A real winner. I just had a hard time."

I thought about this episode most of the way across Tennessee. And of course I thought of all the questions I should have asked him. Like whether he'd been married before, and whether he spoke Spanish, and how he got the idea, and how the twenty-five-year-old took the news that she hadn't made the cut. I wasn't meant to be a reporter, obviously.

I thought, too, of a "60 Minutes" special I'd seen on the subject of off-the-rack wives. The predictable people had produced the predictable responses, and I hadn't learned much from it except the extent of the practice. I remembered that my reaction had been to reflect that this kind of thing has been going on for as long as there have been frontiers. Is the problem (say) too few women in Australia, too many in England? Too few in Minnesota, too many in Sweden? The answer suggests itself.

But this is different. The current traffic in wives doesn't result from demographic imbalance. It speaks instead of economic crisis in the Third World and cultural—well, shall we say "strain"?—at home. There's obviously a U.S. market for old-fashioned girls, and the Third World is well on the way to cornering it. Do I hear calls for protectionism?

This is a sad business, in so many ways. It's sad, obviously, that a young Costa Rican woman is so desperate to get even to Alaska (Alaska!) that she'd invest three days and what's left of her pride in cuddling with a physically repulsive gringo old enough to be her father—hell, in Costa Rican terms, old enough to be her grandfather.

But spare some sympathy, if you can, for a lonely and unattractive man who wants someone to help him face old age and the long Alaska nights—a man with so little going for him that he's surprised and delighted when women treat him nice, even though he knows perfectly well why they do it. A guy, moreover, who has no one with whom to share his surprise and delight but a perfect stranger in the Memphis airport. That's sad, too.

(November 1987)

～ Ora Pro Nobis ～

On the tenth anniversary of Elvis's death, a reporter called to ask the usual question: What does it all mean? Ah, that took me back.

To be precise, it took me back to that August of 1977. We were living in England when Elvis died, and I noticed at the time that the BBC didn't ring up the local sociologists for foolish observations about the meaning of it all; they turned instead to South London vicars. When it comes to ancient, expensive havens for shabby-genteel idlers (usually left-wing) who will bloviate about the larger significance of any subject whatsoever, universities don't have a patch on the Church of England. But since lazy American journalists have no underemployed Establishment clergymen at hand, they have to turn to—well, to people like me, which strikes me as one of the many arguments for rethinking the establishment clause, but never mind.

In a single day recently I had two of these callers. One wanted to know why *Friday the 13th, Part 6* was doing so well at the box office; the other asked what the doubling of vanity license plate sales told us about life in North Carolina today. I should have said that both phenomena suggest that North Carolinians have more money than is good for them, but I merely referred these seekers to younger colleagues who haven't learned yet how silly you look in print when you answer questions like these off the cuff.

The call about Elvis shouldn't have surprised me, but I wasn't ready for it. I couldn't even remember what those parsons had said back in '77—just something about "bringing us together," and I think "Lord of the Dance" was mentioned—so I referred the reporter to my buddy Charles, an Ole Miss historian, who once wrote a wonderful piece on Bear Bryant's funeral (in the *South Atlantic Quarterly*, just before that venerable journal was hijacked by post-structuralists). Charles also keeps a vial of Elvis's sweat in his office, so I thought he'd do.

After the reporter rang off, I got to thinking about that sweat. I also thought about another friend, a Memphis pathologist who told me once after a couple of drinks that he has a fragment of liver. Relics.

At Graceland, in the garden where Elvis is buried with his parents, candles burn, pilgrims pray, tears flow. On the wall of the public men's room, there are (I swear it) messages to Elvis. Votives, honest.

On the wall of my office is a picture of Elvis ascending a golden staircase to a heavenly Graceland where his mother waits for him and Hank Williams extends a hand in greeting. An icon of the apotheosis.

And—are you ready for this?—a book published in 1987 cataloged the King's apparitions in the preceding decade.

Listen, if this were the Middle Ages, there'd be a cult. Heck, there *is* a cult: what more does it take?

Now, the license plates in the Graceland parking lot suggest that this craziness is not exclusively or even mostly a Southern phenomenon; when I was there, at least, Southern plates were a decided minority. Lots of us down here are fond of Elvis, but he's a homeboy—one of us—and certainly no saint. We find Elvisolatry amusing, and try to figure a way to make some money off it, as I'm doing right now. (One of my favorite efforts is an amazing song by a former North Carolina Bible-college student named Mojo Nixon; call your local radio station and request "Elvis is Everywhere," because I can't even begin to summarize it.)

Besides, Evangelical Protestantism is rather stern in these matters. Some time ago, the Gallup Poll showed that Southerners are less likely than other Americans to believe that it's possible to communicate with the dead, despite the fact that we're more likely to believe in an afterlife in the first place. Pilgrimages, relics, shrines, apparitions—no, this isn't really our kind of thing.

But orthodox Catholics (if there are any left) probably aren't heavily represented among Elvis's more extreme devotees either. With the mellow wisdom of the ages, their church takes all this stuff in stride, but Rome has routinized it, organized it, introduced some quality control.

A few years ago, a group of us, Episcopalians and Roman Catholics, got together to read and discuss a highly touted book called *A Common Catechism*, written by an ecumenical group of Continental theologians. It quickly became clear that the important distinction in our group was not between Protestants and Catholics, but between those who were orthodox and proud of it, or unorthodox and ashamed of it, or who-knows-how-orthodox but committed to the proposition that orthodoxy exists and the church should teach it, and those (call them "liberals") who felt that truth is in the seeking, or is whatever works for you, or is something we all have a piece of—those, in other words, who found the concept of orthodoxy quaint, if not alarming.

Now the interesting thing is that these liberals have far less reason than traditionalists to make fun of the credulous. When

Tennessee country folk see the Holy Face on the side of a freezer, or a mother tells the tabloid *Star* that "Rock Hudson's Ghost Cured My Son of AIDS," or some poor soul thinks Elvis answers prayers written on a men's room wall, liberals have no basis for ridicule other than intellectual snobbery. On what grounds can they say these people are not just tacky, but wrong? How do they know? If it's every man for himself in matters of belief, why shouldn't some middle Americans beatify a small-town Southern boy who liked peanut-butter-and-banana sandwiches? Hey, it works for them.

We'll be seeing a lot more of this kind of thing. As Flannery O'Connor tactfully implied from time to time, the absence of ecclesiastical authority means the efflorescence of credal and devotional extravagance, not its absence. And someone, probably Chesterton, has observed that in a secular age people don't believe nothing, they believe *anything*. The book our group was supposed to be discussing began with a great deal of blather about what "modern man" would and would not believe. Its version of modern man was heavily influenced by nineteenth-century scientism; he looked, as a matter of fact, rather like a Continental theologian. But I've got news for the book's authors. Last I heard, modern man was out on the West Coast waiting for the harmonic convergence.

The decay of orthodoxy leaves a vacuum that certainly can't be filled by the desiccated rationalism of *A Common Catechism*. And the amorphous, nonjudgmental, sentimental quasi-religion of my liberal friends can't say why it shouldn't be filled by the cult of St. Elvis.

(April 1988)

❧ E.P. Phone Home ❧

My buddy Ben is a newspaperman. Like many in his trade, he's a connoisseur of the grotesque and absurd, and occasionally he sends along a bundle of clippings and wire service bulletins. For Christmas 1988 he sent me a year's worth of Elvisiana, and I thought I'd let you know what has been going on, because I know some of you care deeply about the King.

I hope you don't care as deeply as Jim Tennant, though. The *Weekly World News* (*WWN*)—which seems to have become the newspaper of record for news of Elvis, his doings, and his fans—says that Mr. Tennant, fifty, took his collection of sixteen hundred Elvis records and left his home in Wolverhampton, England, when his wife Joan delivered a me-or-Elvis ultimatum. Tennant had announced that he was changing his name—to "Elvis Presley." Explaining his decision, the new Mr. Presley said: "I've been an Elvis fan for 30 years, and that's a lot longer than I've known Joan."

Speaking of immoderate middle-aged European fans, Jutta Jeuthe, forty-six, of Hamburg, has become one of the few working female Elvis impersonators. The headline accompanying the tabloid story says "She ain't nothin' but a hound dog!" and there are photographs to prove it. The robust Miss Jeuthe, who has visited Graceland eight times and actually met the King in 1977, particularly resembles the later Elvis in torso and chins, perhaps because she eats only his favorite foods: peanut butter, hot dogs, and hamburgers.

Meanwhile, down the road in Baden-Baden, Patricia Sieler's painting of Elvis has begun to cry real tears, or at any rate what a chemist says is "a saline solution that's indistinguishable from the human tear." The painting weeps only when Miss Sieler plays her Elvis records, according to *WWN*. In fact, it cries during "Heartbreak Hotel" and stops when "Jailhouse Rock" is played.

Back in the U.S. of A. we don't have weeping pictures, but we do have all-Elvis radio stations—three of them at last count by the New York Times News Service, one each in Ohio, Washington, and Alabama. And we lead the world in Elvis sightings.

You've heard, of course, about the sightings. Now and again since his alleged death and burial in 1977, Elvis has made his continuing presence manifest to the faithful. An Atlanta barmaid, for instance, claims to have lived with him from 1978 to 1981. *WWN* says that forty-four-year-old Elizabeth Price now wants to write a book about the affair. She passed a polygraph test, which proves at least that she believed her bearded lover when he said he was Elvis. There is also the matter of a strange tape supposedly recorded by Elvis four years after his death in which he explains his need for privacy and his desire to get back on stage. Two hundred and seventy thousand people have paid two dollars each to listen to the tape. That, friends, is upward of a half-million dollars for somebody.

As I say, there have always been signs for those with eyes to see. But in 1988 more people seemed to be seeing Elvis than Dan Quayle. Actually, the first of this new wave of sightings came in late 1987, in Vicksburg, Michigan, when a Kalamazoo housewife saw Elvis buying a fuse in Felspausch's grocery store. Louise Welling told *WWN* that she was speechless. "I mean you're not expecting to run into Elvis Presley in the grocery store." A couple of weeks later, Mrs. Welling saw Elvis again, this time coming out of a Kalamazoo Burger King.

Well, the scoffers had a field day, as you might suppose. A rival Vicksburg grocery store attempted to match Felspausch's publicity windfall with a sign proclaiming "Jimmy Hoffa Shops Here." This kind of Midwestern narrow-mindedness may explain why nobody else in Kalamazoo has let on to having seen Elvis. Mrs. Welling told *WWN* that many others have seen him, but are afraid to say so in public.

Elsewhere, though, Elvis-spotters aren't as reticent. Two California sisters told the *National Examiner* that they saw Elvis outside the Church of Scientology in Hollywood where, unknown to them, Presley's daughter was being married. Then there's Verena Deuble of Bad Nauheim, West Germany. Frau Deuble, eighty-seven, who says she knew Elvis when he was an American GI, showed the German press a letter sent from Memphis in which Elvis explains that he faked his own death to escape from the rat race. The president of Elvis's German fan club suggested cautiously that the letter might be a hoax, but "handwriting experts" were said to have told the press that they are "99 percent sure" the signature is authentic.

After *WWN* broke the Kalamazoo story, readers wrote to say that they'd seen Elvis in a variety of places, some rather unlikely, on the face of it: outside a Las Vegas hotel where a tribute to him was in progress, shopping at a Texas department store, at a car race in Minnesota, fishing in upstate New York, on the beach in Maine, eating lunch in the California wine country, and in a bookstore in Florida.

If the idea of a bookish Elvis sounds farfetched, ponder this story, from Blacksburg, Virginia. At a college party, a fiftyish, balding, bearded man appeared. "At first I thought he was just a professor looking for a good time," one musician told *WWN*. But then he grabbed the mike and joined the band in "Blue Suede Shoes." When the song was over, the crowd stood stunned as the professorial Presley strolled off and vanished into the night.

Could it be that these people are just seeing Elvis imitators or look-alikes? Well, Gail Brewer-Giorgio, author of the book *Is Elvis Alive?*, points out that the proliferation of Elvis imitators makes it easier for Elvis to hide out. Many people who think they're looking at an imitator may actually be seeing the real thing. Think about that.

And stranger things have happened. Consider the final words of Ms. Brewer-Giorgio's book:

> Around the 10th anniversary of the death of Elvis Presley, an Atlanta attorney who had been working in the Gary Hart campaign responded to the rumor that Gary Hart would run again with this statement: "The probability of Gary Hart seeking the nomination for president of the United States is as unlikely as believing Elvis Presley is still alive."
>
> Less than four months after this statement, Gary Hart again announced his candidacy for president of the United States.

Well, there you are. Aren't you?

I should point out that not everyone is buying the Elvis-lives theory. (Note the anagram, incidentally: ELVIS/LIVES.) Not only in Kalamazoo are skeptics to be found. A California woman is writing a book to argue that it isn't Elvis but his twin brother, Jesse, who is alive and being sighted. Laurel King says that Elvis told her that Jesse, who is supposed to have died at birth, was actually hidden with an aunt after he was found to be retarded. Ms. King says she met Jesse at Graceland in 1973, and he looked just like Elvis but "didn't seem to have the intelligence that Elvis had." It's a thought.

Meanwhile, evangelist Rick Stanley, Elvis's stepbrother (his mother married Elvis's father after the death of Elvis's mother) scoffs at the notion that Elvis may still be alive. As an orthodox Protestant Christian, of course, he also rejects the possibility of apparitions. But he told *WWN* last October that he owes his conversion to Elvis. He was just your average drug addict, long-haired hippie, and hanger-on in the Presley entourage when Elvis left us, showing him by example how empty worldly success could be. "Elvis wasn't content," says Stanley. "He was caught in a trap." (Wasn't there a song about that?)

Others claim to have been helped more directly by the deceased. One seventeen-year-old cancer victim from Warrenville, Illinois, told WWN that "I'm alive today by the grace of the Lord and with a lot of help from Elvis," and drag-racer Marion "Tinker" Gladden of Salisbury, Maryland, told the Sun that Elvis "is up there in heaven right now talking to me and other people like me who care so deeply about him." "When I have a problem," Gladden said, "I ask God for guidance and He hands me over to Elvis, who is one of God's right-hand men. Like all angels [!], Elvis inspires people." Gladden's theology may be a little unsound, but he has a theory about why so many people believe Elvis is still alive on earth: they've been fooled by his "vibrations." Elvis is talking to them, "but they don't know where the vibrations are coming from. The vibes are so powerful that folks figure he must be alive in the flesh."

I should point out that some of those who don't believe Elvis is still among us believe much stranger things. Consider, for instance, an Indiana medium named Diana of the Dunes. According to the Star, when Diana last spoke with Elvis, he told her he was happy, but that he had decided to be reincarnated as a baby boy named Vernon (his daddy's name, of course). This will be a sign unto you, says Diana: the baby's first words will not be "mama" or "dada," but "shook up."

Getting back to the question of who (or what) is buried in Elvis's tomb, however, another psychic says that question will soon be settled once and for all. Janos Szabo told the Sun that there's going to be this big earthquake in the Memphis area, see, and hundreds will die, and the tomb at Graceland will open, and . . . its contents will be revealed. Sometime before the year 2000.

Maybe that's OK, for those who can wait, but the rest of us want to know now. What's going on? Is the King still alive? Well, when fifty thousand Americans paid fifty cents each to vote on the subject in one of those dumb telephone polls, they decided that he was, by a two-to-one margin. I doubt that we could get two-thirds of fifty thousand Americans to pay fifty cents to attest that, say, George Bush is alive. Make of that what you will. I call it another nail in the coffin of the case for universal suffrage.

I find that I'm reluctant to say how I'd have voted, if only because those who believe that Elvis walks the earth today are zealous in their belief. Ann Landers lived to regret a column in which she supported the official story that Elvis was buried at Graceland in 1977. She printed a sample from the flood of protesting letters that came in, and *I don't want to hear from you people, understand?* But I have to say, frankly, that I think it's more likely that the casket buried at Graceland contains all that was mortal of Elvis Presley than that Lee Harvey Oswald acted alone, or that the man from Avon wrote Shakespeare's plays.

True, the success of grocery-store tabloids like the *Weekly World News*, the *Sun*, the *Star*, and the *National Examiner* should occasion second thoughts not just about universal suffrage but about universal literacy. When it comes to Elvis, though, the tabloids are sort of like *USA Today* gone mad, just peddling good news: in this case, that the King may actually still be among us—middle-aged, balding, bearded, off drugs but still fighting a weight problem—like one of us, you know? And if our fellow citizens must read, I think they're better served by stories like the one headlined "Statue of Elvis Found on Mars" (I didn't make that up, honest) than by the novels of Judith Krantz, the columns of Tom Wicker, or the opinions of Justice Brennan.

(April 1989)

❧ Beavers, Banners, and Bulls ❧

Here in Chapel Hill we've had a problem with beavers. They've been damming creeks, as is their wont. Unfortunately in the process they've been turning great areas into marsh, creating a mosquito problem, and interfering with our town's principal industry, which is real-estate development. So last year the old boys of our public works department set out to kill the critters, figuring: no beavers = no dams = no flooding = no problem.

Well, anyone who thinks you can murder beavers with impunity in a college town in the waning years of the American Century has been living on another planet. After the predictable outcry in the newspaper, public meetings, and so forth, the decision was solemnly taken to capture the beasts, sterilize the males, and return them to the wild, where the population is supposed to diminish gradually, by attrition.

But wait. We are not simply to neuter these hapless creatures, as one does with steers, or hogs, or geldings. No, such treatment could cause lasting psychological damage, as one dear lady pointed out, and I don't doubt that she was right. Rather than have distressed eunuch beavers on their consciences, my fellow citizens have anted up their tax money and mine to provide—are you ready for this?—vasectomies for the little fellows. So now we are to have beavers with futile but active sex lives, sort of a rodent version of today's college experience.

Those of you who don't live in college towns don't know what you're missing. Being a professor means I have to know. On the other hand, it also means that I don't have to stick around in the summers. Our family spent a couple of weeks in the summer of 1989 in and around Barcelona where (it probably won't surprise you to hear) I had some thoughts about the American South.

To begin with, what can the Confederate flag possibly mean to Europeans? I keep running into it. On this trip I found it on a postcard at a *snack bar* (French for "snack bar") near Montpellier. On an earlier trip, in the market at Conigliano, north of Venice, I found a booth selling posters for the Grateful Dead and lapel pins with a picture of Elvis, the latter superimposed on the battle flag of the CSA (on the back, the legend "Made in Canada"). Later, I came across an Italian factory with an imposing array of flags out front: the Common Market nations, Japan, the U.S.—and the Confederate States of America. Later still, in the Austrian town of Villach, near the Italian and Yugoslav frontiers, an army surplus store obviously catering to flaming youth flew, out front, the Stars and Stripes with a Harley-Davidson roaring out of it—and the rebel flag. Back in Italy, on the autostrada from Venice to Milan, I passed a tractor-trailer cab wallpapered with—a giant Confederate flag. In Paris, in the Latin Quarter, I paused at a shop selling cheap straw hats, pocketbooks, postcards, and—the flag.

What's going on here? Does anybody know? I suspect this display doesn't have much to do with the Confederate States of America. (If it does, though, where were these allies when we

needed them?) Rather, thanks to a motley assortment of white
Southern musicians ranging from Hank Williams, Jr., and Alabama to Lynyrd Skynyrd and the Allman Brothers, on back (yes)
to Elvis and Buddy and Jerry Lee—thanks no doubt to these
ambassadors, for many good old European boys emblems of the
South connote good-timing, beer-drinking, hell-raising freedom
and rebellion. (The Italian factory is another story. I'll bet they just
ordered up a couple of dozen assorted flags from a wholesaler.)

To the point is a group we ran into in Barcelona. "Los Huevos"
at first glance looked like your typical Euro-scum rock band: a
half-dozen long-haired musicians, Jaggeresque lead singer. But
they were cooking in a particularly down-home mode, featuring
a fine harmonica player. No Confederate flags were in evidence,
but the guitarist wore a Jack Daniels T-shirt.

To a newcomer, of course, what is Spanish about Barcelona is
more striking than what is not. On the television at our hotel, for
instance, we encountered bullfighting, complete with slow-motion
instant replay. I was surprised not to find the spectacle more
disturbing. In fact it was riveting, so much so that the next Sunday
evening found my daughter and me at the plaza de toros, me
bareheaded lest a Durham baseball cap that said "Bulls" be thought
in poor taste. In a little over two hours we saw six bulls dispatched
with varying degrees of artistry. So far as I know, no one has ever
proposed to do vasectomies instead, but that could be a heck of a
show, too.

My teenage daughter came away from the bullring with a crush
on a dashing young matador named Rafi de la Viño. I came
away—well, not troubled exactly, but pensive, because ordinarily
I look away from cruelty, and certainly don't seek it out.

It has been remarked that a bullfight is not a sport but a tragedy.
(All right, so I've been reading *Death in the Afternoon*. It makes a
lot more sense now.) To understand why I didn't find the bullfight
revolting, you must understand that the bulls we saw were not
poor, bewildered creatures cruelly goaded into aggressiveness,
but proud, vicious animals bred for assault. Snorting and stamp-
ing and tossing their wicked horns, these beasts came loaded for
matador. If you have ever been chased by a large, ferocious dog,

you may have some idea of what those men were facing. It was only at the corrida that I really came to understand why pit bulls are called that: the reckless, single-minded ferocity is the same.

The picadors and banderilleros didn't have to infuriate these bulls; their job was to weaken them, to even the odds. Even so, the encounters were made contests only by the bullfighters' skill and courage. If you or I had been out there, we'd have been (in my daughter's elegant phrase) dead meat. We saw three matadors. One was gored in the arm; he tied on a tourniquet and finished the fight. Another stumbled and was tossed on the bull's horns, but miraculously escaped without serious injury.

In each fight, in short, two of God's creatures were trying to kill each other. And I, for one, had no trouble choosing sides. (If you want to feel sorry for something, pity the horses—but that's another story.)

Maybe one can question the morality of raising bulls for the ring instead of for, say, the Golden Arches. But I won't. I don't want bullfights in North Carolina, not even satellite television coverage, but I have no problem with the fact that there are places in the world where men fight bulls, and vice versa. There are cultures with worse traditions.

Anyway, as I said, we knew we were in Spain. But we were also constantly reminded that we were in Catalonia, and the distinction Catalans often make between the Spanish "state" and the Catalan "nation" is easily and sympathetically grasped by someone from a place where caps and bumper stickers say "American by birth / Southern by the grace of God."

Moses Hadas remarked once that a subject people's only glories are departed ones. That Catalonia's cultural high-water marks came in the twelfth century and in the first third of this one makes for some fine Romanesque and art nouveau architecture. If you turn your back to Barcelona's harbor, which once served Romans and Phoenicians, and start walking, you come first to the medieval "Gothic Quarter" around the cathedral, then to spacious neighborhoods of boulevards and cafés that feel like Paris without the tourists, finally to execrable high-rise worker-warrens that should merely be passed through as quickly as possible—which is usually not quickly at all, given the gruesome traffic. The city's most famous building, almost its signature, is Gaudí's unfinished sand-castle church of Sagrada Familia. One of the many sculpted figures called for by the original plan was that of Satan in the form of a serpent, handing a bomb to an anarchist worker. Gaudí was an early victim of the Barcelona traffic, run down by a tram before he lived to see the Civil War, but he knew an enemy when he saw one. In the cloister of the old cathedral is a chapel dedicated to 930 priests, monks, and nuns of the diocese murdered in that war, many by anarchists. (If those killed by the Nationalists have a memorial now I didn't see it.)

After the war, Catalan autonomist sentiment was vigorously suppressed by the Franco regime. In particular, the Catalan language was expunged from the schools and public life. Since Franco's death, however, restrictions on Catalan have gone the way of bikini tops on the Costa Brava. Now Castilian Spanish has little more standing in Catalonia than English does in Quebec. A tourist can get along pretty well with Castilian only because most waiters and hotel staff seem to be Spanish-speaking migrants from the impoverished South; as one moves up the economic ladder Barcelonans tend more and more to be bilingual, and some refuse to speak Castilian on principle. Newcomers are encouraged to learn Catalan, and to all appearances are fully accepted once they've done so. Road signs are provided in both Catalan and Castilian, but the Castilian has often been effaced by language vigilantes with spray paint. Meanwhile the Catalan flag is everywhere. (Its four red stripes on a yellow field represent the bloody fingerprints of a national hero.)

Elsewhere—across the French border in "Occitania," for instance—the typical separatist is usually a member of the petit-intelligentsia who dreams of being minister of culture or ambassador to the court of St. James's instead of senior lecturer in sociology at a provincial university. But Catalan nationalism's appeal is both broader and deeper. The major nationalist party is headed by a banker. That may help to explain why Catalans, unreliable Spaniards, seem to be good Europeans. As it's usually presented, "Europe" strikes me as an idea that only a Chamber of Commerce could love, but Barcelona has always been a bourgeois city of merchants and manufacturers, many of whom would prefer to think of their town as a major European metropolis rather than the second city of Spain.

The thought that "Europe" may eventually make Spain obsolete has another, more romantic, attraction. There's an image lurking about of the New Europe as a loose confederation of communities: Catalans, Flemings, Bretons, Alsatians, Basques, Occitans, Welsh—in time maybe Croats, Vlachs, Lapps, Ukrainians, who knows? This vision of all the old, suppressed, organic Nations rising up, shaking free of the artificial strictures of States, becoming fully themselves—this pluralistic vision conflicts with the ambitions of the Eurocrats in Brussels, but it's a lovely idea, and I wish it well. It reminds me of *The Napoleon of Notting Hill*, when the king gives each district of London its independence. Pointing to "old inviolate Notting Hill," he says: "Look up nightly to that peak, my child, where it lifts itself among the stars so ancient, so lonely, so unutterably Notting."

(December 1989)

⮑ Allons, Enfants de la Patrie ⮐

It was years ago that I first read the collection of Donald Davidson's essays called *Still Rebels, Still Yankees*. In one of them, "Some Day, in Old Charleston," the doughty Last Agrarian addressed one of his perennial themes, the trashiness of modern civilization and the inherent superiority of the Old Southern regime, by describing Charleston's Army Day parade of April 6, 1948.

Down King Street that day came "a ceremonious procession stepping to martial music, carrying flags and deadly weapons": columns of helmeted and booted paratroopers, Marines in red and blue, sailors "who looked unhappy as sailors always do when marching as infantry," the old Carolina regiments (Washington Light Infantry, Sumter Guards), the Citadel band, the cadets of Porter Military Academy. Davidson was savoring the parade's order and decorum, "traditional and unalterable," when, suddenly, "more music, with a saucy blare in its horns and drums," and a high-school band from upstart North Charleston appeared, led by a girl dressed as a blue devil and turning cartwheels—

> And behind her pranced a whole squad of drum majorettes. They
> threw their knees high to the beat of the drums. They tossed and

swung their batons, twisted hips and bodies, nodded their heads under their grotesque shakos. They simpered brassily, their girlish features frozen in a Hollywood smile.

Oh, my (I thought). Brassy simpering? Twisted hips? Knees up? Steady, Don.

Davidson went on at length about the horror of "the naked legs of drum majorettes on King Street, in old Charleston." About majorettes "largely without clothes." About "the flesh and the devil" devoid of "any but the crudest meaning." About the traditional drum major displaced by "a follies girl, a bathing beauty, a strip-tease dancer," his baton now "the ornament by which the drum majorette attracts attention to her charms," this for "purposes that will not bear examination."

I've never forgotten this diatribe. A year later I couldn't have told you much else about Davidson's essay, but for twenty years and more every time I've thought about baton-twirling (which isn't often, I admit) I've thought about his revulsion at "the bare flesh of drum majorettes in their quasi-march."

I thought about it, for instance, when I read a snide but hilarious *Esquire* article on the Dixie National Baton Twirling Institute at Ole Miss, by Terry Southern, the author of *Candy*. (What would poor Davidson have thought of his beloved Southland's taking the lead in this activity, and being mocked for it by a pornographer?) I thought about it again when someone joked in the early days of the Carter administration that maybe a Southern president would come across with Arts Endowment grants for twirling schools. (I thought, too, about Davidson's prescient warning in *I'll Take My Stand* against federal cultural programs.) I thought about it when I went to my hometown's Christmas parade and encountered a half-dozen twirling schools, each with its students marching behind a sound-truck. ("The next logical step," Davidson had written, intending sardonic reductio ad absurdum, "would be to abandon the band and to substitute a sound-truck playing phonograph records—a sound-truck which could be preceded by and followed by and covered with a large company of drum majorettes, all twirling batons, all as little clothed as the censor would allow.") Finally, I thought about it when I read somewhere that the principal twirling stance, left hand on hip, is African in origin. (I don't know what else you do with your left hand when your right is engaged with a baton, but if there's anything to this theory I fear it may confirm the old segregationist's worst suspicions.)

My selective memory of Davidson's essay stuck with me, of course, because his disgust was so violent. So Terry Southern thinks twirling is tacky—well, OK. But Davidson almost lost his lunch over it. Not just your average misogynist (I thought). Something of a dirty old man. A *repressed* dirty old man. Yuck.

But on July 14, 1989, the television coverage of the bicentennial Bastille Day parade sent me back to that essay. As the ancient joke has it, it's remarkable how much the old man has learned. I may owe his shade an apology. I'd really lost sight of his point, which was about exploitation and "abstraction" and what would now be called commodification. He saw majorettes not just as an intrusion but as a perversion—perverting the beautiful, just as the big-time sports they often accompany pervert the gallant.

I think I know what Davidson would have made of the French extravaganza.

No doubt you heard that it was expensive. *Newsweek* put the cost at $67 million, more or less. The prime-time parade was put together by a young French-American named Jean-Paul Goude, heretofore best known for his work in advertising and music videos. "We're trying to prove a point," Goude told a television interviewer; he wanted, he said, to produce "a parade with a content." Of course that content had nothing to do with anything as boring as history or as atavistic as patriotism. "The French Revolution," he said (in an accent you can supply yourself), "is only a schoolbook souvenir to me. I mean, just cliché. It's a big cliché." Goude didn't even want to display the Tricolor, but he lost that battle.

He billed his parade as "the Festival of the Planet's Tribes," and its theme was supposedly the Rights of Man. In fact, it began well, with a moving tribute to the Chinese liberation movement smashed by the People's Army shortly before. Chinese acrobats had been supposed to tumble down the Champs Élysées, but after the events of June they were replaced by a hundred or so Chinese students, simply walking their bicycles. Accompanying them was a float bearing a giant Chinese drum, silent. On the drum was a crudely lettered sign: "Nous continuons." The only sound was the spooky ringing of bicycle bells.

But things went downhill swiftly from there. We had the "tribes of France" in Goude's rendition of French coal-miners' costumes and striped stockings, playing a tedious refrain by an African composer on accordions and hurdy-gurdies. (Two tribes, Basques and Bretons, mostly refused to participate.) We had tattered English punks, slouching along in an artificial drizzle, attended by hotel doormen carrying umbrellas. We had a hissing steam railroad, accompanied by sweaty bare-chested drummers (Dutch, I think). We had Soviet soldiers from Lenin's Tomb goose-stepping through artificial snow, and an ice-skating polar bear pursuing a flag-carrying Russian maiden on a rink carried on the shoulders of Soviet sailors. We had a dozen or so giant, deformed women who looked something like Goude's ex-wife Grace Jones, spinning atop what I presume were golf carts hidden in their voluminous skirts and carrying children who wore the costumes and bore the flags of many nations (including, I noticed, Palestine).

Most Europeans in the parade seemed to be militaristic automata or outright degenerates, and perhaps this was no accident. This was clearly the ex-colonies' night. A striking African float held a six-sided pyramid of drummers, limbs akimbo, resembling something off a Hindu temple. The television coverage (which Goude mixed himself) returned again and again to a Senegalese float where spotlights and smoky torches illuminated tribal drummers and dancers: the drummers conducted by a maniacal figure in white tie and tails; the dancers, in tutus, a savage parody of Degas.

After all this the Florida A&M University marching band was downright homey as it moonwalked to James Brown's "I Feel Good." The Brit announcer said that Brown—Mr. Please Please Please, the Godfather of Soul, Hardest Working Man in Show Business—is "one of Goude's great heroes." (This may be the only thing Goude has in common with Lee Atwater.)

The announcer observed that the parade gave full play to Goude's "cartoon sensibility on an epic scale," and there's no denying that it was effective theater. But the message it conveyed to me, at least, wasn't the upbeat, brotherly one Goude had in mind. The dim, smoky, pulsating scene pierced now and again by flashbulbs as if by lightning, the techno-primitivism, the Third World flavor—it was a lot like the New York subway at rush hour.

Sorry. Couldn't resist. Actually it was a nightmare vision straight out of *Blade Runner*, and it gave me the creeps.

The African and Asian and Arab presence, as striking in the parade as it is these days on the streets of Paris, illustrated vividly France's colonial chickens coming home to roost. ("Why are you here?" the Frenchman asks the Algerian immigrant. "Because you were there," the Algerian replies.) This phenomenon can be viewed with the fear and loathing of Jean Raspail's disturbing novel *Camp of the Saints* or with the cheerful equanimity of a *Wall Street Journal* editorial, but for better or for worse the place won't be the same again. I'm sure Goude saw his parade as a celebration of that fact, but I'm afraid I saw it as another half-million votes for the thuggish Jean-Marie Le Pen and his nativist National Front.

"We're all from the Ganges now," some of the less admirable characters in Raspail's novel chirp, and Goude seems to share that view. We were told solemnly that he believes "world music can heal the divisions between nations." This belief "stems from his love of, almost obsession with, rhythms like [those] he heard in Senegal," a "relentless beat" he feels is "at the root of most of today's popular music."

Well, the parade's relentless beat did go on—and on. People paraded to hip-hop, R&B, and rap; to whining Moroccan music; to African drumming; to generic Oriental sounds. But aside from some Scottish bagpiping I heard no martial music. For that matter the only French music I heard was the Marseillaise, at the end. And even that was sung by an American, soprano Jessye Norman. (Miss Norman seems to rank right below Jerry Lewis in the French pantheon of American cultural heroes, so when she asked to sing it her buddy the minister of culture apparently couldn't just say no.) With the possible exception of "Dixie," the Marseillaise is the most stirring national anthem going; it usually makes me want to go sack a church or something. But Goude's lugubrious arrangement resembled that New Age stuff with whale noises. I perked up when Miss Norman was carried off, singing, on some sort of tumbrel, thinking maybe Goude had scheduled a date with the belle dame sans merci as a boffo conclusion. No such luck.

Far be it from me to tell other folks how to mark their historic anniversaries, especially the French. Since it's not my country I don't figure I've got much opinion coming. Besides, anyone who has been in a music video with a midget lady wrestler should probably keep his mouth shut about decadence. But even if you don't think much of the French Revolution, surely its bicentennial deserved better than this. Or did it, perhaps, somehow lead to this? Maybe Donald Davidson could explain.

I must say that it was something of a relief when Goude's festival was over, and replaced by a rerun of the morning's military parade. There was something clean and purposeful about the cadets and fire brigades, the airplanes and APCs. Even the bearded Foreign Legionnaires with their leather aprons and axes looked jolly and wholesome, straight from the village smithy, their sinister half-time tread notwithstanding.

And now I begin to understand how Donald Davidson felt at the Army Day parade in Charleston. As he watched the soldiers he took his characteristic grim pleasure from this "reminder . . . that the processes of government, laboratory science, liberalism, and expertism must be depended upon sometime, somewhere, to reach a breaking point, at which breaking point the army takes over and the ancient battle begins once more."

Not exactly words to stir hearts in Tiananmen Square, but after Goude's jour de gloire one can almost see Davidson's point.

(November 1989)

About the Author

You're entitled to know who has been imposing on your attention, but the possibility that you might not care inhibits me a bit. So, rather than composing a proper autobiographical sketch, I've just collected the identifying squibs that originally went with some of these pieces. Some evening you could try to match details from this description with the essays they once accompanied. That is, if you don't have anything better to do. Sometimes I have evenings like that.

John Shelton Reed is a semi-pro curmudgeon who tracks the decline of the West and the rise of the South at the University of North Carolina in Chapel Hill, where he reads comic books, listens to country music, and comments on public policy from the security of a tenured position in the sociology department. He says Chapel Hill has recently metastasized, but that New Yorkers will still find it a great place to visit (although they wouldn't want to live there).

Reed is a diglossal, middle-aged, bald, bearded, and overweight East Tennessean with relatives on both sides of the Late Unpleasantness, and a registered Republican who knows it's wrong to want to vote Libertarian. Armed but not dangerous, he still believes in waltzes, admires the Tenth Amendment, and recognizes that his crypto-semi-neo-Agrarian opinions put academic freedom to the test.

He is descended from Baptists, but is himself a failed Episcopal Sunday-school teacher. Although known to some admirers as "the gnome of Carrboro," he did not complete the form he received from *Who's Who in Business and Finance.*

As a youth, he worked as a disk jockey at WMCH, "your good neighbor station in Church Hill, Tennessee." From 1961 to 1963 he was the host of "Rock and Roll Memory Time" on MIT's student FM station, playing those great old songs of 1956–1960. He is now an aspiring singer-songwriter whose unrecorded country songs include the classic "My Tears Spoiled My Aim." He has the same birthday as Elvis. (They're both Capricorns.)

He is the founder and executive director of the Save the Hookworm Federation.